# ACKNOWLEDGEMENTS

I want to take this opportunity to especially thank those individuals who so graciously helped in compiling information and editing this book. Their suggestions and advice were warmly welcomed:

William Godwin, Esq.

John McGover,

David Stone, Trustee

Robert Sonnenblick

Karen Johnston

E. Jeffrey Smith

Heidi and Noel Kowenhoven

Martin Garrick

Jimmy O'Loughlin

Jonathan Kirch, Esq.

Patrick Tenore

Howie Gordon

Dennis H. Johnston, Esq.

Deputy Hubert Bernat, Court Services, Real Estate Section, Sheriff's Department

Ms. Deidre Dickey, Chief, Loan Service & Claims, Department of Veteran Affairs

Lieutenant Adam P. Feller, Naval Legal Service Office, Naval Station, Long Beach

Agent Extraordinaire Peter Fleming

Mr. Larry Johnson, HUD Mortgage Assistance Program, Department of Housing and Urban Development

Ms. Debbie Lehr, Cal-Vet Foreclosure Unit, Sacramento

Mr. Richard Miler, CPA

Don Ferris, real estate broker

John Geddis, CPA

Susan Lipsett

And to Lisa Goldoftas and Steve Elias, the two best editors an author could ever have.

This book is dedicated to the loving memory of Richard Sablowsky (1948–1996), an attorney and former law partner, who never stopped encouraging me to achieve the impossible.

FIRST EDITION

**STOP FORECLOSURE NOW IN CALIFONIA**

by Attorney Lloyd M. Segal

NOLO PRESS BERKELEY

# YOUR RESPONSIBILITY WHEN USING A SELF-HELP LAW BOOK

We've done our best to give you useful and accurate information in this book. But laws and procedures change frequently and are subject to differing interpretations. If you want legal advice backed by a guarantee, see a lawyer. If you use this book, it's your responsibility to make sure that the facts and general advice contained in it are applicable to your situation.

## KEEPING UP-TO-DATE

To keep its books up-to-date, Nolo Press issues new printings and new editions periodically. New printings reflect minor legal changes and technical corrections. New editions contain major legal changes, major text additions or major reorganizations. To find out if a later printing or edition of any Nolo book is available, call Nolo Press at 510-549-1976 or check the catalog in the *Nolo News,* our quarterly newspaper.

To stay current, follow the "Update" service in the *Nolo News.* You can get a free two-year subscription by sending us the registration card in the back of the book. In another effort to help you use Nolo's latest materials, we offer a 25% discount off the purchase of your Nolo book when you turn in the cover of an earlier edition. (See the "Recycle Offer" in the back of the book.)

This book was last revised in: JUNE 1997

| | |
|---|---|
| *First Edition* | JUNE 1997 |
| *Editor* | STEVE ELIAS |
| *Illustrations* | MARI STEIN |
| *Book Design* | JACKIE MANCUSO |
| *Manuscript Preparation* | STEPHANIE HAROLDE |
| *Proofreading* | KRISTIN BARENDSEN |
| *Index* | NANCY MULVANY |
| *Printing* | BERTELSMANN INDUSTRY SERVICES, INC. |

Segal, Lloyd, 1948-
    Stop foreclosure now in California / by Lloyd Segal. -- 1st ed.
      p.   cm.
    ISBN 0-87337-383-9
    1. Foreclosure--California--Popular works.  I. Title.
    KFC177.F6S44  1997
    346.79404'364--dc21                97-13533
                                                CIP

*Quantity sales:* For information on bulk purchases or corporate premium sales, please contact the Special Sales department. For academic sales or textbook adoptions, ask for Academic Sales. 800-955-4775, Nolo Press, Inc., 950 Parker St., Berkeley, CA, 94710.

# TABLE OF CONTENTS

## Introduction

### CHAPTER 1

## Develop a Plan to Stop Foreclosure

### CHAPTER 2

## Understanding the Documents Underlying a Foreclosure

### CHAPTER 3

## Nonjudicial Foreclosures

CHAPTER 12

# Help Beyond This Book

# Glossary

# Appendix

# INTRODUCTION

**T**he experience of falling behind on your loan payments and going into foreclosure can be painful, humiliating and stressful. And if you're like most people, your emotional distress is aggravated by a lack of knowledge as you are cast into unknown territory. But, please be assured—you are not alone. Foreclosures are at an all-time high across America and especially in California.

To minimize your anxiety and maximize your understanding, this book provides a thorough discussion of what you will likely encounter once your property goes into foreclosure. But before we leap into the fray, there are several pointers that you should consider as you start your journey.

## A. What Is Foreclosure?

Let's start with a clear definition of foreclosure. Your lender has the legal right to sell your property at a public auction if you fall behind on loan payments and don't bring your loan current within a specified period of time. This process, known as foreclosure, can be conducted though the court system (judicial foreclosure) or without going to court (nonjudicial foreclosure).

*Learning the lingo.* If you're facing a foreclosure, you're going to run into a lot of unfamiliar legal terminology. Along the way, this book will try to explain the most common jargon in plain English. For a quick reference, you can also check the Glossary at the back of the book.

## B. When Will This Book Help You?

If you are reading this book, there's a good chance your lender has already started foreclosure proceedings. This book will help you understand the foreclosure process and figure out what you can do to stop it. But this book will also be helpful if you've missed payments on a real estate loan and your lender is threatening to start foreclosure, or you are struggling to keep current on a real estate loan but expect that you won't be able to keep up the payments for much longer. In addition to learning about foreclosure methods, you'll find valuable information on how to negotiate with your lender or use other strategies to avoid a foreclosure.

Your goal should be to learn all you can about foreclosure so you can anticipate what might happen and develop a strategy to stop it. The book will also help you analyze whether or not to keep your property, by taking a long, hard look at your options and deciding what ultimately will be of benefit to you.

## C. What Types of Property Does This Book Cover?

In this book, we use the generic word "property" to refer to all types of real estate. In other words, the information in this book applies to any real property, regardless of whether you own a single-family home, condominium, duplex, triplex, apartment building, shopping center, office building, commercial building, industrial park or raw land.

## D. What Types of Foreclosures Does This Book Cover?

This book covers foreclosure by a lender who holds a written lien against your property (called a deed of trust) as security for repayment of its loan. This lender could be the financial institution that originally gave you a loan to purchase your property, someone who later lent you money backed by secu-

rity in your property (such as a bank that granted you a home equity loan), the seller of the property who accepted a portion of the sale's price in the form of a promissory note and deed of trust, or a third party that subsequently purchased the loan from your original lender.

*Foreclosures not covered by this book.* This book does not cover tax, court judgment or mechanic's lien sales, which are not technically foreclosures. If you are involved with any of these sales, you should consult an attorney. Nevertheless, many of the strategies described in this book can be applied to involuntary sales as well.

### ICONS USED IN THIS BOOK

Throughout this book, we have included special icons to help organize the material and underscore particular points:

Legal or common-sense tip to help you understand or comply with legal requirements.

A caution to slow down and consider potential problems.

A suggestion to seek the advice of a lawyer, tax advisor or other specialist.

An indication that you may be able to skip some material.

A cross-reference to another section of this book, or a suggestion to consult another book or resource.

## E. Don't Panic

Property owners in foreclosure are like deer caught in the headlights of an approaching automobile. Panicked, they freeze with inaction. Misunderstanding the process, they often use the word "foreclosed" in the past tense as though they have already lost their property. Or worse, some people assume their properties are already gone and move out without putting up a fight. Don't let this happen to you!

Although easier said than done, it is important not to panic simply because a foreclosure has started. As you will learn in this book, foreclosure is a lengthy process—not a single event. The process takes a minimum of four months (nonjudicial foreclosure), and often as long as two to three years (judicial foreclosure). Additionally, in a judicial foreclosure, you may have the right to buy back (redeem) your property for an additional three months to one year after the foreclosure sale.

So, whatever you do, don't think all is lost and give up without a fight. You have time to develop and implement a plan to stop the foreclosure, and this book will help you.

## F. Can You Really Do It Yourself?

Unless your foreclosure is unusually complex, the answer is yes—a resounding yes. You simply need to have common sense, the willingness to learn about foreclosure procedures and the commitment to deal with your lender. In other words, your everyday life experience is the foundation of what you need to know.

For the most part, the techniques described in this book do not require legal knowledge. Forget the notion that you have to act or sound like an experienced lawyer to be successful in dealing with lenders. As you will discover, the vast majority of people you'll deal with during the foreclosure will not be lawyers.

Realize that no matter how many times you read this book and how carefully you prepare, you will probably be nervous when you approach your lender, trustee or sheriff. But, rest assured, you're

not the only one feeling uneasy. Most people (including lawyers) feel anxious when they begin a new task.

So take a deep breath and gather up your courage. As long as you combine your common sense with the principles and techniques described in this book, and are not afraid to ask people questions if you need help, you should be able to represent yourself competently and effectively.

## G. Will This Book Help You If You Do Have an Attorney?

Finally, if you are already represented by an attorney, this book can still help you. Keep in mind that your property belongs to you—not your lawyer. Based upon this simple fact, no lawyer will ever be able to give as much attention to stopping your foreclosure as you can. But, a good lawyer can do a better job of representing you if you are informed and knowledgeable about the foreclosure process and can participate in making critical decisions.

## H. How to Use This Book

This book is designed to increase your overall understanding of the foreclosure process (including procedures and strategies that may initially seem peculiar or foreign), and to provide specific techniques you can use to stop the foreclosure. Here's the best way to use this book.

### Step 1. Read Chapter 1 and Decide Whether or Not to Keep Your Property

Chapter 1 orients you to the world of foreclosure law and helps you decide whether to keep your property. Based on your decision, you'll begin to develop a plan to stop foreclosure in Chapter 1, Section E.

*If you're in the midst of a foreclosure.* If you do not have the time to read large portions of this book, read Chapter 1, then proceed to those method(s) of dealing with foreclosure that apply to your particular situation.

### Step 2. Learn About the Legal Documents Underlying a Foreclosure

Chapter 2 explains the underlying documents in a foreclosure: the promissory note and deed of trust. Understanding these documents, which you signed when you took out your loan, is fundamental to dealing with a foreclosure.

### Step 3. Read About the Kind of Foreclosure You're Facing

There are two kinds of foreclosures:
- nonjudicial—where the lender follows an out-of-court procedure to foreclose, and
- judicial—where the lender files a lawsuit to foreclose.

Each type of foreclosure follows different procedures, and you need to be concerned only with those procedures that apply to your particular circumstances. Most likely, your foreclosure will be nonjudicial, covered in Chapter 3. Although less common, you may face a judicial foreclosure, covered in Chapter 4. Occasionally, a lender may file both kinds of foreclosures and then decide later which foreclosure to pursue. (If you don't know which kind of foreclosure applies to you, the difference is explained in Chapter 1, Section C.)

### Step 4. Pursue Strategies to Stop Foreclosure

Depending on whether you've decided to keep or give up your property, you need to read only those chapters with strategies that interest you. Chapter 1, Section E, summarizes your options and refers you to the appropriate chapters. (Chapters 5 through 9 describe strategies to keep your property. Chapters 10 and 11 cover strategies to get rid of your property.)

### Step 5. Seek Additional Help If You Need It

In Chapter 12, you'll learn how to find a lawyer or foreclosure consultant to help you. Chapter 12 also gives helpful information on doing your own legal research.

# 1

# DEVELOP A PLAN TO STOP FORECLOSURE

**M**ost people believe that foreclosure laws are designed to hurt rather than help them. Not so. The truth is, foreclosure laws have evolved to protect the borrower—not the lender. The foreclosure process gives you, the borrower, specific periods of time in which to:

- bring your loan current by making up the missed payments (known as reinstatement), or
- pay off your loan in its entirety (called redemption).

If neither of these options is feasible, you will still have time to prevent your property from being sold at a public auction (the foreclosure sale).

You will get the most benefit out of the foreclosure process if you come to see it as a window of opportunity to resolve your financial problems. During this period, you have time to learn about the foreclosure process and implement a strategy to stop the foreclosure.

Another basic misconception about foreclosure is that lenders want to foreclose. Nothing could be further from the truth! Lenders are in the business of loaning money—not owning real estate. Lenders are also reluctant to incur the costs of a foreclosure. For example, if your lender is forced to foreclose, it will not only lose your back payments, but it will also incur foreclosure expenses, taxes, insurance, wear and tear while you (or your tenant) live in the property, rehabilitation expenses to refurbish the property for sale and a real estate agent's commission once the property is sold. As a result, many lenders will go out of their way to work out a resolution—short of actually foreclosing—if given the opportunity to avoid paying these costs.

# A. Communicate With Your Lender

At the heart of stopping your foreclosure is communicating with your lender. Don't shy away because you've missed payments, you're concerned that you will miss some payments, or your property has already gone into foreclosure. Whether you communicate by telephone, letter, fax or in person, you will have a much easier time stopping (or at the very least, delaying) the foreclosure if you talk to your lender than if you adopt a code of silence.

The first step is to determine who your lender actually is. If your property has already gone into foreclosure, the first person you will be dealing with is the foreclosing trustee. The trustee is responsible for handling the foreclosure process. (For more on the trustee, read Chapter 2, Section B). But you need to communicate with your lender, not the trustee. So you should request from the trustee the name, telephone number and address of the foreclosing lender. In the unlikely event that the trustee refuses to disclose the name of your lender, you can look on the Notice of Default or telephone the customer service department of a local title insurance company.

Another situation may occur where you discover the name of your lender, but it turns out to be a servicing agent rather than the party that actually holds the promissory note and deed of trust. A servicing agent is a company (sometimes it can be a bank, mortgage company, or private corporation) that is hired by the actual lender to "service" the loan, including the collection of payments, issuing of payment coupons and late notices, monitoring the insurance and tax payments, and handling foreclosures if necessary. Most servicing agents will disclose the name of the lender. If they won't, you may be forced to negotiate with the servicing agent. In either event, follow the guidelines in this book to communicate and negotiate with them.

Do not under any circumstance ignore your lender's contacts. Your goal should be to respond to every phone call or letter. Difficult as it may be to talk about your financial problems, be polite and cooperative. Follow up all telephone calls with a letter to the person you spoke to, confirming what was said. If you're not in when a call comes, return it as soon as you can.

When you receive a letter from your lender, immediately write a letter in response. It is important to establish a paper trail so you can prove to your lender (or a court, if necessary) that you have been cooperative, especially during the initial stages of the foreclosure process.

It is also important to send copies of all of your letters to:
- the lender's CEO
- the branch manager (if applicable)
- the loan officer who helped you obtain your loan, and
- any other person you know by name at your lender's office.

## CONTACTING PEOPLE YOU KNOW AT THE LENDER'S OFFICE

Make sure your letter indicates you are sending copies by typing "cc:" and the name of the person(s) below your signature. Please don't be hesitant to send copies of your letters to these individuals, as they can't do anything to help you if they aren't informed of your predicament. At the very least, the person you sent the letter to won't be able to ignore your letter because he or she knows that supervisors have received copies of your letter.

## 1. Keep a Log of Contacts (Communications Chart)

Catalog all communications on a Communications Chart (a sort of log), including the date and time of the communication, the method (by letter, telephone call, fax or meeting), the name of the person you spoke to, what she said or promised, and what

you said or promised. A self-explanatory Communications Chart you can use appears below. A tear-out
copy of this form is also included in the Appendix.

---

## COMMUNICATIONS CHART

| | |
|---|---|
| Date of contact: | Time: |
| ☐ Telephone    ☐ Letter    ☐ Fax    ☐ Meeting/location | |
| Name of contact person: | |
| Who initiated communication? | |
| What we discussed: | |
| Agreements we reached, if any: | |

| | |
|---|---|
| Date of contact: | Time: |
| ☐ Telephone    ☐ Letter    ☐ Fax    ☐ Meeting/location | |
| Name of contact person: | |
| Who initiated communication? | |
| What we discussed: | |
| Agreements we reached, if any: | |

| | |
|---|---|
| Date of contact: | Time: |
| ☐ Telephone    ☐ Letter    ☐ Fax    ☐ Meeting/location | |
| Name of contact person: | |
| Who initiated communication? | |
| What we discussed: | |
| Agreements we reached, if any: | |

## 2. How to Respond to Lender's Initial Contacts

Typically, in its initial letters and telephone calls, your lender will state that it has not received your payment(s) and inquire innocently whether or not you have mailed a payment. What you say in response to your lender's inquiry is another matter. If you already mailed your payment, give your lender the date. If you have not, tell the truth. Your lender in turn will want to know why you haven't paid, and what date you will be sending a payment. Acknowledge that you are having temporary financial problems and that you won't be able to make the payments for the next couple of months. Provide a good explanation of your financial difficulties (layoff, medical emergency, death in the family, loss of business, divorce). Contrary to popular misconceptions, sharing this information will not speed up the foreclosure process. Each lender has its own foreclosure timetable, regardless of what you say. Nevertheless, what you say may make the lender more sympathetic to your situation and foster a positive atmosphere for negotiations later in the process. (For more on negotiating with your lender, see Chapter 5.)

Your lender may warn you that if payments are not made, your loan will go into default. It may also threaten to start foreclosure proceedings unless you bring all of your payments current immediately. But don't be intimidated. Stay calm and understand that the person you're dealing with is simply doing his job. At this point, write a letter explaining your financial problem and requesting an appointment with a senior loan officer to discuss your loan. (See the sample letter below.)

September 6, 199X

William Blackman
Acme Savings Bank
1000 First Street
San Diego, CA 91600

Re: Property at 1234 Highland Avenue,
San Diego, California

Loan No. 15400

Dear Mr. Blackman:

I own the property listed above. On September 5, you threatened to start a foreclosure against my property because I missed several loan payments.

I am having severe financial problems which will not be resolved for several months. Although several collection representatives of your bank have called me, they are not authorized to help me resolve my loan. Accordingly, I would like to schedule an appointment with an authorized officer of your bank who can discuss my options and assist me during this temporary crisis.

Please have a representative contact me as soon as possible. I am eager to resolve this problem and bring my loan current.

Sincerely,

David Stone

cc: Leslie Bernton, Bank President

---

### RESOURCES FOR HELP WITH FINANCIAL PROBLEMS

If your financial problems go beyond just one loan in foreclosure, you may want to read *Money Troubles: Legal Strategies to Cope With Your Debts*, by Robin Leonard (Nolo Press). Essential for anyone who is feeling overwhelmed by debts, this book shows you how to deal with credit bureaus, negotiate with creditors, challenge wage attachments, decide whether to file for bankruptcy and rebuild your credit.

If you confronting a tax debt, *Stand Up to the IRS*, by Fred Daily (Nolo Press), provides excellent information for surviving a tax audit and resolving your tax problems.

### 3. Find Someone With Authority to Stop the Foreclosure

As you develop a strategy to stop your foreclosure, you will want to be in close touch with someone at your lender's office who has authority to stop the foreclosure. Don't waste your time dealing with a lower-level collections person who has little interest in your hardship or the reasons you are not making the monthly payments. All he or she wants to know is when you are going to pay. Collection personnel have no authority to negotiate with you or stop your foreclosure.

If a collection person calls, politely say goodbye and hang up. Then call the main office of your lender. Ask for the names of the branch manager and the senior loan officer. When you get the information, thank the person you're speaking to and hang up again. Wait one hour, call back and ask for the branch manager or senior loan officer by name. Once you are connected, request an appointment.

If you can't get through and no one returns your call, send a letter such as the one on the previous page. Be sure you send a copy to the president of your lender. Wait several days and call again. Sooner or later, you'll reach someone with authority. This is the person you will want to meet with. (For more information on negotiating with your lender, see Chapter 5.)

## B. Get Organized

It is important to gather together all the documents that relate to your property and your loan. In a typical real estate transaction, you signed an offer to purchase, escrow instructions, a promissory note and a deed of trust. Organize and review as many of these documents as you can in order to understand how the foreclosure process applies to you and develop a strategy to stop the foreclosure. Here's what you should get:

- Copies of the promissory note and deed of trust.
- Copies of any documents and letters in your escrow (contact the escrow company that handled the purchase of your property to get copies).
- A "property profile" which contains information on all documents recorded against your property. You can obtain a free copy of a property profile from the title insurance company that originally insured your purchase of the property. Also ask the company for copies of all documents recorded against your property in the county recorder's office.
- Your Communications Chart (see Section A above).
- Copies of all letters you sent to and received from your lender, along with the envelopes the letters from your lender came in, if you have them.
- Copies of your loan payment stubs or any other billing and payment information.
- Copies of all foreclosure documents you've received, if any. Also save the envelopes of documents you've received, if available.

Label one file folder for each group of documents and put them in the folders in chronological order. You will refer to these documents as you read this book and fight your foreclosure.

## C. Learn the Clock

Foreclosure involves very specific timetables in which notices and procedures must be carefully served, mailed, recorded, posted and published before your lender can legally foreclose. For example, in a nonjudicial foreclosure, a Notice of Default and Election to Sell will be posted on your property and mailed to you. After three months, a Notice of Trustee's Sale will be issued. 21 days thereafter, a trustee's sale may be conducted. As you can see, a nonjudicial foreclosure will take a minimum of 111 days, if not slightly longer.

Knowing the foreclosure clock is crucial to successfully using the strategies in this book to stop your foreclosure. Chapters 3 and 4 explain the timetables in detail.

Once you understand the time constraints within which you are working, you can customize a strategy that fits your particular situation. For example, if you have less than three months until the foreclosure sale, you have some time to bring your loan current, negotiate with your lender or refinance your property. On the other hand, if only four days remain before the sale, your only option to stop the sale may be to file for bankruptcy.

Remember, these time periods are for your benefit—not your lender's. This is your opportunity to apply a strategy that can most effectively stop the foreclosure.

---

**UNDERSTAND THE DIFFERENCE BETWEEN JUDICIAL AND NONJUDICIAL FORECLOSURES**

In California, foreclosures can be conducted either judicially or nonjudicially. Each kind of foreclosure has its own procedural rules, so you need to know whether you are facing a nonjudicial or judicial foreclosure. Here are the particulars:

*Nonjudicial foreclosure.* Most California foreclosures are nonjudicial. Your lender avoids the court system entirely by having a trustee (a third party who conducts the foreclosure) follow a specific series of notice procedures, then sell your property. If you are involved in a nonjudicial foreclosure, read Chapter 3.

*Judicial foreclosure.* This kind of foreclosure starts when your lender files a lawsuit in the Superior Court of the county in which your property is located. You must be served (provided with) with a copy of the Summons and Complaint for foreclosure. A judicial foreclosure can take anywhere from one to three years. Judicial foreclosures are covered in Chapter 4.

---

# D. Decide Whether or Not to Keep Your Property

Before you can settle on a strategy to stop foreclosure, you should clearly and wisely assess whether you really want, and can afford, to keep your property. This may be the most difficult and important decision you'll make.

This is a critical decision because you don't want to spend your precious time and money saving a property that you really can't afford, or that may only cause you more financial problems in the future. Although it may be difficult to accept, you simply may have to cut your losses.

Rather than fighting the foreclosure to the bitter end, the wiser approach might be to apply one of the strategies described in this book to get rid of the property (quick sale, short sale, or deed in lieu of foreclosure) and buy (or rent) another less expensive property, with more affordable monthly payments. Of course, this is a decision only you can make. For most people, this decision rests on four important questions:
- Is there any equity in the property?
- Does the property have economic value apart from the equity?
- Are you emotionally attached to the property?
- Are there any other factors that may affect your decision?

Let's look at each of these questions in detail.

## 1. Is There Any Equity in the Property?

From an economic standpoint, you may think your property is worth keeping. It may therefore come as a surprise to find that the cost to stop the foreclosure and keep your property may outweigh the benefits. Whether or not you try to keep your property should be based on a realistic assessment of the amount of equity (or lack of equity) you have in your property. This is often a very painful task, especially if the value of your property has dropped significantly. But it must be done.

For starters, understand that equity refers to the market value (or possible sales price) of your property less (a) the balance owed on all of the liens (legal claims) against it and (b) the costs of sale. If you have equity in your property, then it is economically worth saving.

## a. Changes in Property Values

If property values in your area have remained stable or increased over the past years, the equity in your property has probably gone up. In contrast, if property values in your area have gone down over the past several years, your equity may have decreased too. As a result, you may have less equity in your property than you believe, even if you have dutifully made payments to your lender on time. This knowledge may hurt, but you are not alone. The harsh reality is that for a number of reasons, property values and equity have dropped for many Californians during much of the 1990s. In some communities, exorbitant real estate values have simply fallen back to reality. Elsewhere, industry downsizing, base closings and other economic conditions have made those communities less attractive to live in. Still other Californians have just had bad luck.

*Example: Steve and Karen purchased their Eureka home for $200,000, making a down payment of $40,000 and financing $160,000. Eight years later, property values in their area have declined by 20%. Their home now has a present market value of $160,000. Their have made approximately $120,000 in interest payments and $20,000 in principal payments, and incorrectly assume that the total equity in their property is $60,000 (down payment $40,000 + principal paid $20,000). Due to the decline in property values, however, they have only $20,000 in equity, and this is before deducting costs of selling their property.*

## b. Calculate Your Equity Using the Equity Worksheet

Use the following Equity Worksheet and accompanying instructions to figure out if you have salvageable equity in your property. You'll find much of the information requested in the worksheet on your loan documents and any foreclosure notices you may have received.

### EQUITY WORKSHEET

1. Estimated sales price:

2. List estimated costs of sale:

   a. Real estate agent's commission (6% of sales price):

   b. Closing costs (2% of estimated sales price):

   c. Balance due on first deed of trust:

   d. Balance due on additional deeds of trust:

   e. Balance due on any other loans by property:

   f. Missed payments on first deed of trust:

   g. Missed payments and late fees on additional deeds of trust:

   h. Any other liens:

   i. Unpaid property taxes:

   j. Foreclosure costs:

3. Total estimated costs of sale:

4. Your equity (1-3):

1. *Estimated sales price.* You need a reasonable estimate of how much your property would sell for on the open market. The basic methods are to ask a real estate agent, hire an appraiser or look at comparable properties in your area. For now, just use a good ballpark figure. (For a more detailed discussion on how to estimate the fair market value of your property, see Chapter 10, How to Sell Your Property Quickly to Stop Foreclosure.)

2. *Estimated costs of sale.* Next, you need to estimate the costs of selling your property.

- *Real estate agent's commission.* If you decide to use a real estate agent (almost always advisable in foreclosure situations), he or she will charge a commission of approximately 6% of the sales price. Even if you think you won't use an agent, it is prudent to include this cost at this point.

- *Closing costs.* Closing costs include such expenses as the title insurance policy, escrow fees, document fees, transfer tax, termite inspection, tax prorations and loan payments. You can use a rough estimate of 2% of the estimated sales price.

- *Outstanding liens and taxes.* Next, you'll list the outstanding balances on your deeds of trust (mortgages) and home equity loans, as well as back payments owed and any late fees. To determine what these fees will be, you can contact your lender or the trustee directly and ask; they should have no problem giving you this information. Also list the amount of any other liens recorded against your property, such as judgment liens, tax liens and mechanic's liens.

- *Foreclosure costs.* If any foreclosure costs have already been incurred, these must be paid regardless of whether your property actually sells in a foreclosure sale. The foreclosure trustee (the person conducting the foreclosure) will have an estimate of these costs, but they are generally about 1–2% of the balance of the foreclosing deed of trust.

3. *Total estimated costs of sale.* Add up the costs of sale above and fill in this amount.

4. *Your equity.* Finally, deduct all of the estimated costs of sale from the estimated sales price (1–3). The result is your estimated equity in your property.

## c. How Much Equity Is Worth Saving?

After completing the Equity Worksheet, you may be rudely surprised to find you have little or no equity in your property. In fact, it is not uncommon to find that the costs associated with selling your property can eliminate most of the equity you thought you had.

*Example: Let's continue with Steve and Karen, who you'll remember have only $20,000 of estimated equity remaining in their property. They decide to sell their property to avoid foreclosure. If they sell their house for $165,000, here's what they'll pocket:*

| | |
|---|---|
| *Estimated sales price* | $165,000 |
| *First deed of trust* | -140,000 |
| *Back payments on first* | |
| *(4 at $1,200/month)* | - 4,800 |
| *Foreclosure costs* | - 1,500 |
| *Commission (6%)* | - 9,900 |
| *Closing costs (2%)* | - 3,300 |
| *Total costs of sale* | 159,500 |
| *Seller's equity* | $ 5,500 |

On the other hand, if you have no equity, your lender may require you to pay money into escrow before allowing you to sell. If this sounds unbelievable, consider the following example.

*Example: If Steve and Karen sell their property for $150,000 to avoid foreclosure, they will actually lose money on the sale:*

| | |
|---|---|
| *Estimated sales price* | $150,000 |
| *First deed of trust* | -140,000 |
| *Back payments on first* | |
| *(4 months at $1,200/month)* | - 4,800 |
| *Foreclosure costs* | - 1,500 |
| *Commission (6%)* | - 9,000 |
| *Closing costs (2%)* | - 3,000 |
| *Total costs of sale* | $ 158,300 |
| *Seller's equity* | <8,300> |

In the above example, not only did Steve and Karen lose all of their equity, but they had out-of-pocket costs of $8,300 to sell their property. While this may be hard to believe, it frequently occurs in depressed real estate markets.

Unfortunately, there is no simple answer to the question: How much equity is worth saving? As difficult as it may seem, you'll need to take a good hard look at your property and the accuracy of your financial calculations. As a general rule, if your equity is worth at least 8% of the value of your property it is probably worth saving. On the other hand, if your equity is under 8% of your property's value, all else being equal, consider letting go of it. But if the thought of giving up your property is just too painful to accept, the next section may address your predicament.

## 2. Does the Property Have Economic Value Apart From the Equity?

Even though you don't have any equity, your property may still be worth keeping if it has "economic value." Economic value can best defined as collateral for junior liens. For example, if your property is foreclosed upon by the senior lienholder, you will still be liable for payment of the junior liens. On the other hand, if you stop the foreclosure, you can sell or refinance your property to pay off the junior liens. This economic value is an important reason to stop the foreclosure before you lose the property.

For example, let's say you own a property worth approximately $200,000. Your property is encumbered with a first deed of trust for $150,000, a second deed of trust for $35,000 and a tax lien for $15,000. In this example, although you don't have any equity in your property, it nevertheless has economic value worth saving. If you lose the property in foreclosure to the holder of the first deed of trust, you will still be liable to the second deed of trust holder ($35,000) and the taxing authority ($15,000). In contrast, if you stop the foreclosure and sell (or refinance) your property, you will be able to use its economic value to pay off the second deed of trust and tax lien.

## 3. Are You Emotionally Attached to the Property?

Even if you have no equity in your property, strong emotional ties may make the thought of losing it unbearable. For instance, if you've lived in your home for many years, your children were born and raised in the home or you've made significant renovations and customized improvements, your property may be worth the sacrifice it will take to save it. On the other hand, if you own income-producing property, such as a rental house, apartment building or commercial building, it probably has no sentimental value to you. In that case, you have no reason to fight for property in which you have no equity.

This decision is very personal. If you decide your property has value to you that money cannot replace, and if you're willing to put in the time and energy it will take to save your property, pursue the strategies in this book.

## 4. Other Considerations

Other considerations may affect your decision to stop the foreclosure. For example, if you believe your financial situation will improve in the next few months, you may want to fight to keep your property. Or if you need additional time to sell your property, it is worth stopping the foreclosure. On the other hand, if your financial future looks bleak, spending your time and money to fight foreclosure may not be wise. You don't want to fight to keep your property now, only to lose it because you can't really afford the loan payments.

Carefully consider the extent of your other debts and their effect on your financial situation. Perhaps you can trim your budget, sell a car or come up with other ways to bring your loan current and meet your ongoing expenses. Or maybe your other unpaid bills could be eliminated in bankruptcy, leaving you with enough cash each month to easily afford the payments on your property. (See Chapter 9 for a detailed discussion of bankruptcy.)

Another important consideration may be your credit rating. Although your credit report may already indicate missed or late payments to your property's lender (and possibly other creditors), this may not be so bad because you can usually explain why you have missed payments. However, most people want to avoid a foreclosure—or bankruptcy—from appearing on their credit reports because most creditors will not give credit when they see these more serious blemishes.

## 5. Tax Effects of Giving Up or Selling Your Property

It may come as shock to discover that by giving up your property in foreclosure, or selling it, you could actually incur a personal income tax obligation. This section gives you a general overview of income tax liability issues to watch out for, and suggests some ways you may be able to get out of such a predicament.

*Get advice before you give up your property.* No area of the law experiences more revisions and invites more questions than the tax code. Check with an accountant, tax attorney or other tax specialist to learn more about whether taxes will be due in your particular circumstance.

### a. Tax Liability If You Sell Your Property

What if you sell your property during the foreclosure to pay off your foreclosing lender? If you pay taxes, it depends on whether you make a profit (called capital gain) or suffer a loss (called capital loss).

If the sales price exceeded the "adjusted cost basis" of your property, you have capital gains which will be taxable by the Internal Revenue Service. Adjusted cost basis is defined as the price you paid for your property plus any capital improvements you put into it over the years (such as replacing the roof or adding a bathroom), plus costs of sale, minus any depreciation, casualty losses and

postponement of gain from a previous sale. If the sales price is greater than the adjusted cost basis, you have a capital gain which is taxed by the IRS.

*Example: Jean purchased a $100,000 home in Stockton which she financed with a $80,000 loan with Olympic Federal Savings Bank. Over the years, Jean improved the home with a $10,000 swimming pool and jacuzzi, which adjusted her cost basis from $100,000 to $110,000. When Jean could no longer afford the payments, Olympic started foreclosure proceedings. To avert foreclosure, Jean sold her residence for $150,000, its current market value. The difference between $150,000 (sale price) and $110,000 (adjusted cost basis) is $40,000, which is her taxable gain.*

However, you will not have to pay income taxes on your capital gains if the property is your personal residence and if, within 24 months of the sale, you purchase and occupy a new residence that costs at least as much as the old residence. Also, if you are over 55, you may qualify for a one-time $125,000 exclusion.

If you have a loss on the sale of your property, you can deduct the capital loss from any capital gains in order to reduce your tax liability only if the property is a rental or income-producing property. If it is your personal residence, your capital loss is not deductible.

### b. Tax Liability If You Lose Your Property in Foreclosure

The IRS treats a foreclosure like any other sale of your property. In other words, if you lose your property in a foreclosure sale, you will be liable to the IRS for taxes if the adjusted cost basis of your property is less than the sales price at the foreclosure sale.

*Example: Merv and Kathy own a property in Yosemite, which they purchased several years ago for $190,000 with a $160,000 loan. Today, the loan balance is down to $150,000. When they default on the loan payments, their lender forecloses selling the property for $150,000. As a result, Merv and Kathy will have a capital gain of $10,000 (the difference between the original loan balance of $160,000 and the sale price of $150,000) which is taxable.*

On the other hand, if their property had depreciated to $130,000, there would have been taxable ordinary income of $20,000 from the foreclosure sale (the difference between the sales price of $150,000 and the $130,000 depreciated value), which Merv and Kathy could offset against other ordinary losses provided the property was not their personal residence.

You may even face a tax bill for capital gains if your lender forecloses and sells your property for more than you originally paid (plus capital improvements), even if you don't get a penny back.

*Example: Yvette bought a $180,000 summer home in Santa Barbara, making a $30,000 down payment and taking a $150,000 loan. The house significantly increased in value (although Yvette made no improvements to the property) and she took out a home equity loan for $75,000. Several years later, property values dropped drastically, Yvette lost her job and her lender foreclosed, selling the property at a trustee's sale for $195,000. Yvette owed her first lender $140,000 and her second lender $65,000—a total of $205,000—so she received nothing from the sale. Unfortunately for Yvette, the IRS rules that she has "discharge of debt" taxable income of $25,000 (the difference between the loans in the amount of $205,000 and the original purchase price of $180,000).*

### c. Tax Liability If You Sell Your Property in a Short Sale

As an alternative to foreclosure, some property owners reach agreement with the foreclosing lender to sell the property in a "short sale" (for less than the balance of the loan). When your lender releases you from paying the deficiency, it is known as "discharge of debt" and is considered taxable income by the IRS. In fact, your lender will submit a Form 1099A to the IRS which will reflect the amount of the discharge.

*Example: Mark and Tom own a property in Chula Vista encumbered with a $100,000 deed of trust held by Unity Mortgage Company. Over the years, the market value of the property has fallen from $120,000 to $80,000. Mark and Tom are able to convince Unity Mortgage to accept $80,000 as payment in full as part of a short sale. When the property is sold, although Mark and Tom are forgiven for repaying the $20,000, it is considered "discharge of debt" income by the IRS and taxable.*

### d. Income Tax Liability Exceptions

Several IRS exceptions may relieve you of tax liability for a discharge of debt:

- *Bankruptcy exception.* Under the Internal Revenue Code, any amount unpaid on a property loan (discharge of debt) is not recognized as taxable income if you are in bankruptcy. (IRS § 108(a)(1)(A).)
- *Insolvency exception.* Should your secured and unsecured debt exceed the value of your assets at the time the discharge of debt occurs, the discharge of debt income may not be taxable (known as the "balance sheet test"). You will need to file documents with the IRS (Form 982) substantiating your insolvency.
- *Business losses.* Any property that isn't your primary residence is considered investment property—a summer cottage, rental house, store or apartment building. If you have investment property, you can offset discharge of debt income with business losses.
- *Senior exception.* If you are over 55, you may qualify for a one-time $125,000 exclusion, which means that up to $125,000 of the profit will be exempt from taxation as capital gains income.

## E. Develop a Plan of Action

As you read this book and decide which strategies are most suitable to your situation, you can develop a concrete plan of action. The various approaches described in this book are not mutually exclusive, and like most people, you'll probably want to pursue more than one strategy. For example, if you want to keep your property, you may try to refinance your loan at the same time you negotiate with your lender (Chapter 5) or file a lawsuit to enjoin the foreclosure (Chapter 8). Similarly, if you decide to get rid of your property, you may try to sell it while simultaneously preparing to give your lender a deed in lieu of foreclosure if you can't sell it (Chapter 11).

## 1. Options to Keep Your Property

After reading Section D, above, if you decide to keep your property, you can pursue the options listed below.

### a. Negotiate With Your Lender (Chapter 5)

Your first strategy should always be to negotiate with your lender. Chapter 5 explains the basic rules for negotiating and suggests common solutions to resolve a defaulted loan, such as workouts for the arrears or future monthly payments. Chapter 5 also explains the special programs available to you if your loan was insured by the Federal Housing Association (FHA), the Veterans Administration (VA), or is covered by the California Department of Veteran Affairs. You'll also find information on how to negotiate with a private mortgage insurance company (PMI).

### b. Refinance Your Property (Chapter 6)

Another important strategy is to refinance your property so you can bring your loan current or pay off your foreclosing lender before the foreclosure sale. Chapter 6 covers sources of refinancing and distinguishes among various kinds of lenders. Chapter 6 also discusses the advantages and disadvantages of using a mortgage broker to obtain a new loan, rather than dealing directly with potential lenders.

### c. Use Your Military Connection (Chapter 7)

You may not realize it, but if you are in the military (or dependent on someone in the military), you may have the automatic right under the Soldiers and Sailors Civil Relief Act to stop the foreclosure. Chapter 7 explains who qualifies for military relief, who can provide military relief and what you must ask for to obtain assistance. You'll also learn when you may qualify for a reduction in your interest rate.

### d. File a Lawsuit to Stop a Nonjudicial Foreclosure (Chapter 8)

If you have grounds to do so, you can file a lawsuit to stop (enjoin) a pending nonjudicial foreclosure. Chapters 3 and 8 explain how to spot common procedural errors that occur during the nonjudicial foreclosure process as well as the most frequent mistakes lenders make when granting loans, which can be grounds for stopping the foreclosure. You'll also get a brief overview of the ins and outs of filing a lawsuit, and instructions on how to obtain an order from the court to stop the foreclosure, called a temporary restraining order. (Of course, if you are facing a judicial foreclosure, you will have the opportunity to respond in court without initiating the process yourself. We explain judicial foreclosures in Chapter 4.)

### e. File for Bankruptcy (Chapter 9)

If all else fails, bankruptcy may be your most viable option. Chapter 9 discusses the advantages and disadvantages of the different types of bankruptcy. You'll find out how bankruptcy automatically stops foreclosure (at least temporarily), and how to use bankruptcy to resolve the impasse with your lender and keep your property.

## 2. Options to Get Rid of Your Property

If you decide to get rid of your property, but want to do it on your own to stop the foreclosure, here are your options:

### a. Sell Your Property (Chapter 10)

The most expedient strategy is to sell your property as quickly as possible. Chapter 10 discusses how to use a real estate agent, prepare your property for sale, price your property for a quick sale, market your property, negotiate offers and counter-offers and remove contingencies so that escrow closes in time to beat the foreclosure. You'll also learn how to structure a "short sale," where your lender accepts less than the amount of your outstanding loan as payment in full. Finally, if you can't find a buyer willing to pay market value for your property in time to avoid the foreclosure sale, Chapter 10 covers sales to equity purchasers—individuals who pay you a fraction of your equity to get title to your property—and the pitfalls you need to guard against.

### b. Give Your Lender a Deed in Lieu of Foreclosure (Chapter 11)

One strategy is to deed your property to your lender in exchange for ending the foreclosure. Giving a deed in lieu of foreclosure may be the most efficient method of giving up your property, although it has pitfalls you need to guard against. For example, many lenders will refuse to accept a deed in lieu if there are junior liens on your property. Chapter 11 helps you assess the advantages and disadvantages of a "deed in lieu" (as it's called) and how to negotiate with your lender to accept one.

# 2

# UNDERSTANDING THE DOCUMENTS UNDERLYING A FORECLOSURE

**R**eal estate transactions rely heavily on paperwork. Think back to your own closing day—you probably felt like you were signing an endless stream of documents and that you should have brought a suitcase to carry them all home.

The first two documents you will need to review to learn how to stop the foreclosure are the promissory note and deed of trust. These documents describe the rights and responsibilities of you and your lender. When you fail to adhere to your responsibilities, these documents provide the mechanism for your lender to foreclose. They also provide a basis for you to stop a foreclosure if there are any inconsistencies between your note or deed of trust and the foreclosure documents.

*If you understand the significance of these documents and the provisions they contain.* Skip this chapter and proceed to either Chapter 3 (if yours is a nonjudicial foreclosure) or Chapter 4 (if yours is a judicial foreclosure).

## A. Promissory Note

Your promissory note is the document in which you promised to repay the money that was loaned to you. The note sets forth the amount you borrowed, the interest rate and the particulars of how the loan is to be repaid. Typically no more than one or two pages in length, a promissory note is relatively easy to understand.

## 1. Parties to a Promissory Note

There are two parties to a promissory note:

### a. Borrower

The borrower is the person or persons who borrowed the money. The borrower is sometimes referred to as the payor or obligor. This includes you and anyone who co-signed the loan, such as a spouse, non-marital partner or business partner.

### b. Lender

The lender is the person or financial institution that originally loaned you money and any person or financial institution to whom your original lender sold your note. The lender is sometimes referred to as the payee, obligee or holder. When you borrowed money to purchase or refinance your property, the lender was probably a bank, savings and loan association, savings bank, mortgage company, credit union, insurance company, family member or friend, or perhaps, the seller of the property. The current lender may be a company or person that specializes in buying up promissory notes from the original lenders.

## 2. Reviewing Your Promissory Note

To stop the foreclosure, you'll need to understand the terms and conditions of your particular promissory note. You will also need to determine:
- the amount you have already paid on the note
- the amount you are in arrears, and
- the balance of your loan.

If the foreclosure documents recorded against your property are inaccurate, you'll probably have a basis to stop the foreclosure.

When you purchased or refinanced your property, your original lender (or the escrow officer) had you sign a promissory note and gave you a copy. If you don't have a copy of your signed note, get one as soon as possible. Your current lender should have a copy and your original lender should have the original. However, if you don't want to ask your current lender, or aren't sure who it is, you can request a copy from the escrow company. If the escrow company can't help you, send a written request to your original lender similar to the sample letter set out below. Before sending the letter, telephone the lender's office and get the name of an officer that you can specifically send the letter to. Make sure you keep a copy of the letter.

January 10, 19XX

Mr. Neal Brown
Branch Manager
Pacific Hills Bank
1234 Hill Street

Hillsdale, California

Re: Loan No. 34-44356

To Whom It May Concern:

I own the property located at 245 Pacific Coast Highway, in the City of Malibu, California. In July of 199X, I borrowed $155,000 from your bank.

The original promissory note securing my property was given to you. However, I don't have a copy.

Could you please provide me with a photocopy of my promissory note? I will call and arrange to pick up the document at your office.

Thank you in advance for your anticipated cooperation.

Sincerely,

William Scher

Carefully review your note.

## Promissory Note Breakdown

1. Amount of indebtedness: The principal—actual—amount of money you borrowed on this note.

2. Location of execution: The city where you signed the note.

3. Date of execution: The date the promissory note was signed.

4. Name of lender: The name of the person or company that lent you the money.

5. Address of lender: The mailing address of your lender.

6. Amount of indebtedness: The principal amount of money you borrowed is repeated here.

7. Interest effective date: The date when interest began to accrue on the principal.

8. Interest rate: The amount charged by your lender for loaning the money. The interest rate will be expressed as either fixed (interest rate remains the same during the entire term of your loan) or adjustable (interest rate will fluctuate on a semi-annual or annual basis).

9. Installment amount: For a fixed-rate loan, the payment amount typically is shown in both written and numeric form. (If you have an adjustable interest rate, the installment amount will not be shown on the note, but will typically appear on your payment coupons.)

10. Installment due date: The date of the month that each payment is due (the vast majority of notes are paid monthly).

11. Commencement date: The date your first payment on your promissory note is due.

12. Final payment date: The date the final payment on your promissory note is due.

13. Signature of borrower: You and your co-borrowers signed the note here. Your lender does not sign the note.

A sample Promissory Note Worksheet appears below, and a blank tear-out copy is included in the Appendix. Use it to record the relevant terms and conditions in your deed of trust.

| PROMISSORY NOTE WORKSHEET | |
|---|---|
| Date note is signed: | July 10, 199X |
| Borrower(s): | John and Susan Ross |
| Lender: | First Bank |
| Principal amount borrowed: | $175,000 |
| Interest rate: | 9% adjustable |
| Term (number of months, years or other arrangement): | 25 Years |
| Payment frequency (monthly or other arrangement): | monthly |
| Commencement date (date payments begin): | August 1, 199X |
| Payment amount: | $1,123 |
| Is there a reference in the note to the deed of trust? | Yes |

## 3.  Understanding the Promissory Note

There are seven basic components in every promissory note:

- principal
- interest
- term
- payment
- security
- acceleration, and
- negotiability.

The first four are financial components. If you disagree with the amount your lender is claiming you owe—as set out in the foreclosure documents—it may become important for you to figure out whether your lender has calculated correctly the financial information, particularly the default amount ("arrears"). You will need to add up your missed payments, late fees and penalties to determine your arrears. If you are unable to make these calculations, you may need to hire an accountant or bookkeeper. As we point out in Chapter 8, Using the Courts to Stop a Nonjudicial Foreclosure, lenders frequently make mistakes, especially if the note has a variable interest rate or unusual terms. A sample promissory note appears on pages 2/5-6. An explanation of its important terms follows.

### a.  Principal

The principal is the amount of money you borrowed from your lender. This amount does not include any interest, points or other fees. If you refinanced your loan, it is the amount of the refinanced loan, not the amount of your first loan.

### b.  Interest

Interest is the fee a lender charges to loan money. Interest is calculated as a percentage of the unpaid principal, on a yearly (per annum) basis. The interest rate will be computed on a 365-day year, unless otherwise specified in the promissory note. The interest rate can be either:

- fixed, meaning your interest rate will remain the same during the entire term of your loan, or
- variable, meaning that your interest rate will fluctuate on a semi-annual or annual basis as described in your promissory note. For example, this might be a 9% adjustable rate. Lenders can select from a variety of formulas for a given variable rate loan. (See the box below.)

---

### VARIABLE RATE FORMULAS

The most common formulas used by lenders are:

- Prime rate, as established periodically by the Federal Reserve Board

- the 11th District Cost of Funds, as established monthly by the Federal Home Loan Bank Board

- London Interbank Offering Rate (LIBOR), which fluctuates daily based upon market forces in the economy

- the rate for one-year treasury bills, which fluctuates semi-annually based upon market forces in the economy, and

- the rate for six-month Certificates of Deposit, which fluctuates daily based upon market forces in the economy.

---

### c.  Term

Term refers to the period of time in which you have to repay the loan. The term can range anywhere from 1 to 30 years.

### d.  Payment

Payment is the amount of interest and/or principal that you promised to repay on a periodic basis. Your promissory note will specify the date when payments are to start, the amount of each payment and the repayment schedule (usually monthly). Some loans call for you to make monthly payments for several years and then a lump sum payment at the end. This lump sum is called a balloon payment. Foreclosures are often precipitated by a borrower's inability to make a balloon payment.

# NOTE

_(City)_                    _(State)_

_(Property Address)_

## 1. BORROWER'S PROMISE TO PAY

In return for a loan that I have received, I promise to pay U.S. $                    (this amount is called "principal"), plus interest, to the order of the Lender. The Lender is

I understand that the Lender may transfer this Note. The Lender or anyone who takes this Note by transfer and who is entitled to receive payments under this Note is called the "Note Holder."

## 2. INTEREST

Interest will be charged on unpaid principal until the full amount of principal has been paid. I will pay interest at a yearly rate of

The interest rate required by this Section 2 is the rate I will pay both before and after any default described in Section 6(B) of this Note.

## 3. PAYMENTS

### (A) Time and Place of Payments

I will pay principal and interest by making payments every month.

I will make my monthly payments on the                    day of each month beginning on                    , 19          I will make these payments every month until I have paid all of the principal and interest and any other charges described below that I may owe under this Note. My monthly payments will be applied to interest before principal. If, on                    I still owe amounts under this Note, I will pay those amounts in full on that date, which is called the "maturity date."

I will make my monthly payments at

or at a different place if required by the Note Holder.

### (B) Amount of Monthly Payments

My monthly payment will be in the amount of U.S. $

## 4. BORROWER'S RIGHT TO PREPAY

I have the right to make payments of principal at any time before they are due. A payment of principal only is known as a "prepayment." When I make a prepayment, I will tell the Note Holder in writing that I am doing so.

I may make a full prepayment or partial prepayments without paying any prepayment charge. The Note Holder will use all of my prepayments to reduce the amount of principal that I owe under this Note. If I make a partial prepayment, there will be no changes in the due date or in the amount of my monthly payment unless the Note Holder agrees in writing to those changes.

## 5. LOAN CHARGES

If a law, which applies to this loan and which sets maximum loan charges, is finally interpreted so that the interest or other loan charges collected or to be collected in connection with this loan exceed the permitted limits, then: (i) any such loan charge shall be reduced by the amount necessary to reduce the charge to the permitted limit; and (ii) any sums already collected from me which exceeded permitted limits will be refunded to me. The Note Holder may choose to make this refund by reducing the principal I owe under this Note or by making a direct payment to me. If a refund reduces principal, the reduction will be treated as a partial prepayment.

## 6. BORROWER'S FAILURE TO PAY AS REQUIRED

### (A) Late Charge for Overdue Payments

If the Note Holder has not received the full amount of any monthly payment by the end of                    calendar days after the date it is due, I will pay a late charge to the Note Holder. The amount of the charge will be                    % of my overdue payment of principal and interest. I will pay this late charge promptly but only once on each late payment.

### (B) Default

If I do not pay the full amount of each monthly payment on the date it is due, I will be in default.

### (C) Notice of Default

If I am in default, the Note Holder may send me a written notice telling me that if I do not pay the overdue amount by a certain date, the Note Holder may require me to pay immediately the full amount of principal which has not been paid and all the interest that I owe on that amount. That date must be at least 30 days after the date on which the notice is delivered or mailed to me.

### (D) No Waiver By Note Holder

Even if, at a time when I am in default, the Note Holder does not require me to pay immediately in full as described above, the Note Holder will still have the right to do so if I am in default at a later time.

### (E) Payment of Note Holder's Costs and Expenses

If the Note Holder has required me to pay immediately in full as described above, the Note Holder will have the right to be paid back by me for all of its costs and expenses in enforcing this Note to the extent not prohibited by applicable law. Those expenses include, for example, reasonable attorneys' fees.

## 7. GIVING OF NOTICES

Unless applicable law requires a different method, any notice that must be given to me under this Note will be given by delivering it or by mailing it by first class mail to me at the Property Address above or at a different address if I give the Note Holder a notice of my different address.

Any notice that must be given to the Note Holder under this Note will be given by mailing it by first class mail to the Note Holder at the address stated in Section 3(A) above or at a different address if I am given a notice of that different address.

## 8. OBLIGATIONS OF PERSONS UNDER THIS NOTE

If more than one person signs this Note, each person is fully and personally obligated to keep all of the promises made in this Note, including the promise to pay the full amount owed. Any person who is a guarantor, surety or endorser of this Note is also obligated to do these things. Any person who takes over these obligations, including the obligations of a guarantor, surety or endorser of this Note, is also obligated to keep all of the promises made in this Note. The Note Holder may enforce its rights under this Note against each person individually or against all of us together. This means that any one of us may be required to pay all of the amounts owed under this Note.

## 9. WAIVERS

I and any other person who has obligations under this Note waive the rights of presentment and notice of dishonor. "Presentment" means the right to require the Note Holder to demand payment of amounts due. "Notice of dishonor" means the right to require the Note Holder to give notice to other persons that amounts due have not been paid.

**10. UNIFORM SECURED NOTE**

This Note is a uniform instrument with limited variations in some jurisdictions. In addition to the protections given to the Note Holder under this Note, a Mortgage, Deed of Trust or Security Deed (the "Security Instrument"), dated the same date as this Note, protects the Note Holder from possible losses which might result if I do not keep the promises which I make in this Note. That Security Instrument describes how and under what conditions I may be required to make immediate payment in full of all amounts I owe under this Note. Some of those conditions are described as follows.

**Transfer of the Property or a Beneficial Interest in Borrower.** If all or any part of the Property or any interest in it is sold or transferred (or if a beneficial interest in Borrower is sold or transferred and Borrower is not a natural person) without Lender's prior written consent, Lender may, at its option, require immediate payment in full of all sums secured by this Security Instrument. However, this option shall not be exercised by Lender if exercise is prohibited by federal law as of the date of this Security Instrument.

If Lender exercises this option, Lender shall give Borrower notice of acceleration. The notice shall provide a period of not less than 30 days from the date the notice is delivered or mailed within which Borrower must pay all sums secured by this Security Instrument. If Borrower fails to pay these sums prior to the expiration of this period, Lender may invoke any remedies permitted by this Security Instrument without further notice or demand on Borrower.

WITNESS THE HAND(S) AND SEAL(S) OF THE UNDERSIGNED.

_____   Borrower          _____   Borrower

_____   Borrower          _____   Borrower
                                                               (Sign Original Only)

MULTISTATE FIXED RATE NOTE-Single Family-FNMA/FHLMC UNIFORM INSTRUMENT          FORM 3200 12/83

## e. Security

Promissory notes are either secured or unsecured. A secured note simply means that you have pledged your property as guarantee for payment of the note (collateral or security). A secured note gives your lender the right to sell your property to pay off the loan if you default. This involuntary sale of your real property is called foreclosure. Secured notes usually use the word "secured" in the title (for example, "Note Secured by Deed of Trust") and in the description ("this note is secured by a deed of trust...) so that the parties to the note, or subsequent purchasers, know that the note is secured by property. (See "Negotiability" below.)

By way of comparison, an unsecured note does not have property as security for its repayment. In that situation, if the borrower fails to pay the note, the lender is required to file a lawsuit in court to collect the note.

## f. Acceleration

An acceleration clause states that in the event you miss a payment (default), your lender has the right to declare the entire balance of principal and accrued interest due. The purpose of an acceleration clause is to relieve your lender of the burden of having to sue you for each late payment one by one until the end of the loan. All promissory notes have an acceleration clause. [However, notwithstanding the acceleration clause, once the foreclosure starts, there is still a period of time (called the reinstatement period) in which you can still stop the foreclosure by simply paying the amount that is in arrears.]

## g. Negotiability

Negotiability refers to your lender's right to sell your promissory note to a third party, such as a private or institutional investor. Investors typically purchase these loans in quantity and at a discount. This industry is called the "secondary market." The three largest purchasers of loans secured by real property are:

- Federal National Mortgage Association, also known as FNMA or Fannie Mae
- Federal Home Loan Mortgage Corporation, also known as FHLMC or Freddie Mac, and
- Government National Mortgage Association, also known as GNMA or Ginnie Mae.

Once your loan is sold, the third party acquires all the rights and obligations of your original lender under the promissory note. This means that even though your original lender's name may appear on your note, someone else may actually own the note and the right to receive your payments. Knowing who owns your note and deed of trust is vital to negotiating and using other strategies in this book. Although the holder may not be your actual original lender, we use the term "lender" to refer to whoever actually holds your note.

A promissory note will typically contain a paragraph describing its negotiability or assignability, or simply state "or order" after the name of the lender, which accomplishes the same purpose.

### IF YOU AREN'T SURE WHETHER YOUR LOAN WAS SOLD

Although not required to do so, lenders usually send out an Assignment of Beneficial Interest or some other written document to borrowers to notify them that the loan has been sold. If you didn't receive written notification but you think your loan may have been sold, contact your initial lender and ask whether it still owns your loan. If it has been sold, get the name, address and telephone number of the current holder of the loan. Or, you can contact a title insurance company and ask them to search for the title in the county recorder's office and determine whether an Assignment of Beneficial Interest was recorded on your property. (Unfortunately, you probably won't be able to gain any leverage in the foreclosure process by claiming you didn't receive notice of the assignment.)

## 4. Types of Promissory Notes

There are three basic types of promissory notes, each of which has endless variations. This information is important if there is a dispute with your lender over the amount owed. The three basic types are:

• amortized (or installment) notes
• interest-only notes, and
• straight notes.

### a. Amortized (Installment) Notes

An amortized promissory note (also referred to as an installment note) calls for regular payments—typically monthly, but sometimes bi-weekly, quarterly, semi-annually or yearly. With a fixed interest rate, these payments are equal amounts. With a variable interest rate, payment amounts are generally adjusted semi-annually or annually.

Amortized notes are the most common type of notes used for single family home purchases. Over the term of an amortized note, you make a set number of payments. A portion of each payment is attributed to interest and another part to principal (as determined by amortization tables). At the end of the term, you will have paid back the entire loan.

*Example 1: Douglas borrows $100,000 from First Federal Bank to purchase a new home in Needles. The interest rate is fixed at 10% per year. The loan is to be repaid with monthly payments of $525, fully amortized over 30 years.*

*Example 2: Judy borrows $345,000 from Buffalo Credit Union to purchase an apartment building in Morro Bay. The interest rate is variable, starting at 7.5% but adjusted annually based upon 3% above the prime rate each year. The loan is to be amortized over 25 years.*

### b. Interest-Only Notes

As its name implies, with an interest-only note you make scheduled interest payments, usually monthly. At the end of the term of your loan, you must repay the entire principal balance in a single (balloon) payment.

*Example: Kathy borrows $85,000 from Grass River Mortgage Company to refinance her home. The interest rate is fixed at 9% per year. The promissory note calls for interest-only monthly payments of $637.50 for five years, with a lump-sum payment of $85,000 (original principal balance) at the end of the five years.*

Typically, an interest-only note is used when a borrower cannot afford high payments of principal and interest. The risk, however, is that when the note matures, the borrower will not be able to afford the balloon payment. To avoid default, most property owners arrange to sell or refinance their property when the balloon payment comes due.

### c. Straight Notes

A straight note requires the borrower to repay the entire principal amount, plus interest, in one payment when the term of the note expires. Typically, these notes are for relatively short periods and small amounts. Straight notes are frequently used when an owner remodels or fixes his or her property or uses it as security for a personal loan.

*Example: Benjamin borrows $15,000 from First National Bank to remodel his kitchen. The annual interest rate is 10.25%. The promissory note calls for a single payment of $16,537.50 ($15,000 principal plus $1,537.50 interest) at the end of one year.*

## B. Deed of Trust

If everything went as planned, borrowers would pay back their loans in full and on time. Lenders know, however, that some borrowers are either unable or unwilling to pay their debts. For this reason, lenders require that borrowers pledge property as security (collateral) for their loans. If the borrower defaults, the lender can force the sale of the property to recover the money owed. As a practical matter, real property cannot be deposited at the bank pending repayment of the loan. Thus, documents were developed as a substitute for the impossibility of delivering property to a lender.

When you signed a promissory note to borrow money from your lender to purchase or refinance your property, you also signed a deed of trust. A deed of trust is evidence of your lender's security interest in your property. To be valid, a deed of trust must be recorded in the county recorder's office for the county in which the property is located.

The deed of trust creates a lien (legal claim) against your property, which remains in force until you repay your loan or your lender forecloses. Although California prescribes no standard form for a deed of trust, these documents have become relatively standardized. A sample of a typical deed of trust used in California is provided below.

Almost all deeds of trust have a "power of sale" clause, which gives your lender the right to foreclosure against your property without first suing you in court. This is known as a nonjudicial foreclosure (covered in Chapter 3).

A sample deed of trust is shown on pages 2/10-15. An explanation of the important terms follows.

### DEED OF TRUST VS. MORTGAGE

A deed of trust is similar to a mortgage, which also documents real property as security for a loan. However, a mortgage is a two-party document (mortgagor and mortgagee), while a deed of trust is a three-party document (trustor, trustee and beneficiary). The significant difference is that if you default on a mortgage, your lender must file a lawsuit to foreclose. In contrast, if you default on a deed of trust, your lender can avoid the courts entirely and file a nonjudicial foreclosure. Mortgages are used primarily in states east of the Mississippi River. Deeds of trust are used primarily in states west of the Mississippi River and almost exclusively in California.

## 1. Parties to a Deed of Trust

As mentioned, there are three people involved in a deed of trust: the trustor (the borrower), the beneficiary (the lender) and the trustee (an individual or company authorized to foreclose if the borrower defaults).

### a. Trustor (You)

The trustor is the person, or persons, who own property, signed the promissory note and pledged the property as security for the loan. The trustor is almost always the borrower, especially where a single family residence is involved. (Although rare, a trustor could agree to use property he or she owns as security for someone else's loan.)

### b. Beneficiary

The beneficiary is initially the person or business that loaned you money to purchase or refinance your property. If the original beneficiary (your original lender) sells your loan, the new beneficiary holder of the loan is the beneficiary.

# DEED OF TRUST

THIS DEED OF TRUST ("Security Instrument") is made on
The trustor is

("Borrower"). The trustee is
("Trustee"). The beneficiary is

which is organized and existing under the
laws of                                          and whose address is
("Lender"). Borrower

owes Lender the principal sum of
Dollars (U S $                    ). This debt is evidenced by Borrower's note dated
the same date as this Security Instrument  ("Note"), which provides for monthly payments, with the full debt, if not
paid earlier, due and payable on                                        . This Security Instrument
secures to Lender : (a) the repayment of the debt evidenced by the Note, with interest, and all renewals, extensions
and modifications of the Note; (b) the payment of all other sums, with interest, advanced under paragraph 7 to protect
the security of this Security Instrument; and (c) the performance of Borrower's covenants and agreements under this
Security Instrument and the Note. For this pupose, Borrower irrevocably grants and conveys to Trustee, in trust, with
power of sale, the following described property located in
County, California:

which has the address of
                                        [Street]                                                    [City]
California                      ("Property Address");
          [Zip Code]

TOGETHER WITH all the improvements now or hereafter erected on the property, and all easements, appurtenances,
and fixtures now or hereafter a part of the property. All replacements and additions shall also be covered by this Security
Instrument. All of the foregoing is referred to in this Security Instrument as the "Property."

BORROWER COVENANTS that Borrower is lawfully seised of the estate hereby conveyed and has the right to grant
and convey the Property and that the Property is unencumbered, except for the encumberances of record. Borrower
warrants and will defend generally the title to the Property against all claims and demands, subject to any encumbrances
of record.

CALIFORNIA---Single Family---Fannie Mae/Freddie Mac UNIFORM INSTURMENT      FORM 3005  9/90 (page 1 of 6 pages)

THIS SECURITY INSTRUMENT combines uniform covenants for national use and non-uniform covenants with limited variations by jurisdication to constitute a uniform security instrument covering real property.

UNIFORM CONVENANTS. Borrower and Lender covenant and agree as follows:

**1.    Payment of Principal and Interest: Prepayment and Late Charges.** Borrower shall promptly pay when due the principal of and interest on the debt evidenced by the Note and any prepayment and late charges due under the Note.

**2.    Funds for Taxes and Insurance.** Subject to applicable law or to a written waiver by Lender, Borrower shall pay to Lender on the day monthly payments are due under the Note, until the Note is paid in full, a sum ("Funds") for: (a) yearly taxes and assessments which may attain priority over this Security Instrument as a lien on the Property; (b) yearly leasehold payments or ground rents on the Property, if any; (c) yearly hazard or property insurance premiums; (d) yearly flood insurance premiums, if any; (e) yearly mortgage insurance premiums, if any; and (f) any sums payable by Borrower to Lender, in accordance with the provisions of paragraph 8, in lieu of the payment of mortgage insurance premiums. These items are called "Escrow Items." Lender may, at any time, collect and hold Funds in an amount not to exceed the maximum amount a lender for a federally related mortgage loan may require for Borrower's escrow account under the federal Real Estate Settlement Procedures Act of 1974 as amended from time to time, 12 U.S.C. § 2601 *et seq.* ("RESPA"), unless another law that applies to the Funds sets a lesser amount. If so, Lender may, at any time, collect and hold Funds in an amount not to exceed the lesser amount. Lender may estimate the amount of Funds due on the basis of current data and reasonable estimates of expenditures of future Escrow Items or otherwise in accordance with applicable law.

The Funds shall be held in an institution whose deposits are insured by a federal agency, instrumentality, or entity (including Lender, if Lender is such an institution) or in any Federal Home Loan Bank. Lender shall apply the Funds to pay the Escrow Items. Lender may not charge Borrower for holding and applying the Funds, annually analyzing the escrow account or verifying the Escrow Items, unless Lender pays Borrower interest on the Funds and applicable law permits Lender  to make such a charge. However, Lender may require Borrower to pay a one-time charge for an independent real estate tax reporting service used by Lender in connection with this loan, unless applicable law provides otherwise. Unless an agreement is made or applicable law requires interest to be paid, Lender shall not be required to pay Borrower any interest or earnings on the Funds. Borrower and Lender may agree in writing, however, that interest shall be paid on the Funds. Lender shall give to Borrower, without charge, an annual accounting of the Funds, showing credits and debits to the Funds and the purpose for which each debit to the Funds was made. The Funds are pledged as additional security for all sums secured by this Security Instrument.

If the Funds held by Lender exceed the amounts permitted to be held by applicable law, Lender shall account to Borrower for the excess Funds in accordance with the requirements of applicable law. If the amount of the Funds held by Lender at any time is not sufficient to pay the Escrow Items when due, Lender may so notify Borrower in writing, and, in such case Borrower shall pay to Lender the amount necessary to make up the deficiency. Borrower shall make up the deficiency in no more than twelve monthly payments, at Lender's sole discretion.

Upon payment in full of all sums secured by this Security Instrument, Lender shall promptly refund to Borrower any Funds held by Lender. If, under paragraph 21, Lender shall acquire or sell the Property, Lender, prior to the acquisition or sale of the Property, shall apply any Funds held by Lender at the time of acquisition or sale as a credit against the sums secured by this Security Instrument.

**3.    Application of Payments.** Unless applicable law provides otherwise, all payments received by Lender under paragraphs 1 and 2 shall be applied: first, to any prepayment charges due under the Note; second, to amounts payable under paragraph 2; third, to interest due; fourth, to principal due; and last, to any late charges due under the Note.

**4.    Charges; Liens.** Borrower shall pay all taxes, assessments, charges, fines and impositions attributable to the Property which may attain priority over this Security Instrument, and leasehold payments or ground rents, if any. Borrower shall pay these obligations in the manner provided in paragraph 2, or if not paid in that manner, Borrower shall pay them on time directly to the person owed payment. Borrower shall promptly furnish to Lender all notices of amounts to be paid under this paragraph. If Borrower makes these payments directly, Borrower shall promptly furnish to Lender receipts evidencing the payments.

Borrower shall promptly discharge any lien which has priority over this Security Instrument unless Borrower: (a) agrees in writing to the payment of the obligation secured by the lien in a manner acceptable to Lender; (b) contests in good faith the lien by, or defends against enforcement of the lien in, legal proceedings which in the Lender's opinion operate to prevent the enforcement of the lien; or (c) secures from the holder of the lien an agreement satisfactory to Lender subordinating the lien to this Security Instrument. If Lender determines that any part of the Property is subject to a lien which may attain priority over this Security Instrument, Lender may give Borrower a notice identifying the lien. Borrower shall satisfy the lien or take one or more of the actions set forth above within 10 days of the giving of notice.

**5.    Hazard or Property Insurance.** Borrower shall keep the improvements now existing or hereafter erected on the Property insured against loss by fire, hazards included within the term "extended coverage" and any other hazards, including floods or flooding, for which Lender requires insurance. This insurance shall be maintained in the amounts and for the periods that Lender requires. The insurance carrier providing the insurance shall be chosen by Borrower subject to Lender's approval which shall not be unreasonably withheld. If Borrower fails to maintain coverage described above, Lender may, at Lender's option, obtain coverage to protect Lender's rights in the Property in accordance with paragraph 7.

All insurance policies and renewals shall be acceptable to Lender and shall include a standard mortgage clause. Lender shall have the right to hold the policies and renewals. If Lender requires, Borrower shall promptly give to Lender all receipts of paid premiums and renewal notices. In the event of loss, Borrower shall give prompt notice to the insurance carrier and Lender. Lender may make proof of loss if not made promptly by Borrower.

Form 3005  9/90 *(page 2 of 6 pages)*

Unless Lender and Borrower otherwise agree in writing, insurance proceeds shall be applied to restoration or repair of the Property damaged, if the restoration or repair is economically feasible and Lender's security is not lessened. If the restoration or repair is not economically feasible or Lender's security would be lessened, the insurance proceeds shall be applied to the sums secured by this Security Instrument, whether or not then due, with any excess paid to Borrower. If Borrower abandons the Property, or does not answer within 30 days a notice from Lender that the insurance carrier has offered to settle a claim, then Lender may collect the insurance proceeds. Lender may use the proceeds to repair or restore the Property or to pay sums secured by this Security Instrument, whether or not then due. The 30-day period will begin when the notice is given.

Unless Lender and Borrower otherwise agree in writing, any application of proceeds to principal shall not extend or postpone the due date of the monthly payments referred to in paragraphs 1 and 2 or change the amount of the payments. If under paragraph 21 the Property is acquired by Lender, Borrower's right to any insurance policies and proceeds resulting from damage to the Property prior to the acquisition shall pass to Lender to the extent of the sums secured by this Security Instrument immediately prior to the acquisition.

**6. Occupancy, Preservation, Maintenance and Protection of the Property; Borrower's Loan Application; Leaseholds.** Borrower shall occupy, establish, and use the Property as Borrower's principal residence within sixty days after the execution of this Security Instrument and shall continue to occupy the Property as Borrower's principal residence for at least one year after the date of occupancy, unless Lender otherwise agrees in writing, which consent shall not be unreasonably withheld, or unless extenuating circumstances exist which are beyond Borrower's control. Borrower shall be in default if any forfeiture action or proceeding, whether civil or criminal, is begun that in Lender's good faith judgment could result in forfeiture of the Property or otherwise materially impair the lien created by this Security Instrument or Lender's security interest. Borrower may cure such a default and reinstate, as provided in paragraph 18, by causing the action or proceeding to be dismissed with a ruling that, in Lender's good faith determination, precludes forfeiture of the Borrower's interest in the Property or other material impairment of the lien created by this Security Instrument or Lender's security interest. Borrower shall also be in default if Borrower, during the loan application process, gave materially false or inaccurate information or statements to Lender (or failed to provide Lender with any material information) in connection with the loan evidenced by the Note, including, but not limited to, representations concerning Borrower's occupancy of the Property as a principal residence. If this Security Instrument is on a leasehold, Borrower shall comply with all the provisions of the lease. If Borrower acquires fee title to the Property, the leasehold and the fee title shall not merge unless Lender agrees to the merger in writing.

**7. Protection of Lender's Rights in the Property.** If Borrower fails to perform the covenants and agreements contained in this Security Instrument, or there is a legal proceeding that may significantly affect Lender's rights in the Property (such as a proceeding in bankruptcy, probate, for condemnation or forfeiture or to enforce laws or regulations), then Lender may do and pay for whatever is necessary to protect the value of the Property and Lender's rights in the Property. Lender's actions may include paying any sums secured by a lien which has priority over this Security Instrument, appearing in court, paying reasonable attorneys' fees and entering on the Property to make repairs. Although Lender may take action under this paragraph 7, Lender does not have to do so.

Any amounts disbursed by Lender under this paragraph 7 shall become additional debt of Borrower secured by this Security Instrument. Unless Borrower and Lender agree to other terms of payment, these amounts shall bear interest from the date of disbursement at the Note rate and shall be payable, with interest, upon notice from Lender to Borrower requesting payment.

**8. Mortgage Insurance.** If Lender required mortgage insurance as a condition of making the loan secured by this Security Instrument, Borrower shall pay the premiums required to maintain the mortgage insurance in effect. If, for any reason, the mortgage insurance coverage required by Lender lapses or ceases to be in effect, Borrower shall pay the premiums required to obtain coverage substantially equivalent to the mortgage insurance previously in effect, at a cost substantially equivalent to the cost to Borrower of the mortgage insurance previously in effect, from an alternate mortgage insurer approved by Lender. If substantially equivalent mortgage insurance coverage is not available, Borrower shall pay to Lender each month a sum equal to one-twelfth of the yearly mortgage insurance premium being paid by Borrower when the insurance coverage lapsed or ceased to be in effect. Lender will accept, use and retain these payments as a loss reserve in lieu of mortgage insurance. Loss reserve payments may no longer be required, at the option of Lender, if mortgage insurance coverage (in the amount and for the period that Lender requires) provided by an insurer approved by Lender again becomes available and is obtained. Borrower shall pay the premiums required to maintain mortgage insurance in effect, or to provide a loss reserve, until the requirement for mortgage insurance ends in accordance with any written agreement between Borrower and Lender or applicable law.

**9. Inspection.** Lender or its agent may make reasonable entries upon and inspections of the Property. Lender shall give Borrower notice at the time of or prior to an inspection specifying reasonable cause for the inspection.

**10. Condemnation.** The proceeds of any award or claim for damages, direct or consequential, in connection with any condemnation or other taking of any part of the Property, or for conveyance in lieu of condemnation, are hereby assigned and shall be paid to Lender.

In the event of a total taking of the Property, the proceeds shall be applied to the sums secured by this Security Instrument, whether or not then due, with any excess paid to Borrower. In the event of a partial taking of the Property in which the fair market value of the Property immediately before the taking is equal to or greater than the amount of the sums secured by this Security Instrument immediately before the taking, unless Borrower and Lender otherwise agree in writing, the sums secured by this Security Instrument shall be reduced by the amount of the proceeds multiplied by the following fraction: (a) the total amount of the sums secured immediately before the taking, divided by (b) the fair market value of the Property immediately before the taking. Any balance shall be paid to Borrower. In the event of a partial taking of the Property in which the fair market value of the Property immediately before the taking is less than the amount of the sums secured immediately before the taking, unless Borrower and Lender otherwise agree in writing or unless applicable law otherwise provides, the proceeds shall be applied to the sums secured by this Security Instrument whether or not the sums are then due.

If the Property is abandoned by Borrower, or if, after notice by Lender to Borrower that the condemnor offers to make an award or settle a claim for damages, Borrower fails to respond to Lender within 30 days after the date the notice is given, Lender is authorized to collect and apply the proceeds, at its option, either to restoration or repair of the Property or to the sums secured by this Security Instrument, whether or not then due.

Unless Lender and Borrower otherwise agree in writing, any application of proceeds to principal shall not extend or postpone the due date of the monthly payments referred to in paragraphs 1 and 2 or change the amount of such payments.

**11. Borrower Not Released; Forbearance By Lender Not a Waiver.** Extension of the time for payment or modification of amortization of the sums secured by this Security Instrument granted by Lender to any successor in interest of Borrower shall not operate to release the liability of the original Borrower or Borrower's successors in interest. Lender shall not be required to commence proceedings against any successor in interest or refuse to extend time for payment or otherwise modify amortization of the sums secured by this Security Instrument by reason of any demand made by the original Borrower or Borrower's successors in interest. Any forbearance by Lender in exercising any right or remedy shall not be a waiver of or preclude the exercise of any right or remedy.

**12. Successors and Assigns Bound; Joint and Several Liability; Co-signers.** The covenants and agreements of this Security Instrument shall bind and benefit the successors and assigns of Lender and Borrower, subject to the provisions of paragraph 17. Borrower's covenants and agreements shall be joint and several. Any Borrower who co-signs this Security Instrument but does not execute the Note: (a) is co-signing this Security Instrument only to mortgage, grant and convey that Borrowers's interest in the Property under the terms of this Security Instrument; (b) is not personally obligated to pay the sums secured by this Security Instrument; and (c) agrees that Lender and any other Borrower may agree to extend, modify, forbear or make any accommodations with regard to the terms of this Security Instrument or the Note without that Borrower's consent.

**13. Loan Charges.** If the loan secured by this Security Instrument is subject to a law which sets maximum loan charges, and that law is finally interpreted so that the interest or other loan charges collected or to be collected in connection with the loan exceed the permitted limits, then: (a) any such loan charge shall be reduced by the amount necessary to reduce the charge to the permitted limit; and (b) any sums already collected from Borrower which exceeded permitted limits will be refunded to Borrower. Lender may choose to make this refund by reducing the principal owed under the Note or by making a direct payment to Borrower. If a refund reduces principal, the reduction will be treated as a partial prepayment without any prepayment charge under the Note.

**14. Notices.** Any notice to Borrower provided for in this Security Instrument shall be given by delivering it or by mailing it by first class mail unless applicable law requires use of another method. The notice shall be directed to the Property Address or any other address Borrower designates by notice to Lender. Any notice to Lender shall be given by first class mail to Lender's address stated herein or any other address Lender designates by notice to Borrower. Any notice provided for in this Security Instrument shall be deemed to have been given to Borrower or Lender when given as provided in this paragraph.

**15. Governing Law; Severability.** This Security Instrument shall be governed by federal law and the law of the jurisdiction in which the Property is located. In the event that any provision or clause of this Security Instrument or the Note conflicts with applicable law, such conflict shall not affect other provisions of this Security Instrument or the Note which can be given effect without the conflicting provision. To this end the provisions of this Security Instrument and the Note are declared to be severable.

**16. Borrower's Copy.** Borrower shall be given one conformed copy of the Note and of this Security Instrument.

**17. Transfer of the Property or a Beneficial Interest in Borrower.** If all or any part of the Property or any interest in it is sold or transferred (or if a beneficial interest in Borrower is sold or transferred and Borrower is not a natural person) without Lender's prior written consent, Lender may, at its option, require immediate payment in full of all sums secured by this Security Instrument. However, this option shall not be exercised by Lender if exercise is prohibited by federal law as of the date of this Security Instrument.

If Lender exercises this option, Lender shall give Borrower notice of acceleration. The notice shall provide a period of not less than 30 days from the date the notice is delivered or mailed within which Borrower must pay all sums secured by this Security Instrument. If Borrower fails to pay these sums prior to the expiration of this period, Lender may invoke any remedies permitted by this Security Instrument without further notice or demand on Borrower.

**18. Borrower's Right to Reinstate.** If Borrower meets certain conditions, Borrower shall have the right to have enforcement of this Security Instrument discontinued at any time prior to the earlier of: (a) 5 days (or such other period as applicable law may specify for reinstatement) before sale of the Property pursuant to any power of sale contained in this Security Instrument; or (b) entry of a judgment enforcing this Security Instrument. Those conditions are that Borrower: (a) pays Lender all sums which then would be due under this Security Instrument and the Note as if no acceleration had occurred; (b) cures any default of any other covenants or agreements; (c) pays all expenses incurred in enforcing this Security Instrument, including, but not limited to, reasonable attorneys' fees; and (d) takes such action as Lender may reasonably require to assure that the lien of this Security Instrument, Lender's rights in the Property and Borrower's obligation to pay the sums secured by this Security Instrument shall continue unchanged. Upon reinstatement by Borrower, this Security Instrument and the obligations secured hereby shall remain fully effective as if no acceleration had occurred. However, this right to reinstate shall not apply in the case of acceleration under paragraph 17.

**19. Sale of Note; Change of Loan Servicer.** The Note or a partial interest in the Note (together with this Security Instrument) may be sold one or more times without prior notice to Borrower. A sale may result in a change in the entity (known as the "Loan Servicer") that collects monthly payments due under the Note and this Security Instrument. There also may be one or more changes of the Loan Servicer unrelated to a sale of the Note. If there is a change of the Loan Servicer, Borrower will be given written notice of the change in accordance with paragraph 14 above and applicable law. The notice will state the name and address of the new Loan Servicer and the address to which payments should be made. The notice will also contain any other information required by applicable law.

**20. Hazardous Substances.** Borrower shall not cause or permit the presence, use, disposal, storage, or release of any Hazardous Substances on or in the Property. Borrower shall not do, nor allow anyone else to do, anything affecting the Property that is in violation of any Environmental Law. The preceding two sentences shall not apply to the presence, use, or storage on the Property of small quantities of Hazardous Substances that are generally recognized to be appropriate to normal residential uses and to maintenance of the Property.

Borrower shall promptly give Lender written notice of any investigation, claim, demand, lawsuit or other action by any governmental or regulatory agency or private party involving the Property and any Hazardous Substance or Environmental Law of which Borrower has actual knowledge. If Borrower learns, or is notified by any governmental or regulatory authority, that any removal or other remediation of any Hazardous Substance affecting the Property is necessary, Borrower shall promptly take all necessary remedial actions in accordance with Environmental Law.

As used in this paragraph 20, "Hazardous Substances" are those substances defined as toxic or hazardous substances by Environmental Law and the following substances: gasoline, kerosene, other flammable or toxic petroleum products, toxic pesticides and herbicides, volatile solvents, materials containing asbestos or formaldehyde, and radioactive materials. As used in this paragraph 20, "Environmental Law" means federal laws and laws of the jurisdiction where the Property is located that relate to health, safety or environmental protection.

NON-UNIFORM COVENANTS. Borrower and Lender further covenant and agree as follows:

**21. Acceleration; Remedies. Lender shall give notice to Borrower prior to acceleration following Borrower's breach of any covenant or agreement in this Security Instrument (but not prior to acceleration under paragraph 17 unless applicable law provides otherwise). The notice shall specify: (a) the default; (b) the action required to cure the default; (c) a date, not less than 30 days from the date the notice is given to Borrower, by which the default must be cured; and (d) that failure to cure the default on or before the date specified in the notice may result in acceleration of the sums secured by this Security Instrument and sale of the Property. The notice shall further inform Borrower of the right to reinstate after acceleration and the right to bring a court action to assert the non-existence of a default or any other defense of Borrower to acceleration and sale. If the default is not cured on or before the date specified in the notice, Lender at its option may require immediate payment in full of all sums secured by this Security Instrument without further demand and may invoke the power of sale and any other remedies permitted by applicable law. Lender shall be entitled to collect all expenses incurred in pursuing the remedies provided in this paragraph 21, including, but not limited to, reasonable attorneys' fees and costs of title evidence.**

**If Lender invokes the power of sale, Lender shall execute or cause Trustee to execute a written notice of the occurrence of an event of default and of Lender's election to cause the Property to be sold. Trustee shall cause this notice to be recorded in each county in which any part of the Property is located. Lender or Trustee shall mail copies of the notice as prescribed by applicable law to Borrower and to the other persons prescribed by applicable law. Trustee shall give public notice of sale to the persons and in the manner prescribed by applicable law. After the time required by applicable law, Trustee, without demand on Borrower, shall sell the Property at public auction to the highest bidder at the time and place and under the terms designated in the notice of sale in one or more parcels and in any order Trustee determines. Trustee may postpone sale of all or any parcel of the Property by public announcement at the time and place of any previously scheduled sale. Lender or its designee may purchase the Property at any sale.**

**Trustee shall deliver to the purchaser Trustee's deed conveying the Property without any covenant or warranty, expressed or implied. The recitals in the Trustee's deed shall be prima facie evidence of the truth of the statements made therein. Trustee shall apply the proceeds of the sale in the following order: (a) to all expenses of the sale, including, but not limited to, reasonable Trustee's and attorneys' fees; (b) to all sums secured by this Security Instrument; and (c) any excess to the person or persons legally entitled to it.**

**22. Reconveyance.** Upon payment of all sums secured by this Security Instrument, Lender shall request Trustee to reconvey the Property and shall surrender this Security Instrument and all notes evidencing debt secured by this Security Instrument to Trustee. Trustee shall reconvey the Property without warranty and without charge to the person or persons legally entitled to it. Such person or persons shall pay any recordation costs.

**23. Substitute Trustee.** Lender, at its option, may from time to time appoint a successor trustee to any Trustee appointed hereunder by an instrument executed and acknowledged by Lender and recorded in the office of the Recorder of the county in which the Property is located. The instrument shall contain the name of the original Lender, Trustee and Borrower, the book and page where this Security Instrument is recorded and the name and address of the successor trustee. Without conveyance of the Property, the successor trustee shall succeed to all the title, powers and duties conferred upon the Trustee herein and by applicable law. This procedure for substitution of trustee shall govern to the exclusion of all other provisions for substitution.

**24. Request for Notices.** Borrower request that copies of the notices of default and sale be sent to Borrower's address which is the Property Address.

**25. Statement of Obligation Fee.** Lender may collect a fee not to exceed the maximum amount permitted by law for furnishing the statement of obligation as provided by Section 2943 of the Civil Code of California.

**26. Riders to this Security Instrument.** If one or more riders are executed by Borrower and recorded together with this Security Instrument, the covenants and agreements of each such rider shall be incorporated into and shall amend and supplement the covenants and agreements of this Security Instrument as if the rider(s) were a part of this Security Instrument.
[Check applicable box(es)]

| | | |
|---|---|---|
| ☐ Adjustable Rate Rider | ☐ Condominium Rider | ☐ 1-4 Family Rider |
| ☐ Graduated Payment Rider | ☐ Planned Unit Development Rider | ☐ Biweekly Payment Rider |
| ☐ Balloon Rider | ☐ Rate Improvement Rider | ☐ Second Home Rider |
| ☐ Other(s) [specify] | | |

BY SIGNING BELOW, Borrower accepts and agrees to the terms and covenants contained in this Security Instrument and in any rider(s) executed by Borrower and recorded with it.

_____ (Seal)
                                                                    -Borrower

_____ (Seal)
                                                                    -Borrower

_____ (Seal)
                                                                    -Borrower

_____ (Seal)
                                                                    -Borrower

————————————————— [Space Below This Line For Acknowledgment] —————————————————

**State of California,**                                          **County ss:**

        On                              , before me,
personally appeared

known to me (or proved to me on the basis of satisfactory evidence) to be the person(s) whose name(s) is/are subscribed to the within instrument and acknowledged to me that he/she/they executed the same in his/her/their authorized capacity(ies), and that by his/her/their signature(s) on the instrument the person(s), or the entity upon behalf of which the person(s) acted, executed the instrument.

        WITNESS my hand and official seal.

Signature _____            (Seal)

                                                                    _____
                                                                    Name (typed or printed)

My commission expires:            **REQUEST FOR RECONVEYANCE**

TO TRUSTEE:
    The undersigned is the holder of the note or notes secured by this Deed of Trust. Said note or notes, together with all other indebtedness secured by this Deed of Trust, have been paid in full. You are hereby directed to cancel said note or notes and this Deed of Trust, which are delivered hereby, and to reconvey, without warranty, all the estate now held by you under this Deed of Trust to the person or persons legally entitled thereto.

    Dated:                                                _____

### c. Trustee

Legally, the trustee is a party to whom you transferred title (when you purchased or refinanced your property) to hold as security for repayment of the loan. Obviously, the trustee hasn't moved in and really exists only on paper. The trustee serves two practical functions:

• to conduct a foreclosure of your property if you default on your loan, or

• to return the deed of trust to you when you repay your loan in full (called "reconveyance").

To conduct a foreclosure or to reconvey (return) a deed of trust, a trustee will not act on his or her own. A trustee will become involved only upon the request of the beneficiary—your lender. Institutional lenders, such as banks or savings and loan associations, typically name their own subsidiary corporations as trustees in their deeds of trust. Private lenders often have title companies or independent foreclosure companies act as their trustees.

## 2. Reviewing Your Deed of Trust

If you do not have a copy of the recorded deed of trust, request one from your lender or the foreclosing trustee. If neither has a copy readily available, call a local title insurance company and request a copy. If you can't afford the fee or are in a do-it-yourself mood, visit the county recorder's office in the county where your property is located. You can obtain a copy of the deed of trust for a nominal fee.

### Deed of Trust Breakdown

1. Lender's name and address: The lender's name, street address, city and state are entered here so that the recorded deed is returned to the lender.

2. County recorder identification: This area contains the county recorder's stamp, which reflects the time and date the deed was recorded and the fee paid to have it recorded. If this is blank, you probably have a copy of the deed before it was recorded. It is possible the deed was never recorded, but unlikely.

3. Date of execution: This is the date you signed the deed of trust.

4. Trustor(s): This blank contains the name(s) of the borrower(s).

5. Trustor's address: This is where your address goes. If you move, it is your responsibility to notify the trustee and beneficiary of your address.

6. Trustee: The name of the trustee.

7. Beneficiary: The name of your lender.

8. Location of real property security: The county in which your property is located.

9. Legal description of your property: The full legal description of your property typically includes the lot, block and tract, metes and bounds, or a government survey description.

10. Principal amount of loan: This is the principal amount you borrowed.

11. Acknowledgment: A formal written declaration, before a notary public, that you signed the deed of trust willfully.

12. Signature(s) of trustor(s): Your signature (and that of any co-property owners) is here.

13. Boilerplate language: Every deed of trust refers to the promissory note, the amount it secures and the location in each county (book and page number) of a document of legal requirements you must adhere to.

A sample Deed of Trust Worksheet appears below, and a tear-out copy is included in the Appendix. Use it to record the relevant terms and conditions in your deed of trust.

| DEED OF TRUST WORKSHEET | |
|---|---|
| Date recorded: | July 13, 199X |
| Date signed: | July 10, 199X |
| Trustor: | John and Susan Ross |
| Trustee: | California Reconveyance Corp. |
| Beneficiary: | 9% adjustable |
| County in which property is located: | Humboldt County |
| Legal description: | Lot 5, Parcel 23, Page 356, Book 465 |
| Principal amount borrowed: | $175,000 |
| Date notarized: | July 10, 199X |
| Did you sign the deed of trust? yes/no | Yes |

## 3. A Deed of Trust Is Recorded

Each county in California has a recorder's office, which keeps files on all real property in that county. The recorder's office tracks who owns property, who claims any interest in a piece of property (such as an easement—a claim of a right to use a portion of someone's property), and what liens (including deeds of trust) have been recorded against each piece of property. Any property that has one or more liens recorded against it is said to be "encumbered." The recorder's office is open to the public and you can review the county records with respect to your property at no cost (photocopies will cost you, however). To get started, the only information you will need is your street address. If you have difficulty, there are clerks available to help you. If you don't want to bother with the recorder's office, you can contact a title insurance company that will do it for you for free or a small fee.

## 4. Multiple Lienholders

More than one deed of trust can encumber your property. In fact, it is not unusual to see several deeds of trust recorded against a single property.

The lender holding the first deed of trust is considered the "senior" lienholder and has the first right to be paid in a foreclosure sale or if you sell or refinance your property. All other lenders holding subsequently recorded deeds of trust (or any other type of lien) are called "junior lienholder."

*Example: John owns a house in Los Angeles. Two deeds of trust encumber his property. The first is held by Los Angeles Savings Bank, which loaned John the money to purchase the house. The second deed of trust is held by Second Home Loan Company, which loaned money to John to remodel his kitchen. If John defaults on his payments and Los Angeles Savings conducts a foreclosure sale, Los Angeles Savings will be paid first as the senior lienholder. Any excess proceeds from the sale will go towards paying off Second Home Loan, the junior lienholder.*

## 5. Your Obligations Under a Deed of Trust

When you signed the deed of trust, you agreed to undertake five obligations. If you default on any of these, the property may legally be foreclosed upon. The five requirements are to:
- pay the promissory note according to its terms
- insure the property and keep insurance payments current

- maintain and keep the property in good repair
- pay property taxes assessed against the property, and
- get consent from the lender before selling the property.

### a. Paying the Promissory Note

A deed of trust requires that you repay your loan according to the terms of your promissory note. Most importantly, you must make your payments on time. Late or missed payments are the most common causes of foreclosure.

*Reality check.* In most situations, one late payment will not cause your lender to initiate foreclosure. More likely, your lender will send you a threatening letter and report the late payments to a credit reporting agency (credit bureau). Typically, lenders wait until payments are at least three to four months in arrears before initiating foreclosure. Nevertheless, a single late payment provides your lender with the legal right to start a foreclosure.

### b. Maintaining and Repairing the Property

Most property owners diligently maintain their property and keep it in good repair no matter what their deeds of trust require. As long as you are current on your payments, if your lender becomes aware of some deterioration, you would probably receive a phone call or letter demanding that you maintain your property as you agreed to in the deed of trust. People who do not maintain their property also tend to default on payments, which would inevitably lead to foreclosure.

### c. Paying Property Taxes

Your deed of trust requires you to promptly pay all taxes and related charges assessed against your property. Here's why lenders include this provision.

The most common taxes are property taxes (assessed by the county on a semi-annual basis) and special tax liens (assessed by cities, counties, water districts and other government bodies). These property and special tax liens always take priority over deeds of trusts and other liens, regardless of when the tax liens are recorded. If you don't pay these taxes and your property is foreclosed on or you sell or refinance, the taxing authority will be paid before your lender. If the sale doesn't cover both the tax lien and what you owe on your note, your lender won't get all that is owed.

To avoid this problem, lenders will typically pay your past due taxes if your property is already in foreclosure. In that event, the amount you need to bring your loan current will include the amount of taxes your lender paid on your behalf.

### d. Insuring Your Property

Your obligation to keep your property insured protects your lender in the event you abandon your property—perhaps after a fire or flood. Without insurance in such a situation, your lender would have a worthless piece of property and could collect only by suing you. With insurance, if you abandon the property, your lender can use the proceeds to either pay off your loan or rebuild the structure.

Virtually all deeds of trust require that you maintain hazard insurance for at least the amount of your loan, to protect against damage to your property caused by fire or other destruction. Check your deed of trust for other requirements. Institutional lenders generally require fire and extended coverage insurance, which covers most damage to your property except flood and earthquakes. Few lenders require earthquake insurance because of the high cost. Similarly, lenders rarely require flood insurance unless your property is located in a designated flood-hazard zone.

Lenders will typically purchase insurance for your property if they discover it is not insured during the foreclosure. They then add the insurance cost to the amount you need to cure the default.

### e. Selling Your Property Only With Lender Approval

Almost all deeds of trust today include what is known as a "due-on-sale" clause. The due-on-sale clause requires that you notify your lender when you sell your property. In most situations, this situation resolves itself because the buyer will obtain a new loan to pay off your existing lender. However, there may be a problem if you sell your property without your lender's permission. This is because the due-on-sale clause allows your lender to declare the entire balance immediately due and payable even though you may have years left on your loan. Keep in mind that a due-on-sale clause does not prohibit you from selling your property. It simply requires that you either pay off your existing loan or have the new buyer assume the loan when you sell your property. If you don't, your lender has the right to foreclose.

Due-on-sale clauses are used by lenders to protect themselves in case interest rates rise after the loan is taken out. By forcing you to notify your lender when you sell your property, your lender can have the old lower interest loan paid off, or demand that the buyer assume the existing loan by paying the current (presumably higher) market rate of interest. In addition, by using a due-on-sale

clause, the lender can earn fees for processing the new loan.

*Example: Shirley and Edward own a single-family residence in San Diego. San Diego Savings Bank holds the first deed of trust, which secures a $75,000 loan at 6.5% interest. The deed of trust has a due-on-sale clause. Without notifying San Diego Savings, Shirley and Edward sell their property to Henry, who agrees to purchase the property with the existing low interest rate loan. Although Henry will make the payments, Shirley and Edward remain liable on the loan. After escrow closes, San Diego Savings discovers the sale and immediately notifies Shirley and Edward that it has accelerated their loan because they violated the due-on-sale clause. If Shirley and Edward do not pay off their loan within 30 days, San Diego Savings will begin foreclosure proceedings. Henry must pay off San Diego Savings by using his own funds or obtaining a new loan from another bank, or he will risk losing the property in foreclosure.*

*chapter*

# 3

# NONJUDICIAL FORECLOSURES

A nonjudicial foreclosure is a procedure in which your lender has your property sold to recover money you owe after you've defaulted on your loan. The conditions under which your lender may institute a nonjudicial foreclosure are addressed in your deed of trust. (Refer back to Chapter 2, Section B, for information on the deed of trust.)

## A. Overview of Nonjudicial Foreclosure

The main feature of a nonjudicial foreclosure is that your lender can have your property auctioned without going to court. Because courts do not oversee the foreclosure process, state law requires the trustee—the person authorized by your lender to conduct the foreclosure—to follow strict procedures before selling your property. (Cal. Civil Code [CC] § 2924.) If the trustee sells the property for less than the full amount of its loan, your lender must accept whatever is received and cannot pursue you for the difference (deficiency).

*Judicial foreclosures are covered in Chapter 4.* Another type of foreclosure, called a judicial foreclosure, is used much less frequently in California. Judicial foreclosures use the court system and allow deficiency judgments (the lender may collect the balance due on the loan if the sale doesn't cover it). In California, lenders can initiate both a judicial and nonjudicial foreclosure.

### 1. Nonjudicial Foreclosures Can Be Stopped

Property owners often misunderstand the nonjudicial foreclosure process. Most believe once it begins, it can't be stopped and that it happens quickly. A nonjudicial foreclosure takes at least 111 days, however, and frequently longer. During this period, you have the right to stop the foreclosure and save your property. You must receive adequate and timely notice of the upcoming foreclosure sale. If the trustee does not properly conduct the procedures, you have grounds to stop the foreclosure by filing a lawsuit in court and obtaining a temporary restraining order. (See Chapter 8 for more on temporary restraining orders.)

What is crucial for you to understand is that even after a nonjudicial foreclosure has begun, you still have a period of time to stop it. Rather than throwing in the towel, you should envision this time period as a "window of opportunity" to either save your property or sell it! In this chapter, you will learn various strategies you can use to accomplish these goals while the foreclosure is pending.

### 2. The Nonjudicial Foreclosure Timetable

A nonjudicial foreclosure consists of five basic steps, summarized below in the Nonjudicial Foreclosure Timeline and covered in detail in the rest of this chapter. Once you learn each of the steps, you will better understand how and when to utilize the strategies described in this book.

## B. Notice of Default and Election to Sell

A nonjudicial foreclosure begins when the trustee issues a document called a Notice of Default and Election to Sell (or simply a Notice of Default). The Notice of Default, which must be mailed to you, notifies you that because you have defaulted on

## NONJUDICIAL FORECLOSURE TIMELINE

| ACTION | WHEN | PURPOSE |
| --- | --- | --- |
| Trustee sends borrower a Notice of Default and Election to Sell ("Notice of Default") | Sometime after loan has gone into default—usually several months. Trustee must comply with time requirements for recording and giving notice | Gives borrower notice that loan is in default and trustee has begun judicial foreclosure proceedings |
| Reinstatement period | A minimum of three months and 16 days from date trustee issues Notice of Default | Gives borrower opportunity to bring loan current by paying arrears, lender's costs and expenses |
| Notice of Trustee's Sale | Trustee sends notice to borrower a minimum of three months from date trustee issued Notice of Default | Informs borrower where and when property will be sold (a minimum of 20 days after Notice of Trustee's Sale was issued) |
| Redemption period | Last 5 business days before trustee's sale | Borrower may stop foreclosure by paying off entire balance of loan plus foreclosure costs |
| Trustee's sale | Date listed on Notice of Trustee's Sale, which must be at least 20 days after Notice of Trustee's Sale was issued | Trustee sells property at a public auction. Trustee gives buyer a Trustee's Deed Upon Sale and distributes proceeds within about a week |

your loan a nonjudicial foreclosure has started to sell your property to pay off your loan. The trustee prepares the Notice of Default only upon the request of your lender.

## 1. Contents of the Notice of Default

Although the Notice of Default may be a few pages long, you are primarily interested in the following important information:

- your name (you're the trustor)
- the book and page number in the county recorder's office where your deed of trust was recorded

- a statement that your promissory note or deed of trust is in default
- a cursory description of your defaults, such as missed payments, delinquent property taxes and unpaid insurance, and
- a statement that your lender has elected to sell your property to satisfy the debt.

A sample Notice of Default and Election to Sell appears below (in italics). Each paragraph in this sample is followed with an explanation. Use this information to review any Notice of Default you receive.

RECORDING REQUESTED BY

California Trustee Corporation
1234 Wilshire Blvd.
Los Angeles, California 90012

WHEN RECORDED MAIL TO
California Trustee Corporation       TRUSTEE'S SALE NO. 3422
1234 Wilshire Blvd.
Los Angeles, CA 90012

SPACE ABOVE THIS LINE FOR RECORDER'S USE

## NOTICE OF DEFAULT AND ELECTION TO SELL UNDER DEED OF TRUST
### IMPORTANT NOTICE

IF YOUR PROPERTY IS IN FORECLOSURE BECAUSE YOU ARE BEHIND IN YOUR LOAN PAYMENTS, IT MAY BE SOLD WITHOUT ANY COURT ACTION, and you may have the legal right to bring your account in good standing by paying all of your past due payments plus permitted costs and expenses within the time permitted by law for reinstatement of your account, which is normally five business days prior to the date set for the sale of your property.

*[This paragraph explains that your property is in foreclosure because you did not make your loan payments to your lender and that it may be sold without any court action. It states that you have the legal right to bring your loan current by paying all of your past due payments plus the costs your lender and the trustee incurred in foreclosing. You can pay this until five days prior to the foreclosure sale.]*

No sale date may be set until three months from the date this Notice of Default may be recorded (which date of recordation appears on this notice). This amount is $ 178,000 as of July 1, 199X, and will increase until your account becomes current.

*[The date of the foreclosure sale cannot be scheduled until three months after the Notice of Default was recorded. The amount needed to reinstate the loan is calculated as of the date of the Notice. The amount will increase, because of interest and foreclosure fees, until you bring your loan current.]*

While your property is in foreclosure, you still must pay other obligations (such as insurance and taxes) required by your note and deed of trust. If you fail to make future payments on the loan, pay taxes on the property, provide insurance on the property, or pay other obligations as required in the note and deed of trust or mortgage, the beneficiary or mortgagee may insist that you do so in order to reinstate your account in good standing. In addition, the beneficiary may require as a condition to reinstatement that you provide reliable written evidence that you paid all senior liens, property taxes, and hazard insurance premiums.

*[Even though your property is in foreclosure, you must still pay insurance, taxes and senior liens (if any) as they come due. If you fail to make any of these payments, the trustee may pay these expenses and add them to the amount you must pay to bring your loan current.]*

Upon your written request, the beneficiary or mortgagee will give you a written itemization of the entire amount you must pay.

*[You have the right to request that your lender send a "beneficiary statement," in which your lender itemizes the amount you must pay to reinstate your loan. See paragraph below.]*

You may not have to pay the entire unpaid portion of your account, even though full payment was demanded, but you must pay all amounts in default at the time payment is made. However, you and your beneficiary or mortgagee may mutually agree in writing prior to the time the Notice of Sale is posted (which may not be earlier than the end of the three-month period stated above) to, among other things, (1) provide additional time in which to cure the default by transfer of the property or otherwise; (2) establish a schedule of payments in order to cure your default; or both (1) and (2).

*[This paragraph explains that although your lender may have accelerated your loan and demanded full payment, you do not have to pay the full amount. To reinstate (bring your loan current), you have to pay the amount in default plus any additional interest and foreclosure costs that have accrued since the Notice of Default was recorded. Further, you have the right to negotiate with your lender to either: (1) allow additional time to cure your loan or sell your property, (2) set up a mutually agreeable schedule of payments, or both.]*

Following the expiration of the time period referred to in the first paragraph of this notice, unless the obligation being foreclosed upon or a separate written agreement between you and your lender permits a longer period, you have the legal right to stop the sale of your property by paying only the entire amount demanded by your lender. To find out the amount you must pay, or to arrange for payment to stop the foreclosure, or if your property is in foreclosure for any other reason, contact the trustee listed at the end of this notice.

*[At the end of the reinstatement period (five days before the foreclosure sale), unless you have cured the default or entered into a written agreement with your lender to extend the reinstatement period, you can stop the foreclosure by paying the entire unpaid balance of your loan plus costs.]*

If you have any questions, you should contact a lawyer or the governmental agency which may have insured your loan.

Notwithstanding the fact that your property is in foreclosure, you may offer your property for sale, provided the sale is concluded prior to the conclusion of the foreclosure.

*[Although the foreclosure is pending, you still have the right to sell your property, as long as you do so before the foreclosure sale date. We explore the option of selling your property in Chapter 11.]*

REMEMBER, YOU MAY LOSE LEGAL RIGHTS IF YOU DO NOT TAKE PROMPT ACTION.

FOR FURTHER INFORMATION, CONTACT:

California Trustee Corporation
0000 Wilshire Blvd.
Los Angeles, CA 90012
213-222-2345

## 2. Notice Requirements for Notice of Default

The trustee must follow strict time formalities for recording, mailing and publishing the Notice of Default to ensure that you receive adequate legal notice of the pending foreclosure. If the trustee fails to follow any of these procedures, you will probably have a legal basis to stop the foreclosure.

*There's no requirement that you receive actual notice of the foreclosure.* The foreclosure remains valid as long as the trustee carried out the notification process properly. It doesn't matter if you were out of the country, in the hospital or for some other reason didn't get a copy of the Notice of Default.

### a. Recording Notice of Default

The trustee must record the Notice of Default in the county recorder's office for the county in which your property is located. Occasionally, a trustee will forget to record the Notice of Default or mistakenly record it against the wrong property.

You can find out if the Notice of Default was properly recorded by searching the property records at the recorder's office or asking the customer service department of a local title insurance company for assistance.

If the Notice of Default was not recorded or was improperly recorded, the foreclosure is invalid. In that case, you can demand that it be stopped until the trustee starts the foreclosure all over again from the beginning by issuing a new Notice of Default. To do this, send a letter to the trustee advising her of the failure to properly record the Notice of Default and demanding that she start over.

Some property owners wait until late in the foreclosure process before advising the trustee of its mistake. Since the trustee will have to reissue the Notice of Default, which requires that a 3-month period elapse before the Notice of Trustee's Sale can be issued, the property owner will have that much more time to navigate the situation.

### b. Mailing Notice of Default to You

Within ten business days of recording the Notice of Default, the trustee must mail you two copies—one copy by registered or certified mail and the other copy by regular first-class mail. They will be sent to your address listed in your original deed of trust, or to your last known address, if it is different.

If the trustee sends the Notices to the wrong address, and you are certain you gave the lender your current address, the trustee must start over.

*Example: Trudy owns a rental home in Salinas. Trudy's old address appears on the recorded deed of trust. Trudy moved and notified her lender, California Savings Bank, of her new address. When Trudy missed several monthly loan payments, California Savings instructed its trustee to start a nonjudicial foreclosure. The trustee mailed a copy of the Notice of Default to Trudy at the address listed in the deed of trust, but didn't send a copy to her new address. When Trudy's tenant revealed that a foreclosure had been started, Trudy wrote a letter to the trustee demanding that the foreclosure be stopped. The trustee had no choice but to comply and start the foreclosure process over.*

*Make sure your lender has your current address.* This is particularly important if you don't live in or receive mail at the property that is in foreclosure. The trustee is only obligated to send a Notice of Default to the address listed in the deed of trust or the last address you gave your lender. If the trustee doesn't have your current address, he or she can simply mail the Notice of Default to the address on the deed of trust and publish a copy of the Notice of Default in a local newspaper (once a week for at least four weeks). In this event, there's a good chance you'll never see the notice.

### c. Mailing Notice of Default to Others Affected

Within 30 days of recording, the trustee must also mail, by first-class and certified mail, a Notice of Default to:

- tenants living on your property
- any creditors who hold a deed of trust on your property junior to your foreclosing lender
- anyone claiming an interest in your property (by recording a lien, such as mechanic's lien, tax lien, or judgment lien in the county recorder's office), and
- anyone else who would be affected by the foreclosure, including people who purchased your property from you (if you're still liable to pay the promissory note, as explained in Chapter 2, Section B4e) and people who are under contract to buy your property.

### d. Publishing Notice of Default

The trustee is not ordinarily required to publish the Notice of Default. However, if either the first-class mailing or certified mailing of the Notice of Default is returned by the post office and the trustee has no other current address, he or she must publish the Notice of Default in a newspaper of general circula-tion in the county where your property is located once a week for at least four weeks. The publication must commence within 10 business days after the recording of the Notice of Default.

### e. Posting Notice of Default Is Optional

Although not required to do so, trustees frequently post a copy of the Notice of Default on the front door or another conspicuous place on the property. Such posting often takes place even before you receive the Notice of Default in the mail.

## 3. Complete a Notice of Default Worksheet

Assemble your promissory note, deed of trust and Notice of Default. Then use the following self-explanatory Notice of Default Worksheet to make sure the trustee complies with all notice and mailing requirements. Remember, if the trustee makes a mistake along the way, you have grounds to stop the foreclosure. A tear-out copy of the worksheet is included in the Appendix.

## NOTICE OF DEFAULT WORKSHEET (NONJUDICIAL FORECLOSURE)

ARE THE FOLLOWING CORRECT ON THE NOTICE OF DEFAULT,
AND CONSISTENT WITH INFORMATION ON YOUR PROMISSORY NOTE AND DEED OF TRUST?

| | | | |
|---|---|---|---|
| Name of trustor (you and any co-signers)? | ☐ No | ☐ Yes | Name: |
| Name of beneficiary (lender)? | ☐ No | ☐ Yes | Name: |
| Name of trustee? | ☐ No | ☐ Yes | Name: |
| Information about recording of deed of trust? | ☐ No | ☐ Yes | Date: |
| Legal description of the property? | | Document No.: | Book/Page No.: |
| Amount of original indebtedness? | | | |
| Amount in default? | ☐ No | ☐ Yes | Amount: |

RECORDING REQUIREMENTS

| | | | |
|---|---|---|---|
| Was the Notice of Default recorded in the recorder's office for the county in which your property is located? | ☐ No | ☐ Yes | When: |

MAILING REQUIREMENTS

| | | | |
|---|---|---|---|
| Was a copy of the Notice of Default mailed to you by certified or registered mail within ten business days of recording? | ☐ No | ☐ Yes | When: |
| Was a copy of the Notice of Default mailed to you by first-class mail within ten business days of recording? | ☐ No | ☐ Yes | When: |
| Within 30 days of recording, was a copy of the Notice mailed by first-class mail to everyone entitled to receive the Notice—including tenants, junior beneficiaries and anyone who recorded a Request for Notice? (You will need to call them and ask them if they received the Notice.) | ☐ No | ☐ Yes | When: |

PUBLICATION REQUIREMENTS

| | | | |
|---|---|---|---|
| If the trustee did not have your correct address, was the Notice of Default published in a newspaper of general circulation once a week for at least four weeks? (You have the right to ask the trustee to see its Affidavit of Publication and copies of the newspapers.) | ☐ No | ☐ Yes | 1st Date: |
| | | | 2nd Date: |
| | | | 3rd Date: |
| | | | 4th Date: |

## 4. Request Beneficiary Statement From Your Lender

You have the legal right to get information from your lender about your defaulted loan. In legal jargon, this is known as your right to receive a beneficiary statement. (CC § 2943.) As soon as you receive a Notice of Default, write to the foreclosing lender (also send a copy to the trustee) and request a beneficiary statement. Follow the guidelines of the sample letter below.

This request will show your lender that you are serious about avoiding foreclosure and saving your property. In addition, the information will help you confirm the accuracy of the Notice of Default and other documents you receive during the foreclosure process. Your lender must respond to your written request for a beneficiary statement within two months after the Notice of Default was filed and within 21 days of your written request.

September 10, 199X

Foreclosure Department
Submarine Savings and Loan
21 May Avenue
Eureka, California

Loan Number: 645-567

Property: 3434 Laurel Street, Mendocino, California

To whom it may concern:

Your company holds a deed of trust recorded against my property securing a promissory note in the original amount of $125,000. On September 1, I received a Notice of Default and Election to Sell from your trustee.

Pursuant to California Civil Code Section 2943, please send me a beneficiary statement, including the following information, as soon as possible:

(1) Copy of my promissory note.

(2) Copy of recorded deed of trust.

(3) Unpaid balance of my loan.

(4) Current fixed or variable interest rate.

(5) Total amount of all overdue installments of principal and interest.

(6) The end of the term of the loan.

(7) Date through which real estate taxes and assessments have been paid by you, if any.

(8) Amount of hazard insurance and the premium you paid, if any.

(9) Balance of any tax or insurance impound accounts in your possession.

(10) Amount of any additional costs and expenses you have paid, including trustee's expenses.

(11) Whether or not I can transfer the loan to a new borrower (that is, whether or not the loan is assumable).

Please send me this information as soon as possible. If you have any questions, please call me at (707)544-8787.

Very truly yours,

Susan Young
3434 Laurel Street
Mendocino, CA

## C. The Reinstatement Period

The reinstatement period starts as soon as the Notice of Default is issued and ends five business days prior to the foreclosure sale. During the reinstatement period, you can stop the foreclosure by simply bringing your loan current (CC § 2924c) by paying the following:

- the amount of overdue principal, interest and late fees stated in the Notice of Default
- monthly payments that come due after the Notice of Default was recorded
- attorney fees incurred by your lender to collect your payments
- any tax or insurance payments advanced by your lender, and
- trustee's fees (the cost to process the nonjudicial foreclosure, including expenses to record, mail, publish and post notices).

---

**LIMITATION ON TRUSTEE'S FEES**

In California, the trustee can't charge more than the total of all of the following:

- $200 on the first $50,000 or less of the unpaid principal of your loan
- 0.5% of the unpaid principal sum between $50,000 and $150,000
- 0.25% of any portion of the unpaid principal between $150,000 and $500,000, plus
- 0.125% for any amounts over $500,000. (CC §§ 2924c(a), 2924c(d) and 2924(d).)

---

As the foreclosure continues, the amount needed to reinstate your loan will increase daily as interest accrues and the trustee incurs additional expenses.

*Example: Albert owns a condominium in Los Angeles, and makes monthly payments of $1,400 on his $150,000 promissory note. Albert missed three monthly payments before First Fidelity started a nonjudicial foreclosure by having its trustee record a Notice of Default on April 1. The Notice of Default states that Albert owes $5,200. He is behind his payments by $4,200 and has incurred $1,000 in foreclosure fees, for a total of $5,200 as of April 1. Albert wants to stop the foreclosure by bringing his loan current. However, the longer he waits, the more he will have to pay to reinstate his loan as it continues to accrue interest and the trustee incurs more costs:*

| Date | Monthly Payment | Trustee Fees | Total to Reinstate |
|---|---|---|---|
| *May 1* | $1,400 | $250 | $6,850 |
| *June 1* | 1,400 | 250 | 8,500 |
| *July 1* | 1,400 | 250 | 10,150 |

### 1. Contact the Trustee

If you can reinstate your loan, your first step is to contact the trustee. Find out exactly how much you'll need to reinstate your loan as of a certain date. The trustee is required to give you this information.

If you agree with the trustee's figures, purchase a cashier's check for that amount. If you disagree with the amount, you may need to contact your lender to get the correct payoff or file a lawsuit to determine the correct amount. (See Chapter 8 for more about filing a lawsuit to stop the foreclosure.)

Once you purchase a cashier's check, take it to the trustee's office and exchange it for a receipt. If the trustee is out of town, send the cashier's check by certified or registered mail.

Assuming it is for the right amount, the trustee must accept your payment and stop the foreclosure. If the trustee refuses to accept, you have grounds for asking a judge to enjoin the foreclosure (see Chapter 8).

Once the trustee accepts your payment, request that he record a Notice of Rescission in the county recorder's office (which officially withdraws the Notice of Default and terminates the foreclosure) and mail a copy of the recorded notice to you.

## 2. Partial Payments During the Reinstatement Period

In general, lenders will not accept partial payments of arrears during the reinstatement period. If a lender accepts a partial payment, it becomes susceptible to later claims that you paid because your lender agreed to delay or stop the foreclosure. Courts tend to view with suspicion a lender that accepts a partial payment and then continues with foreclosure.

With that said, some lenders will accept partial payments and agree to temporarily postpone the foreclosure. You will, however, need to convince your lender that you can bring the loan current within a reasonable period of time. Of course, you won't know whether your lender is open to this suggestion until you ask. (See Chapter 5 for more on negotiating with your lender.)

If your lender agrees to accept a partial payment during the reinstatement period, keep in mind that it will not extend the reinstatement period, or stop the foreclosure, unless it specifically agrees in writing to do this. If you convince your lender to extend the foreclosure to give you extra time to bring your loan current, you should document the agreement in a letter similar to the sample below.

February 9, 199X

Advanced Savings Bank
2345 Main Street
Oxnard, California

Loan: 45289M

Property: 21 Hill Street, Oxnard, California

Dear Mr. Sanchez:

As you know, a foreclosure is currently pending against my property. The total amount to bring my loan current is approximately $31,300. As I previously explained to you, I cannot afford to pay the full amount at this time.

You have agreed to accept a partial payment in the amount of $12,000 (enclosed with this letter) and postpone the foreclosure sale for 90 days. I understand that if I fail to bring my loan current by May 9, you will conduct a foreclosure sale.

If this letter accurately reflects our agreement, please sign in the space below and return one copy of this letter to me. If this letter is not accurate, please advise me immediately in writing and return my check.

Very truly yours,

Henry Gold
805-669-4354

AGREED AS TO FORM AND CONTENT:

ADVANCED SAVINGS BANK

By: _____

Authorized Officer

# D. Notice of Trustee's Sale

If you do not bring your loan current within three months after the Notice of Default was issued, the trustee will issue a Notice of Trustee's Sale, or simply a Notice of Sale. (CC § 2924.) The Notice of Sale gives the date, time and location of the foreclosure sale of your property.

The foreclosure sale must be scheduled at least 20 calendar days after the Notice of Sale was issued. (CC § 2924f(b).) Because of this, trustee's sales are typically scheduled 21–25 days after the Notice of

Sale is issued to avoid the sale date falling on a weekend or holiday.

*The reinstatement period continues after the Notice of Trustee's Sale is issued.* The issuance of the Notice of Trustee's Sale has no effect on the reinstatement period. The reinstatement period continues to run until five business days before the foreclosure sale.

## 1. Contents of the Notice of Trustee's Sale

When you receive a Notice of Trustee's Sale, you may be inclined to put it aside. Don't. Take the time to read it carefully. If you discover inaccuracies in the Notice of Sale, you can buy yourself some time by demanding that the trustee correct the information and record a new Notice of Sale. Any time a trustee records a corrected Notice of Sale, he or she must reschedule the trustee's sale, which will delay the foreclosure for at least an additional 20 days.

Carefully check the following on the Notice of Sale:

• that the date of the sale is more than 20 calendar days after issuance of the Notice of Sale (not the date you received the notice)

• that it names a specific location where the sale will be conducted, and

• the description of your property is the same as in your note, deed of trust and Notice of Default (your street address need not be provided). (CC § 2924f(b).)

Following is an example of a Notice of Trustee's Sale, with explanations for each paragraph.

## 2. Notice Requirements for Notice of Sale

The trustee must comply with strict procedural requirements for the Notice of Sale to be valid. If the trustee fails to follow the required mailing, recording, publishing and posting procedures, you can demand that she record a new Notice of Sale. If she refuses, you have the right to file a lawsuit in Superior Court to have the foreclosure enjoined. (See Chapter 8).

*There's no requirement that you receive actual notice of the trustee's sale.* The trustee's sale remains valid as long as the trustee carried out the notification process properly. It doesn't matter if you were out of the country, in the hospital or for some other reason didn't get a copy of the Notice.

### a. Mailing Notice of Sale to You

At least 20 calendar days before the scheduled sale date, the Notice of Sale must be mailed to you by certified or registered mail, as well as by first-class mail.

### b. Mailing Notice of Sale to Others Affected

Copies must also be sent by certified (or registered) mail and by first-class mail to anyone else entitled to receive the Notice of Default, such as junior lienholders and tenants leasing your property.

### c. Recording Notice of Sale

The Notice of Sale doesn't have to be recorded until 14 days before the sale date, although it may be recorded earlier. (CC § 2924f(b).)

RECORDING REQUESTED BY

WHEN RECORDED MAIL TO
San Diego Reconveyance Co.
1234 Riverfront Drive
San Diego, CA

NOTICE OF TRUSTEE'S SALE
NO. 2651-002-011

SPACE ABOVE THIS LINE FOR RECORDER'S USE

## NOTICE OF TRUSTEE'S SALE

YOU ARE IN DEFAULT UNDER A DEED OF TRUST, <u>May 3</u>, 199X. UNLESS YOU TAKE ACTION TO PROTECT YOUR PROPERTY, IT MAY BE SOLD AT A PUBLIC SALE. IF YOU NEED AN EXPLANATION OF THE NATURE OF THE PROCEEDING AGAINST YOU, YOU SHOULD CONTACT A LAWYER.

*[This paragraph explains that you are in default under your deed of trust and that unless you do something, your property will be sold at a public auction.]*

On _____ September 26, _____ at _____ 10:00 a.m. _____ ,

_____ San Diego Reconveyance _____ ,

as duly appointed Trustee under and pursuant to Deed of Trust recorded on __ May 28, 199X __ , as Instrument No. <u>9X-875890</u>, in book N/A, page N/A, of Official Records in the office of the County Recorder of San Diego County, State of California, WILL SELL AT PUBLIC ACTION TO HIGHEST BIDDER FOR CASH (payable at time of sale in lawful money of the United States) at the <u>front entrance to the San Diego Municipal Courts Building, 350 W. Harbor Blvd., San Diego, California</u> , all right, title and interest conveyed to and now held by it under said Deed of Trust in the property situated in said County and State described as:

COMPLETE DESCRIPTION IN DEED OF TRUST

*[This paragraph specifies the date, time and location where the trustee will sell your property to the highest bidder.]*

The street address and other common designation, if any, of the real property described above is purported to be:

_____ 655 Miller Street, La Jolla, CA _____

The undersigned Trustee disclaims any liability for any incorrectness of the street address and other common designation, if any, shown herein.

*[The trustee gives the legal description of your property, and sometimes the street address, and states that she is not responsible for the street address or property description, if it later turns out to be wrong.]*

Said sale will be made, but without covenant or warranty, express or implied, regarding title, possession, or encumbrances, to pay the remaining principal sum of the note(s) secured by said Deed of Trust, with interest thereon, as provided in said note(s), advances, if any, under the terms of said Deed of Trust, fees, charges and expenses of the Trustee and of the trusts created by said Deed of Trust.

*[The property will be sold without any warranty or promises about the condition of the property, or the title to the property, or whether there are any senior liens on the property.]*

The total amount of the unpaid balance of the obligation secured by the property to be sold and reasonable estimated costs, expenses and advances at the time of the initial publication of the Notice of Sale is ___$175,454.34___ .

*[This paragraph gives the total outstanding amount of your loan, plus expenses, on the date of the Notice of Sale.]*

The beneficiary under said Deed of Trust heretofore executed and delivered to the undersigned a written Declaration of Default and Demand for Sale, and a written Notice of Default and Election to Sell. The undersigned caused said Notice of Default and Election to Sell to be recorded in the county where the real property is located.

*[Your lender (the beneficiary) notified the trustee that you were in default and asked the trustee to sell your property. The trustee then followed proper procedures by recording a Notice of Default in the county where your property is located.]*

Date: ___May 3, 199X___

San Diego Reconveyance Co., as said trustee

1234 Riverfront Drive

San Diego, California

(619) 204-6400, Extension 336

By: _____

Alice Stahls

Authorized Officer

*Don't confuse deadlines.* Borrowers sometimes mix up requirements for Notices of Default and Notices of Trustee's Sale and incorrectly think a foreclosure may be voided because the trustee didn't record the Notice of Sale on time. Remember, a Notice of Trustee's Sale need be recorded only 14 days before the sale.

### d. Publishing Notice of Sale

The Notice of Sale must be published in a newspaper of general circulation in the city, county, or judicial district where your property is located. Publication must take place at least three times between the date the trustee issues the Notice of Sale and the date of the trustee's sale. (CC § 2924f(b).) Because 20 days does not fit into a weekly publication schedule, there may be a spread of as little as 14 days between the first and third publication. You can find out if the trustee correctly followed this requirement by asking the trustee for its Affidavit of Publication. Then get copies of the newspapers from those dates and see if the Notice of Sale was indeed published. If the trustee refuses, you have grounds to file a lawsuit to stop the foreclosure. (See Chapter 8 on filing a lawsuit to enjoin the foreclosure.)

### e. Posting Notice of Sale

The Notice of Sale must be posted—that is, displayed in a conspicuous location so that you (and your tenants) and the public can be made aware of the pending sale—at least 20 days prior to the sale date. Posting is required in two locations (CC § 2924f(b)):

- a public place, such as a courthouse or city hall (which have special bulletin boards for such purposes), and
- on your property.

The Notice of Sale will be posted on your front door, or, if that is not possible, in another conspicuous place on your property. If your property is undeveloped land, the notice will probably be attached to a post or stake driven into the ground.

## 3. Complete Notice of Trustee's Sale Worksheet

Use the following worksheet to make sure the trustee complies with all notice and mailing requirements for the Notice of Sale. A tear-out copy is in the Appendix. Remember, if the trustee makes a mistake along the way, you have grounds to stop the foreclosure by demanding that the trustee start the process all over again from the beginning.

## NOTICE OF TRUSTEE'S SALE WORKSHEET (NONJUDICIAL FORECLOSURE)

ARE THE FOLLOWING CORRECT ON THE NOTICE OF TRUSTEE'S SALE, AND CONSISTENT WITH INFORMATION ON YOUR NOTICE OF DEFAULT, PROMISSORY NOTE AND DEED OF TRUST?

| | | | |
|---|---|---|---|
| Name of trustor (you and any co-signers)? | ☐ No | ☐ Yes | Name: |
| Name of beneficiary (lender)? | ☐ No | ☐ Yes | Name: |
| Name of trustee? | ☐ No | ☐ Yes | Name: |
| Information about recording of deed of trust? | ☐ No | ☐ Yes | Date: |
| | | | Document No.: |
| | | | Book/Page No.: |
| Description of the property? | ☐ No | ☐ Yes | |
| Total amount of outstanding indebtedness? | ☐ No | ☐ Yes | Amount: |
| Date, time and location of sale | ☐ No | ☐ Yes | Date: |
| | | | Time: |
| | | | Location: |
| Is the date of sale at least 20 calendar days from date the Notice of Sale was issued? | ☐ No | ☐ Yes | |
| MAILING REQUIREMENTS | | | |
| Did the trustee wait at least three months after recording a Notice of Default before mailing you a Notice of Sale? | ☐ No | ☐ Yes | When? |
| Was a copy of the Notice of Sale mailed to you by registered or certified mail at least 20 calendar days before the scheduled sale date? | ☐ No | ☐ Yes | When? |
| Was a copy of the Notice of Sale sent to you by first-class mail at least 20 days before the scheduled sale date? | ☐ No | ☐ Yes | When? |
| At least 20 days before the scheduled sale date, was a copy of the Notice of Sale sent by registered or certified mail to everyone entitled to receive notice— including tenants, junior beneficiaries and anyone who recorded a Request for Notice? (Ask the trustee for proof.) | ☐ No | ☐ Yes | When? |

## NOTICE OF TRUSTEE'S SALE WORKSHEET (NONJUDICIAL FORECLOSURE)

RECORDING REQUIREMENTS

Was the Notice of Sale recorded in the county
recorder's office where your property is located
at least 14 days before the scheduled date?          ☐ No   ☐ Yes   When? _____

PUBLICATION REQUIREMENTS

Before the sale date, was the Notice of Sale
published in a newspaper of general circulation
in the county where the property is located
three times over 20 days? (As the trustee for proof.)   ☐ No   ☐ Yes   1st Date: _____

2nd Date: _____

3rd Date: _____

POSTING REQUIREMENTS

Was a copy of the Notice of Sale posted in
a public place?                                       ☐ No   ☐ Yes   Where? _____

Was a copy of the Notice of Sale posted

## 4. If the Trustee Made a Mistake

If the trustee failed to comply with any of the requirements shown on your worksheet, send the trustee a letter, such as the sample below, demanding that a new Notice of Sale be issued using proper procedures. Be sure to send a copy of the letter to your lender so that it is also put on notice of the trustee's mistake.

When should you send the letter? You can wait until the last week or so before the scheduled sale, but don't miss the deadline or neglect to leave yourself enough time to file a lawsuit if the trustee ignores your request. You may even want to hand-deliver the letter or send it by overnight mail. If you send the letter by U.S. mail, send it certified, return receipt requested. If the trustee ignores your request, you have the right to file a lawsuit to stop the sale. (We give instructions in Chapter 8.)

*Example: Thomas fell several months behind on payments for his condominium in San Francisco, and his bank had its trustee start a nonjudicial foreclosure. The Notice of Trustee's Sale was defective because it scheduled the sale for less than 20 days after the date of the Notice of Trustee's Sale. Thomas wrote to the trustee and demanded that the Notice of Sale be canceled and the foreclosure stopped. The trustee agreed, canceled the defective Notice of Trustee's Sale and issued a new one, which delayed the sale for almost a month. If the trustee had ignored Thomas's request, he would have had to quickly file a lawsuit in San Francisco County Superior Court to stop the foreclosure.*

May 3, 199X

Trustee Service Corporation
25 Heaven Highway
San Diego, California

By certified mail, return receipt requested

Re: 453 Summa Lane, San Diego, California

Dear Trustee:

I own the above-referenced property, on which you are conducting a nonjudicial foreclosure as trustee for National Mortgage Company.

You recorded a Notice of Default on January 20 and recorded a Notice of Trustee's Sale on April 15. I noticed that the Notice of Trustee's Sale is defective because you did not wait a full three months after issuing the Notice of Default before issuing the Notice of Trustee's Sale.

As a result, I respectfully request that you immediately rescind the defective Notice of Trustee's Sale and issue a new one. If you refuse and proceed with this illegal foreclosure, I will have no choice but to file a lawsuit in Superior Court to enjoin your foreclosure. In such event, I may be allowed to collect my costs plus punitive damages against Trustee Service Corporation.

Please advise me on or before May 8, 199X in writing or telephone of your response.

Very truly yours,

John Heacock
453 Sumac Lane
San Diego, California

cc: National Mortgage Company

## E. Extending the Reinstatement Period

You may reinstate your loan up until five business days before the scheduled foreclosure sale. (CC 2924c(e).) However, if the sale is postponed for any reason—for example, your lender agrees to a postponement or you file a lawsuit enjoining the foreclosure—the reinstatement period extends to five business days before the new sale date.

*Example: Lisa falls behind on her monthly house payments to First National Bank, which starts a nonjudicial foreclosure proceeding. After receiving the Notice of Default, Lisa meets with representatives of First National and explains that she is expecting payment of a substantial commission within three months, and will be able to reinstate the loan. First National agrees in writing to postpone the sale for 110 days. Because of the postponement, the reinstatement period is extended until five business days before the new sale date.*

## F. The Redemption Period

Assuming you haven't brought your loan current before the expiration of the reinstatement period (five business days before the the date of the scheduled foreclosure sale), the redemption period begins. The redemption period consists of the last five business days before the trustee's sale. (CC § 2924c(e).) The redemption period ends the moment bidding starts at the trustee's sale.

During the redemption period, you no longer have the right to reinstate your loan by simply bringing it current. You are permitted, however, to "redeem" your property (which will stop the foreclosure) by paying off the entire unpaid balance of your loan, plus late fees, penalties, attorney fees and the trustee's costs. (CC §§ 2903 and 2905.)

If you have the funds to pay off your loan in full—perhaps through refinancing, a loan from friend or family, or some other method—call the trustee and ask them to calculate the total amount due. Make an appointment to meet with the trustee as soon as possible. Take a cashier's check for the correct amount and exchange it for a signed Full Reconveyance document, which is then recorded. The Full Reconveyance cancels the deed of trust and terminates the foreclosure.

*Some lenders will let you reinstate your loan during the redemption period.* Although your legal right to reinstate your loan ends during the redemption period (the last five calendar days before the trustee's sale), lenders are sometimes amenable to accepting payment of the arrears during the redemption period. Be forewarned, however—this is unpredictable territory. Once the redemption period kicks in, get any agreement to reinstate your loan in writing from your lender.

## G. Trustee's Sale

The last step in the nonjudicial foreclosure process is the actual trustee's sale of your property.

If you haven't reinstated or redeemed your loan by the date scheduled for the trustee's sale, the trustee will conduct a public auction of your property. The sale must be conducted on a weekday between 9 a.m. and 5 p.m. in the county where your property is located. (CC §§ 2924g(a).) The sale normally will be conducted in front of the county courthouse or another government building.

### 1. Attend the Trustee's Sale

It might cross your mind to avoid the public auction as a way to preserve dignity in the face of foreclosure, but you have other priorities at this juncture. Although it may be humiliating to attend a trustee's sale of your own property, you should nevertheless make an effort to attend. There is always the possibility that the trustee or auctioneer may conduct the auction improperly or something else may occur that would give you grounds to file an action to set aside (overturn) the trustee's sale.

At the sale, you need to be an eagle-eyed observer and your own best advocate. Take a friend along, if possible, to help you keep track of the sale and help you through the rough spots. Be prepared to take copious notes of everything that occurs. Later, you may need a good record of events during the sale if you wish to file a lawsuit to set it aside. (If you need to set aside a trustee's sale that has already occurred, you will need to consult an attorney.)

## 2. Trustee's Sale May Be Postponed

Trustee's sales may be postponed for a variety of reasons. For example, your lender may agree to postpone the sale if you are negotiating to cure your loan, or the trustee may belatedly find out that one of the notices was defective or was not mailed to everyone entitled to get notice. If no one bids on the property at the trustee's sale, the trustee may postpone and reschedule it.

At the time and place of the scheduled sale, the trustee must show up and announce that the sale has been postponed and why. He must also give the new sale date. (CC § 62924g(a).) If the trustee doesn't show up and disclose the new sale date, the Notice of Sale will be automatically canceled and the trustee will be required to issue a new Notice of Sale. That, of course, would temporarily stop the foreclosure and give you at least another 20 days before the next trustee's sale.

The trustee's sale may also be postponed by court order, such as a state court injunction, temporary restraining order or because you filed for bankruptcy (which automatically prohibits the sale from legally occurring without the bankruptcy court's permission). However, if the order or bankruptcy stay terminates, the trustee must wait at least seven more days before conducting the trustee's sale. (CC § 2924g(d).) (Injunctions and temporary restraining orders are covered in Chapter 8 and bankruptcy is discussed in Chapter 9.)

*No automatic postponement.* Californians used to be entitled to one automatic 24-hour postponement of the trustee's sale. However, on January 1, 1993, this right was stricken from the law. (CC § 2924g(c)(1).)

### a. Promises to Postpone Sale Must Be in Writing

As a number of unfortunate property owners have discovered, a trustee may proceed with a properly noticed sale regardless of what the lender or trustee verbally promised. Get any agreement with your lender or the trustee in writing. Only a written agreement for postponement is enforceable. The agreement must clearly state that the trustee's sale has been postponed to a specific date in the future.

### b. New Notice of Sale After Three Postponements

After three postponements of a scheduled trustee's sale, the trustee must mail, record, publish and post a new Notice of Sale, following the rules discussed in Section D2, above. (CC § 2924g(c)(1).) Note, however, that the following kinds of postponements do not count towards the total:

- postponements by court order, such as an automatic stay issued by a bankruptcy court or a temporary restraining order issued by a state court
- postponements by mutual agreement between you and the lender or trustee, and
- postponements caused by the required seven-day waiting period after an injunction, restraining order or stay has terminated.

## 3. Overview of the Auction

Anyone may bid at the foreclosure sale. In other words, you, your lender, junior lienholders and perfect strangers all may bid. Even the trustee may bid on his or her own behalf, although this is extremely unlikely. So, if you suddenly have the money and want to save your property, you can always bid at the sale.

To begin the sale, the trustee or a hired auctioneer will announce that your property is for sale. He or she will describe the terms of sale (such as all bids must be cash or cashier's check) and say that the condition and title of your property are "without warranties or representations." This means that the trustee makes no promises about your property's physical condition or title status (whether it has liens encumbering it).

## a. Foreclosing Lender's Opening Bid

The auctioneer will give your lender the opportunity to make the opening bid. Your lender always bids first because it holds the deed of trust that is being foreclosed and wants to protect its interest up to the value of its deed of trust.

Your lender is not required to bring cash to back its bid, as it would make little sense for your lender, to whom you already owe money, to produce cash at the sale to pay itself. Instead, the lender can "credit bid" up to the outstanding balance of its loan.

*Example: A representative of Stockton Federal Savings Bank attends a trustee's sale of a house on which it holds a first deed of trust. Several potential bidders are present. Stockton Federal starts the bidding by credit bidding $225,000, the outstanding balance of its loan. All subsequent bidders must have cash (or cashier's checks) for the amount of their bids.*

## b. Bidding Procedures

After the opening bid, the trustee or auctioneer will solicit bidding from the group of people assembled. Each bid constitutes an irrevocable offer to purchase your property at the named price. A bid is automatically canceled by the next higher bid. (CC § 2924h(a).) If the bidder does not have the money in cash or cashier's checks, his or her bid is automatically canceled. (Auctioneers generally inspect bidders before starting the auction to determine how high each person can bid.)

The trustee is expected to keep the sale fair and equitable between the various bidders. If there is anything improper in the bidding, you may have grounds to set aside the trustee's sale. For instance, if one person tries to prevent another person from bidding, the trustee will stop the bidding until everyone who wants to bid is given an opportunity to do so. Your property will be sold to the highest bidder, even if the bid is below the property's fair market value.

You'll want to pay attention to any irregularities in the bidding process. For example, under no circumstances may bidders at a trustee's sale:
- accept money in exchange for not bidding
- offer to accept money for not bidding or to withdraw from bidding
- fix bidding, or
- restrain bidding in any way.

Any of these acts would defraud you of your right to a "public" auction of your property at the highest price.

Maybe you're wondering why you should care about the sales price of property you're losing. First of all, if you have any junior lienholders, you'll be personally liable to them after the sale, unless there are sufficient sale proceeds to cover debts owed to them. Second, there is the possibility that your property could sell for more than you owe to the lienholders, meaning that you could receive some of the excess proceeds after everyone else is paid.

If you can prove that the trustee's sale was illegally conducted, the wrongdoer can be fined, imprisoned, or both. (CC § 2924h(g).) In addition, the sale can be set aside (canceled) and the trustee forced to conduct a new sale. For these reasons, it pays to be alert and observant during the entire auction. Situations like the following have been known to happen.

*Example: Robert attends the trustee's sale of his apartment building in Palm Springs, with a current market value of $400,000. Five people attend the sale. Robert observes one man quietly handing money to each of the other potential bidders. When the sale begins, Cochella Savings, his lender, credit bids $275,000, the amount due on the loan. The man who paid off the other potential buyers bids $276,000. When no one makes a higher bid, the trustee declares this man to be the purchaser of Robert's property for $276,000. Because of the obvious irregularity and disparity in the sale price, Robert may have grounds to have the trustee's sale set aside.*

## 4. Trustee Finalizes Sale and Disburses Proceeds

The trustee will give the highest bidder a Trustee's Deed Upon Sale document, also known as a Trustee's Deed, which is then recorded in the county recorder's office. The Trustee's Deed officially transfers title to your property to the new owner.

The Trustee's Deed also conveys title free and clear of the foreclosing deed of trust. Because the proceeds of the trustee's sale are used to satisfy that lien, the foreclosing deed of trust is extinguished after the sale, even if the sale proceeds do not satisfy the total claim. (CC § 2910 and CCP § 726.)

*Example: Bianca owes $150,000 on her home. The trustee's sale takes in $140,000. Bianca is no longer liable for the $140,000 or for the $10,000 shortage. Because the trustee's sale extinguishes the note and deed of trust, the lender cannot subsequently sue Bianca for the deficiency.*

Within about a week of the trustee's sale, the trustee will disburse the sale proceeds in the following order, until the money is exhausted:

- The trustee is reimbursed for its costs and expenses to conduct the foreclosure.
- The foreclosing lender receives the sale proceeds up to the balance of its promissory note, plus costs.
- If there are any funds remaining, they are disbursed to any junior lienholders in order of priority.
- Finally, the owner (you) receive any surplus funds remaining, which is extremely unlikely.

The trustee prepares a settlement sheet that describes how the sale proceeds were distributed. As soon as possible, call or write the trustee and ask for a copy of the trustee's settlement sheet. If you find errors in the calculations, you can write to the trustee (and send a copy to your lender), describing the mistake and demanding that the trustee rectify the problem within 30 days. Of course, you should only go this far if you believe that you (or one of your junior lienholders) will receive a portion of the sale proceeds if they are redistributed. If the trustee ignores your letter, you have the right to file a lawsuit in Superior Court to have the sale proceeds redistributed. (This would require further research or a lawyer's help. See Chapter 12.)

## 5. What Happens to Liens After Trustee's Sale

When the trustee gives a Trustee's Deed to the buyer at the trustee's sale, it grants title to your property as of the date you signed the deed of trust—not the date of the trustee's sale. This is legally important because normally only those liens that were recorded before the foreclosing lienholder's deed of trust continue to encumber the property after the trustee's sale. For example, if a senior lienholder forecloses, all junior liens would be eliminated because they were recorded after the date the foreclosing lienholder recorded its deed of trust. In contrast, if a junior lienholder forecloses, the new owner acquires the property subject to the senior lien.

*Example: Ted owns a single-family home in Vallejo. There are two loans encumbering the property. First National Bank holds a first deed of trust and Second Mortgage Company holds a second deed of trust. While remaining current with First National, Ted defaults on his monthly payments to Second Mortgage. Second Mortgage initiates a nonjudicial foreclosure and sells Ted's house at a trustee's sale. First National is unaffected by Second Mortgage's foreclosure. The end result is that the purchaser owns property that is still encumbered by a first deed of trust in favor of First National.*

### a. Junior Lienholders

All deeds of trust, abstracts of judgments and judicial liens that were recorded after the date the foreclosing lienholder recorded its deed of trust are eliminated ("wiped out") by the trustee's sale. The successful bidder at the trustee's sale takes title to your property free of junior liens.

Even though their deeds of trust are extinguished by the foreclosure, you are still liable to pay those junior lienholders what you owe them (provided they are not purchase money loans). Because a junior lienholder's interest in the property is now unsecured, if you don't pay, the junior lienholder may file a lawsuit to recover the unpaid debt, obtain a judgment and then record a judgment lien against your other property.

*Example: Telly owns a triplex in Sacramento. There are two loans encumbering his property: First National Bank holds a first deed of trust, and Second Credit Union holds a second deed of trust. Telly fell behind on both of his loans and First National filed a foreclosure and sold the property for less than the amount due on the loan. Second Credit Union's deed of trust was wiped out by the trustee's sale because it was junior to First National's deed of trust. Nevertheless, Telly continues to be liable to Second Credit Union for the full balance of the loan, and Second Credit Union may sue him if he doesn't pay it off.*

### b. Special Lien Situations

Certain liens on your property are unaffected by a trustee's sale, regardless of when they were recorded. The new owner will receive title to your property subject to these remaining liens and you will continue to remain liable. Here are the particulars.

- Property tax liens: Liens for real property taxes cannot be eliminated by a foreclosure sale. For example, if you owe the county property taxes for your home, the taxes become a senior lien against your property, regardless of when the lien was recorded. Although you will remain liable, the tax liens will remain on the property even if you don't own it anymore, unless they are paid off at the trustee's sale.

*IRS and Franchise Tax Board liens.* These liens are considered to be personal in nature. As such, even though you continue to remain personally liable, they are automatically removed from the property after a foreclosure sale.

- Mechanic's liens: Mechanic's liens may be placed on your property by persons who worked on your property and did not get paid (plumbers, contractors and the like). Mechanic's liens are eliminated by a trustee's sale only if the date on which the work commenced—not the date the lien was recorded—was before the date the foreclosing lienholder recorded its deed of trust. (CC § 3134.) Even if the lien is eliminated, you are still liable to the workers for the amount of the lien.

## 6. Buyer May Take Possession of Your Property

Although it may seem severe and unfair, once the new owner receive a Trustee's Deed, he or she is entitled to take possession of your property and you are expected to immediately move out. Of course, some lenders or buyers have no intention of moving into the newly purchased property and may consider leasing it to you if you want to live there. If you are interested in leasing the property after the trustee's sale, get the name and phone number of the new owner from the trustee and contact the owner immediately.

If you refuse to leave the premises voluntary, the new owner may serve you with a Notice to Quit, which states that you must move out within three days. (CCP § 1161a(b).) If you still don't move out, the new owner has the right to file an eviction action (called an unlawful detainer) against you in court. You may defend an unlawful detainer by challenging the purchaser's title and/or the validity of the trustee's sale. However, with the foreclosure completed, it will be very difficult to win.

If you have tenants on your property, you won't be able to collect rents after the trustee's sale. From that date forward, the tenants will be required to pay rent directly to the new owner.

# 4

# JUDICIAL FORECLOSURES

If you default on the terms of your promissory note or deed of trust (covered in Chapter 2), your lender may foreclose on your property. Your lender may elect to initiate a judicial foreclosure, which is covered in this chapter, or a nonjudicial foreclosure (Chapter 3). In a few circumstances, lenders file both kinds of foreclosures and later stop one of them.

With a judicial foreclosure, your lender files a lawsuit in Superior Court seeking the sale of your property to repay your loan. Although the thought of being involved in a lawsuit may at first intimidate you, you'll have plenty of time to get your bearings, respond to the lawsuit and explore ways to bring your loan current.

Only if you can't work things out with your lender will a judge allow the county sheriff to conduct a foreclosure sale. If the sale doesn't produce enough cash to pay off your debt, you may owe your lender the deficiency—the difference between the balance of your loan and the amount received at the foreclosure sale. The entire process, from the initiation of the lawsuit to the actual sale, may take several years.

You may sensibly ask yourself, "What should I be doing during the judicial foreclosure process?" The answer to that question is simple. Develop a plan to stop the foreclosure, as discussed in Chapter 1. This is the time when you should apply various strategies to stop the pending foreclosure, covered in Chapters 5 through 11 of this book.

*Judicial foreclosures are complex and lengthy.* This chapter shows you how to respond to a lawsuit and summarizes the judicial foreclosure process. Because we cannot provide comprehensive step-by-step instructions on all phases of Superior Court lawsuits (an in-depth analysis would take up an entire book!), you should probably hire a lawyer. If you cannot afford an attorney, try contacting a local legal services organization for assistance or referrals. Look in your local yellow pages or contact your city's bar association.

# A. Why Lenders Occasionally Choose Judicial Foreclosures

The vast majority of foreclosures in California are nonjudicial, which bypass the court system entirely (see Chapter 3.) Lenders usually prefer nonjudicial foreclosure because they are quicker (approximately four months), less expensive (no attorney fees, and trustee fees are limited by law), and the property owner will not have the right to purchase the property after the trustee's sale (post-sale redemption rights). Nevertheless, there are two distinctive situations in which lenders may opt to foreclose judicially.

## 1. Lender May Want a Deficiency Judgment

When your lender anticipates that your property will sell for less than the balance you owe, it may choose to file a judicial foreclosure. Only a judicial foreclosure enables a lender to obtain a court judgment for the deficiency. (CCP § 726.) Remember, the "deficiency" is the difference between the un-paid balance of your loan and the amount received at the foreclosure sale.

Fortunately, however, for a lender to get a deficiency judgment, it must show all of the following to be true:

- You do not live in the property—for example, it is rental property or an empty lot.
- The property in question was not purchased with the loan issued by the foreclosing lender. For example, the debt may have been incurred when you refinanced your property or took out a loan secured by raw land you bought several years ago.
- The debt was secured by your property. You signed a deed of trust as security for the debt.
- . The promissory note provides that you are personally liable to repay the loan (known as "recourse").

## 2. Lender May Want Rental Income From the Property

Even if it cannot obtain a deficiency judgment against you, your lender may still file a judicial foreclosure if your property is income-producing (multi-residential or commercial). If you have defaulted on your loan, your lender may file a judicial foreclosure and ask a judge to appoint a receiver— someone who is legally empowered to take over management of your property and collect the rents.

*Don't be surprised if your lender files both judicial and nonjudicial foreclosures.* That way, a court-appointed receiver will manage your property and collect the rents while the nonjudicial foreclosure is pending. Using this strategy, once the nonjudicial trustee's sale is completed, your lender will dismiss (cancel) the judicial foreclosure.

# B. Overview of a Judicial Foreclosure

A judicial foreclosure is a lengthy, court-supervised procedure that consists of 12 basic steps, summarized in the Judicial Foreclosure Timeline below and covered in detail in the rest of this chapter.

## JUDICIAL FORECLOSURE TIMELINE

| ACTION | WHEN | PURPOSE |
|---|---|---|
| Lender files Complaint in court | Sometime after loan has gone into default—usually several months | Starts the lawsuit for judicial foreclosure |
| Lender records lis pendens with county recorder | Soon after lawsuit is filed | Gives public notice of lawsuit; effectively prevents property from being sold or refinanced |
| Borrower files an answer to Complaint | Within 30 days after borrower is served with (personally given) copy of Complaint | Prevents lender from obtaining default judgment and immediately proceeding with foreclosure sale |
| Reinstatement period | From date lawsuit is filed until entry of judgment after trial | Gives borrower opportunity to bring loan current by paying arrears and lender's costs and expenses of filing lawsuit |
| Discovery | From date borrower answers Complaint until case goes to trial | Borrower and lender collect evidence in the case: exchange documents, take depositions and follow other procedures |
| Trial | About two to three years after lawsuit was filed | Resolves lawsuit—judgment is entered; ends reinstatement period |

**NOTE:** IF LAWSUIT IS RESOLVED IN BORROWER'S FAVOR, THE CASE IS DISMISSED AND THE REST OF THIS CHART DOES NOT APPLY.

| | | |
|---|---|---|
| Redemption period | Runs from end of trial (entry of judgment) to foreclosure sale | Borrower may stop foreclosure by paying off entire balance of loan plus foreclosure costs |
| Writ of Sale and Notice of Levy | Starts clock running as to date of foreclosure sale | Gives written notice that sale of property is permitted |
| Notice of Sale | At least 20 days before foreclosure sale if lender seeks deficiency judgment. Otherwise, a minimum of 120 days after Notice of Levy was issued | Informs borrower when property will be sold |
| Foreclosure sale | Date listed on Notice of Sale | Sheriff sells property at a public auction, gives buyer a Certificate of Sale and distributes proceeds within a week |
| Deficiency judgment | Within three months of foreclosure sale | Lender must file application with court that heard trial and get deficiency judgment from the court |
| Post-sale redemption period | Starts the day of the sale and continues for either one year (if lender seeks deficiency judgment) or three months (if no deficiency judgment) | Borrower may get property back by paying foreclosure sales price plus foreclosure costs |

## 1. Lender Files Complaint

Your lender starts a judicial foreclosure by filing a Complaint (a written document) seeking the foreclosure in the Superior Court for the county in which your property is located. Your lender is known as the plaintiff—the party filing the action (CCP § 725a.) The complaint must list all defendants—the party or parties defending against the lawsuit. Your lender will name as defendants you and everyone who has any interest in your property, including all present owners, tenants, senior and junior lienholders (including any former owner that holds a deed of trust), taxing authorities and guarantors.

The Complaint will claim that you signed (executed) a promissory note and a deed of trust securing your promissory note, naming your lender as the beneficiary under the deed of trust. Your lender will state that the documents were delivered to your lender and recorded in the county recorder's office and that you subsequently defaulted under the terms of your promissory note and/or deed of trust.

Your lender will request the court to order that your property be sold to satisfy your debt, and that your lender receive a money judgment for any deficiency remaining after sale proceeds are applied to your debt. (If no deficiency judgment is sought, your lender will insert a statement in the Complaint waiving a deficiency judgment.) See the sample Complaint for Judicial Foreclosure below.

Your lender will have copies of the Complaint, together with a document called a Summons (announcement of lawsuit), personally served upon (delivered to) you and each of the other defendants. If a process server cannot serve you personally, a copy of the Summons and Complaint will be left with an adult at your residence (or place of business) and copies will be mailed to you.

1  LAW OFFICES OF FAWN AND GREEN
   2525 Main Street
2  Santa Barbara, California
   805-333-6666
3
   Attorney for Plaintiff
4  Old Federal Bank

5

6

7

8              SUPERIOR COURT OF THE STATE OF CALIFORNIA

9                   COUNTY OF SANTA BARBARA

10
   Old Federal Bank,                          )
11                                            )    Case No: 00000
         Plaintiff,                           )
12 v.                                         )    COMPLAINT FOR
                                              )    JUDICIAL FORECLOSURE
13 Betty Bush, Does 1 to 10, Inclusive,       )
                                              )
14       Defendant.                           )
   _____        )
15

16              COMPLAINT FOR JUDICIAL FORECLOSURE

17       Plaintiff, Old Federal Bank ("Bank") complains and alleges as follows:

18                              VENUE

19       1. Venue in the Superior Court for the County of Santa Barbara is proper under Code of Civil

20 Procedure Section 392(l)(b) because all the property subject to this action is located within Santa

21 Barbara County.

22                           THE PARTIES

23       2. Bank is, and at all times mentioned herein was, a California bank, chartered by the Federal

24 Deposit Insurance Corporation, and doing business in the State of California.

25       3. Bank is informed and believes, and thereon alleges that Defendant Betty Bush ("Borrower" or

26 "Defendant") is, and at all relevant times herein was, an individual residing in the State of California.

27       4. Bank is ignorant of the true names and capacities of the defendants sued herein as DOES 1

28 through 10, inclusive, and therefore sues these defendants by such fictitious names.  Bank will amend the

1   Complaint to allege their true names and capacities when the DOE defendants have been ascertained.

2   Bank is informed and believes and on that basis alleges that DOE 1 through DOE 10, inclusive, are

3   creditors of Defendant or others, and are named as beneficiaries or assignees of the beneficiaries in

4   deeds of trust recorded on the Property.  Said defendants are creditors junior, subsequent and subject to

5   Bank liens as previously described, and each of them is responsible in some manner for the events,

6   occurrences, and obligations herein alleged and for the losses incurred by Bank as a result of the

7   nonpayment of the loan obligations.

8                                    THE LOAN DOCUMENTS

9          5. On or about April 8, 199X, Borrower, for valuable consideration, made, executed and

10  delivered to Bank a written promissory note ("Note") in the amount of $200,000, a true and correct

11  copy of which is attached hereto as Exhibit "All" and incorporated by this reference with the same force

12  and effect as if set forth in full herein.  Under the terms of the Note, Borrower agreed to make monthly

13  payments of $1,278.82, comprised of principal and interest.  The interest was calculated at the initial

14  rate of 9% per year, payable the first day of each month.  The Note provided that upon default the

15  holder could declare all monies payable thereunder immediately due, owing and payable.  The Note

16  also provided for a default interest rate at 4% plus the contract rate.

17         6. As consideration for the Note, on or about April 8, 199X, Borrower made, executed and

18  delivered to Bank a Deed of Trust (the "Deed of Trust") to secure, among other things, the obligations of

19  Borrower under the Note and the payment of the principal sum and interest due thereunder.  A true and

20  correct copy of the Deed of Trust is attached hereto as Exhibit "B" and incorporated by this reference

21  with the same force and effect as if set forth in full herein.

22         7. By the terms of the Deed of Trust, Borrower as Trustor, irrevocably granted, transferred and

23  assigned to Trustee, for the benefit of Bank as beneficiary, with power of sale, all of its right, title and

24  interest in that certain 7-unit apartment building located at 8500 Foothill Blvd., Santa Barbara, Califor-

25  nia, and legally known by the description set forth in the Deed of Trust as recorded with the Santa

26  Barbara County Recorder (hereinafter, the "Property").  The Deed of Trust was duly acknowledged and

27  recorded in the Official Records of the County Recorder of Santa Barbara on or about April 11, 199X,

28  as Instrument No. 9X-345634.

8. Bank complied with all of its contractual obligations under the Note and Deed of Trust by disbursing the monies required under the Note.

LOAN DEFAULTS

9. Borrower defaulted in its performance of the Note and Deed of Trust when the May 1, 199X payment was not made. All monies payable under the Note have been declared and are now immediately due and payable, with interest thereon from May 1, 199X.

10. Prior to the commencement of this action, demand was made on Borrower for the balance due on the Note, but no part of said balance has been paid. There remains due, owing and unpaid as of May 1, 199X, the principal sum of $185,423 plus accrued interest from January 1, 199X to May 1, 199X in the amount of $6,394.10 and late charges of $319.71. The total amount owing is approximately $192,136.81 as of May 1, 199X. Interest continues to accrue at the daily rate of $90 from May 1, 199X.

11. Under the terms of the Note and the Deed of Trust, Borrower is obligated to pay costs, reasonable attorneys' fees and expenses incurred in the collection of the Note.

FIRST CAUSE OF ACTION

(for Judicial Foreclosure of Deed of Trust)

12. Bank hereby realleges and incorporates by reference the allegations contained in paragraphs 1 through 11, inclusive, as though fully set forth herein.

13. Bank is informed and believes, and thereon alleges, that the defendants sued fictitiously herein as DOE 1 through DOE 10, inclusive, are creditors of Defendant or others, and are named as beneficiaries or assignees of the beneficiaries in deeds of trust recorded on the Property. Said defendants are creditors junior, subsequent and subject to Bank's liens as previously described.

14. Bank is informed and believes, and thereon alleges, that the defendants sued fictitiously herein as DOE 1 through DOE 10, inclusive, are creditors of defendant or others, and claim interest in the Property as judgment creditors, lienholders, mechanic's lienholders, holders of tax liens and/or claim to be creditors and have filed lawsuits and notices of pendency of actions to this effect and/or recorded attachments on the Property. Said defendants are creditors junior, subsequent and subject to the liens of Bank as previously described.

15. Bank is the lawful holder of the Note and the lawful owner of the beneficial interests under the Deed of Trust encumbering the Property.

16. The Note and the Deed of Trust provide that upon default in monthly payments, or in the performance of any obligation, covenant, promise or agreement, Bank may invoke the power of sale and, at its election, declare the entire amount of the principal and unpaid interest to be immediately due and payable.  Such election and declaration of acceleration has theretofore been made by Bank as a result of the defaults described herein.

17. Bank is informed and believes, and thereon alleges that defendants are unwilling to cure the defaults described herein.

18. By reason of the defaults as described herein, pursuant to California Code of Civil Procedure Section 725a, Bank is entitled to a judgment that:

(i) the rights, claims, ownership, liens, titles and demand of Defendant and all persons or entities claiming under any of them are subject to the lien of the Deed of Trust;

(ii) the Deed of Trust is foreclosed and the Property shall be sold according to law by a commissioner or a trustee appointed by the Court, and when the time for redemption lapsed, the commissioner or trustee shall execute and deliver a deed to the purchaser(s) of the Property at the foreclosure sale and that said purchaser(s) be put into possession of the Property upon delivery of said Deed; and

(iii) a judgment against Defendant for any amount of the above obligation left unsatisfied after the foreclosure and sale of the Property in the amount of such deficiency.

19. Due to the Defendant's default, Bank has been forced to employ attorneys and incur other expenses and costs, no part of which have been paid by Defendant.  Under the terms of the Note and the Deed of Trust, Defendant is obligated to pay the reasonable attorneys' fees, expenses and costs incurred by Bank in exercising its powers to protect the security interest.

WHEREFORE, Bank prays for judgment as follows:

1. For judgment that the rights, claims, ownership, liens, title and demands of Defendant are subject to the liens of the Deed of Trust;

2. That all defendants sued herein and each of them, and all persons claiming under them, subsequent to the execution of the Deed of Trust either as lien claimants, judgment creditors, claimants

under a junior mortgage or trustee, purchasers, encumbrances, or otherwise, be barred and foreclosed from all rights, claims, interests or equity in redemption of the premises, if any, in every part of the Property, when time for redemption, if any, has elapsed;

3. That Bank have judgment and execution against Defendant for any amount of the obligation identified in the Note which is left unsatisfied after the foreclosure sale of the Property in the amount of such deficiency, plus any additional amount to which Bank is entitled for any misappropriation of rental income, security deposit, insurance proceeds or condemnation awards and waste or damage caused to the Property by Defendant that may remain after applying all the proceeds of the sale of the Property;

4. For an order adjudging that the Deed of Trust be foreclosed, and that judgment be made for the foreclosure sale of the Property, according to law, by a Sheriff appointed by the Court;

5. For an order permitting Bank, or any other parties to this action, to become a purchaser at the foreclosure sale;

6. For an order declaring that Defendant is liable for a deficiency, if there shall be one, after the sale of the property;

7. That when the time for redemption has elapsed, the Sheriff execute a deed to the party who purchases the Property at the foreclosure sale, and that the Purchaser be put into possession of the Property upon production of said deed;

8. For all costs, charges and expenses incurred in connection with Bank's sale and foreclosure;

9. For such other and further relief as the Court may deem just and proper.

DATED _____     FAWN & GREEN

By: _____
Joseph Fawn
Attorneys for Old Federal Bank

## 2. Lender Records Lis Pendens

Immediately after your lender files a Complaint, it will record a Lis Pendens (Notice of Pending Action) in the recorder's office in the county in which your property is located. A Lis Pendens states that a lawsuit for judicial foreclosure of your property was filed in the county's Superior Court. Your lender doesn't have to attach a copy of the Complaint to the Lis Pendens.

Your lender must then mail a copy of the Lis Pendens to you and each of the other defendants. Once properly prepared, recorded and mailed, a Lis Pendens gives public notice of the foreclosure action. Anyone considering purchasing or refinancing your property will check with the county records and discover that there is a judicial foreclosure pending. The net result is that you won't be able to sell or refinance your property until the judicial foreclosure is resolved and your lender is brought current or paid off. Of course, the purpose of selling or refinancing your property would be to pay off the foreclosing lender.

## 3. Answer the Complaint Within 30 Days

You have 30 days from the date you received the Complaint for judicial foreclosure to file an Answer (written response) to your lender's Complaint with the court. The filing fee varies from county to county, and averages about $100 per defendant. You'll also need to have a copy of your Answer mailed to your lender and its attorney.

If you don't file a written Answer within the 30 days, your lender will be able to obtain an immediate default judgment (ruling in its favor) and proceed with the foreclosure sale. In this event, there won't be a trial.

Your Answer should admit each of the lender's allegations (statements) in the Complaint that are true and deny each allegation that is untrue. Although this may sound complicated, it really isn't. For example, you can admit as true the allegations that you own the property that is being foreclosed, that you borrowed the money from the lender, and that you signed the promissory note and deed of trust. However, if you do not owe the amount your lender states in the Complaint, you would deny that allegation.

It is important for your Answer to include affirmative defenses—brief explanations of why you believe your lender's judicial foreclosure action is improper. For example, if the terms in your promissory note and/or deed of trust are wrong, you should raise these issues as affirmative defenses. Or, if your note is not secured by a deed of trust, or the deed of trust was never properly recorded against your property, you'd make those points as affirmative defenses.

1

2

3

4

BETTY BUSH
2433 McCormick Street
Santa Barbara, California
805-455-3476

Defendant In Pro Per

5

6

7

8

9

SUPERIOR COURT OF THE STATE OF CALIFORNIA

COUNTY OF SANTA BARBARA

10

11

12

13

14

15

| Old Federal Bank, | ) | |
|---|---|---|
| Plaintiff, | ) | Case No: 00000 |
| v. | ) | |
| | ) | ANSWER TO COMPLAINT |
| | ) | FOR JUDICIAL FORECLOSURE |
| Betty Bush, Does 1 to 10, Inclusive, | ) | |
| Defendant. | ) | |
| _____ | ) | |

16

ANSWER TO COMPLAINT FOR JUDICIAL FORECLOSURE

17

18

Defendant, Betty Bush ("Defendant" or "Borrower") admits, denies and/or responds to the

Plaintiff's Complaint for Judicial Foreclosure as follows:

19

VENUE

20

1. Defendant admits the allegations of paragraph 1 of the complaint.

21

THE PARTIES

22

23

24

2. Defendant lacks sufficient information and belief with which to respond to the allegations

contained in this paragraph and, on that basis only, generally and specifically denies each and every

allegation contained in paragraph 2.

25

3. Defendant admits the allegations of paragraph 3 of the Complaint.

26

27

28

4. Defendant lacks sufficient information and belief with which to respond to the allegations of

this paragraph and, on that basis, generally and specifically denies each and every allegation contained

in paragraph 4.

<u>THE LOAN DOCUMENTS</u>

5. Defendant admits that on or about April 8, 199X, Defendant, for valuable consideration, made, executed and delivered to Old Federal Bank ("Bank") a written promissory note ("Note") in the amount of $200,000. Under the terms of the Note, Borrower agreed to make monthly payments of $1,278.82, comprised of principal and interest. The interest was calculated at the initial rate of 9% per year payable the first day of each month. The Note provided that upon default the holder could declare all monies payable thereunder immediately due, owing and payable. The Note also provided for a default interest rate at 4% plus the contract rate.

6. Defendant admits that as consideration for the Note, on or about April 8, 199X, Defendant made, executed and delivered to Bank a Deed of Trust (the "Deed of Trust") to secure, among other things, the obligations of Defendant under the Note and the payment of the principal sum and interest due thereunder.

7. Defendant admits that by the terms of the Deed of Trust, Borrower, as Trustor, irrevocably granted, transferred and assigned to Trustee, for the benefit of Bank as beneficiary, with power of sale, all of its right, title and interest in that certain 7-unit apartment building located at 8500 Foothill Blvd., Santa Barbara, California, and legally known by the description set forth in the Deed of Trust as recorded with the Santa Barbara County Recorder (hereinafter, the "Property"). The Deed of Trust was duly acknowledged and recorded in the Official Records of the County Recorder of Santa Barbara on or about April 11, 199X, as Instrument No. 9345634.

8. Defendant admits the allegations of paragraph 8 of the complaint.

<u>LOAN DEFAULTS</u>

9. Defendant denies each and every allegation contained in paragraph 9 and the whole thereof.

10. Defendant denies each and every allegation contained in paragraph 10 and the whole thereof.

11. Defendant admits the allegations of paragraph 11 of the Complaint.

<u>FIRST CAUSE OF ACTION (for Judicial Foreclosure of Deed of Trust)</u>

12. Defendant hereby realleges and incorporates by reference the admissions and denials contained in paragraphs 1 through 11, inclusive, as though fully set forth herein.

13. Defendant lacks sufficient information and belief with which to respond to the allegations of this paragraph and, on that basis, generally and specifically denies each and every allegation contained in paragraph 13.

14. Defendant lacks sufficient information and belief with which to respond to the allegations of this paragraph and, on that basis, generally and specifically denies each and every allegation contained in paragraph 14.

15. Defendant lacks sufficient information and belief with which to respond to the allegations of this paragraph and, on that basis, generally and specifically denies each and every allegation contained in paragraph 15.

16. Defendant lacks sufficient information and belief with which to respond to the allegations of this paragraph and, on that basis, generally and specifically denies each and every allegation contained in paragraph 16.

17. Defendant denies each and every allegation contained in paragraph 17 and the whole thereof.

18. Defendant lacks sufficient information and belief with which to respond to the allegations of this paragraph and, on that basis, generally and specifically denies each and every allegation contained in paragraph 18.

19. Defendant lacks sufficient information and belief with which to respond to the allegations of this paragraph and, on that basis, generally and specifically denies each and every allegation contained in paragraph 19.

First Affirmative Defense: That Plaintiff has failed to state a proper cause of action.

Second Affirmative Defense: That Defendant does not owe the amount Plaintiff is claiming is owed.

Third affirmative Defense: That Plaintiff agreed to a modification of the promissory note and deed of trust and is now refusing to honor that modification.

WHEREFORE, Defendant prays for judgment as follows:

1. That plaintiff take nothing by its complaint;

2. That Defendant be awarded her costs of suit, including reasonable attorneys' fees;

3. That Defendant be awarded such other and further relief as the Court may deem just and proper.

DATED _____

_____
Betty Bush
Defendant In Pro Per

## 4. The Reinstatement Period

The reinstatement period is a time during which you may stop the judicial foreclosure by bringing your loan current. During the reinstatement period, your lender must accept the amount due and dismiss the lawsuit.

The reinstatement period starts when your lender files a Complaint for judicial foreclosure in court and runs until the trial ends and a judge decides the case. It can take two to three years for a case to go to trial, depending on the court's calendar of cases.

To reinstate your loan, you must pay your lender:

- the amount of payments you have missed (arrears), plus
- foreclosure costs and expenses incurred by your lender, including attorney fees.

The amount needed to reinstate your loan will increase daily as interest keeps accruing. As the lawsuit proceeds, your lender will also incur more legal fees and costs. For these reasons, if you are able, reinstate your loan as soon as possible.

### a. Contact Your Lender

If you can come up with the funds to reinstate your loan, contact your lender and determine the exact amount as of the date you anticipate paying the lender. (If you disagree with the amount, ask your lender for details. If all else fails, you have the right to file a motion in court to order an accounting of your lender's books and records to determine the correct amount owed.)

You'll need to purchase a cashier's check for the reinstatement amount and take it to your lender's office. Don't forget to ask for a receipt for the payment. As mentioned earlier, your lender must accept your payment and stop the foreclosure. Request that your lender file a Request for Dismissal with the Superior Court and record a Notice of Withdrawal of Lis Pendens in the county recorder's office. Ask your lender to mail you copies of these two documents as soon as they are processed.

### b. Partial Payments During the Reinstatement Period

Most lenders will not accept partial payment of the arrears during the reinstatement period. Nevertheless, don't discount your ability to negotiate with your lender. If you can convince your lender that you can bring the loan current within a reasonable period of time, your lender may agree to accept a partial payment and temporarily postpone the foreclosure. (See Chapter 5 for tips on negotiating with your lender.)

Lenders that do accept partial payments will typically have you sign a letter acknowledging that the partial payment does not waive your default or extend the reinstatement period. Even if your lender doesn't require anything in writing, you should document your understanding with a letter, such as the sample below.

January 10, 199X

Hugh Powell
Best West Savings Bank
346 Second Street
Redding, California

Loan: 528977

Dear Mr. Powell:

On December 6, 199X, you filed a Complaint for Judicial Foreclosure in Mono County Superior Court to sell my property. The total amount to bring my loan current is approximately $33,345. As you know, I have explained to you that I cannot afford to pay the full arrears at this time.

You have agreed to accept a partial payment in the amount of $13,000 (enclosed with this letter) and agreed to suspend the judicial foreclosure for four months. I understand that if I fail to bring my loan current by May 10, you will resume the foreclosure.

If this letter accurately reflects our agreement, please sign in the space provided below and return this letter to me. Otherwise, please advise me immediately in writing and return my check.

Sincerely,

Harriet Brown
AGREED AS TO FORM AND CONTENT:
BEST WEST SAVINGS BANK
By: _____
Authorized Officer

## 5. Discovery

Because most court systems are backlogged, it can take anywhere from two to three years for your case to come to trial. During this time, you and your lender are expected to conduct discovery—the process in which the parties gather the evidence to prove their case.

The most common types of discovery include:
- interrogatories: written answers to a series of questions
- depositions: cross-examination by the opposing attorney in front of a court reporter
- requests for admissions: series of written questions that require you to admit or deny specific facts, and
- requests for production of documents: the turnover of relevant documents.

*Discovery resource.* The various types of discovery available to you and the timing of these procedures are beyond the scope of this book. *Represent Yourself in Court*, by Paul Bergman and Sara Berman-Barrett (Nolo Press), gives an excellent explanation of discovery and the procedures leading up to trial.

## 6. Foreclosure Trial

If your case goes to trial, your lender must present evidence that proves all of the following facts:
- You executed (signed) and delivered to your lender a promissory note and deed of trust as security for the promissory note.
- A copy of the deed of trust was recorded in the county recorder's office.
- You defaulted on the promissory note and deed of trust.
- Under the terms contained in the deed of trust and state law, your property may be sold to satisfy the unpaid debt.
- Your lender is entitled to (or waives its right to) a judgment for any deficiency that results after

applying the proceeds from the foreclosure sale to your unpaid debt.

To win the case, you must demonstrate with witnesses and documents that your lender failed to prove at least one of the previous points and that at least one of your affirmative defenses is true.

The trial could last anywhere from several hours to a few weeks, depending on the complexity of the case. At the end of the trial, the judge will either rule immediately or take it under submission for several days to think over the decision. You will receive a copy of the judgment in the mail.

If the judge rules in your favor, the judicial foreclosure will be dismissed. Then, your lender can always start a nonjudicial foreclosure. If, on the other hand, the court finds that your lender proved its case, it will enter a judgment of foreclosure and order the sale of your property by the sheriff to satisfy the debt. Finally, the judgment will specify whether you (or anyone else named in the Complaint) will be personally liable for a deficiency if your property is sold for less than the amount of the unpaid loan.

## 7. Equity of Redemption Period

From the time the judge enters a court judgment in your lender's favor until the actual foreclosure sale, you are in what's known as the equity of redemption period—or redemption period. (CC §§ 2903–2905.) This period can range anywhere from at least 20 days to more than four months, depending upon various factors discussed below.

During the redemption period, you can no longer simply bring your loan current. The only way you can stop the foreclosure is to redeem your property, which consists of paying off the entire unpaid balance of your loan, plus foreclosure costs (including attorneys' fees, interest and whatever other expenses your lender incurred in prosecuting the foreclosure). For various strategies to deal with redemption, read Chapter 5 (Negotiating With Your Lender), Chapter 6 (Refinancing out of Foreclosure), Chapter 10 (How to Sell Your Property Quickly to Stop Foreclosure) and Chapter 9 (Bankruptcy).

If you can raise the funds to pay off your entire loan, call the sheriff and find out the total amount to redeem. Make an appointment to meet with the sheriff and bring a cashier's check for the correct amount. In exchange for payment, the sheriff will give you a document called a Certificate of Redemption.

*Lenders sometimes allow reinstatement during the redemption period.* Although your lender is not obligated to accept your late payments during the redemption period, some lenders will still consider reinstatement if they do not want your property. Be forewarned, however, that this is unpredictable territory, and most lenders will only accept full payment of your loan. (See Chapter 5 for more on negotiating with your lender.)

## 8. Writ of Sale and Notice of Levy

If you haven't redeemed your property, your lender will obtain a Writ of Sale from the court and deliver it to the county sheriff. (CCP § 716.010.) A Writ of Sale orders the sheriff to sell your property according to the instructions in the judgment. The sheriff will prepare a Notice of Levy, which states that the sheriff will seize your property in preparation for a sale, and have this notice personally delivered to you. Although not required, most sheriffs also record a copy of the Notice of Levy in the recorder's office and mail a copy to you.

If the sheriff fails to properly follow these procedures, you can file a motion in the court demanding that the foreclosure be stopped until the sheriff completes the proper procedure.

## 9. Notice of Sale

The next document you will receive in this blizzard of paperwork is the Notice of Sale. The Notice of Sale is issued by the sheriff and advises you (and any junior lienholders) that your property will be sold in 20 days. It gives the date, time and location of the foreclosure sale.

When the sheriff issues a Notice of Sale depends on whether your lender is seeking a deficiency judgment against you:

• If your lender wants to obtain a deficiency judgment against you, the sheriff will simultaneously serve the Notice of Levy (Section B8, just above) and the Notice of Sale. (CC § 729.010(b)(2).) You may have as little as 20 calendar days before the foreclosure sale occurs.

• If a deficiency judgment was waived or is prohibited, after issuing the Notice of Levy, the sheriff must wait at least 120 days before issuing the Notice of Sale. (CCP §§ 700.015 and 701.545.) In that event, you will have at least 140 days' notice before the foreclosure sale. Keep in mind that during this period, you retain the right to stop the foreclosure by redeeming your property—paying off the full amount of the loan plus costs and attorney fees. (CC § 2903.)

### a. Notification Requirements for the Notice of Sale

The sheriff must follow strict notice requirements for the Notice of Sale to be valid. Here are the rules.

• *Service.* The sheriff must serve the Notice of Sale on you personally, or leave a copy of the notice with an adult at your residence or place of business.

• *Mailing.* At least 20 calendar days before the sale date, the sheriff must send the Notice of Sale by first-class mail to you and everyone entitled to receive notice, including any junior lienholders and tenants.

• *Publishing.* The Notice of Sale must be published at least once a week over three weeks, with at least five days between each printing. The first publication must be a minimum of 20 calendar days before the sale. The publishing must be in a newspaper of general circulation in the city, county or judicial district where your property is located.

• *Posting.* The Notice of Sale must be posted both in a public place, such as a courthouse or city hall, and on your property in a conspicuous location.

- *Recording* (optional). Although not required, sheriffs usually record a copy of the Notice of Sale in the county recorder's office to assure that there has been adequate public notice of the foreclosure sale.

## b. Notice of Sale Worksheet

The accompanying Notice of Sale Worksheet will help you determine if the sheriff has made any mistakes in issuing a Notice of Sale. Fill in the worksheet with information from your promissory note, deed of trust and Notice of Sale.

## NOTICE OF SALE WORKSHEET (JUDICIAL FORECLOSURE)

### DID THE NOTICE OF SALE INCLUDE

| | | | |
|---|---|---|---|
| Date of sale? | ☐ No | ☐ Yes | Date: |
| Time of sale? | ☐ No | ☐ Yes | Time: |
| Specific location of sale? | ☐ No | ☐ Yes | Location: |
| Correct legal description of the property, including the street address? | ☐ No | ☐ Yes | |
| Correct name and address of beneficiary (lender)? | ☐ No | ☐ Yes | |

### SERVICE AND MAILING REQUIREMENTS

| | | | |
|---|---|---|---|
| Was the Notice of Sale mailed to you by first-class mail a minimum 20 calendar days before the scheduled sale date? | ☐ No | ☐ Yes | When? |
| Was the Notice of Sale personally served on you? | ☐ No | ☐ Yes | When? |
| At least 20 days before the scheduled sale date, was the Notice of Sale mailed by first-class mail to everyone entitled to receive notice (including tenants and junior lienholders)? | ☐ No | ☐ Yes | When? |

### PUBLICATION REQUIREMENTS

| | | | |
|---|---|---|---|
| Was the Notice of Sale published at least once a week over 3 weeks? | ☐ No | ☐ Yes | 1st Date: |
| | ☐ No | ☐ Yes | 2nd Date: |
| | ☐ No | ☐ Yes | 3rd Date: |
| Was the first publication date at least 20 calendar days before the scheduled sale date? | ☐ No | ☐ Yes | When? |
| Was the Notice of Sale published in a paper in the county where your property is located? | ☐ No | ☐ Yes | District: |

### POSTING REQUIREMENTS

| | | | |
|---|---|---|---|
| Was the Notice of Sale posted in a public place? | ☐ No | ☐ Yes | Where? |
| Was the Notice of Sale posted on your front door or another conspicuous place? | ☐ No | ☐ Yes | Where? |

### c. What to Do If Notice Was Not Properly Given

Sheriffs have been known to make mistakes, so it is wise to closely monitor the sheriff's activities. You may have grounds to stop the foreclosure sale and force the sheriff to start the procedures all over again if he doesn't comply with the notice rules described in Section D2, above.

If the sheriff makes a mistake, immediately write him a letter, such as the sample below. Send it by certified or registered mail, with a copy to your lender.) Demand that the sale either be postponed or rescheduled using proper procedures. If the sheriff ignores your request, you may file a lawsuit to enjoin (stop) the foreclosure. (See Chapter 12 for information on hiring a lawyer or doing your own legal research.)

---

May 22, 199X

Sheriff of Santa Barbara County
Civil Division
23 State Street
Santa Barbara, CA

Re:  Case No. 23456

Sheriff's File No. 612

Dear Sheriff:

Your office is conducting a judicial foreclosure of my property, located at 56 Grande Drive in the city of Isla Vista.

You issued the Notice of Levy on February 10, 199X and recorded the Notice of Sale on May 15, 199X. However, the Notice of Sale was defective because you did not wait the required 120 days.

As a result, I respectfully request that you immediately cancel the pending foreclosure sale and issue a new Notice of Sale. If you refuse and proceed with an illegal sale, I will have no alternative but to file a motion in Superior Court to enjoin the foreclosure sale. In that event, you may be held liable for punitive damages for ignoring my request.

Please advise me immediately in writing of your response.

Very truly yours,

John Freidman
P.O. Box 1234
Isla Vista, CA
(805) 555-2233

cc: First Credit Union

---

## 10. Foreclosure Sale

The next step in the judicial foreclosure process is the actual foreclosure sale. If you can't pay off your loan by the date scheduled for the foreclosure sale, the sheriff will conduct a public auction of your property. The sale will be conducted on a weekday between the hours of 9 a.m. and 5 p.m. (CCP § 701.570(a).) The sale normally will be conducted in front of the county courthouse or another government building in the county where your property is located.

### a. Attend the Foreclosure Sale

It might cross your mind to avoid the public auction as a way of avoiding embarrassment and preserving your dignity, but if you are reading this book, you already appreciate that you have other priorities at this juncture—namely, to stop the foreclosure if possible.

There is always the possibility that the sheriff may conduct the auction improperly or something else may occur to invalidate the sale. For this reason, you should attend the sale and observe the procedures closely. Follow the descriptions below to see if the sheriff violates any of the procedural rules. You need to be an eagle-eyed observer and your own best advocate. If possible, take a friend along to help you keep track of the sale and give you moral support. Take detailed notes of everything that occurs. At some later point, you may need a good record of events during the sale if you wish to set the sale aside. (See Chapter 8.)

### b. The Bidding Process

Because the sheriff will advertise the sale, and the Notice of Levy and Notice of Sale are recorded and posted, there should be plenty of potential buyers present. (See Chapter 3, Section G, for what to watch out for at a foreclosure sale.)

Anyone but the sheriff may bid at the foreclosure sale, including you, your lender and any junior lienholders. With the exception of the foreclosing lender, all bids must be backed by cash or cashier's checks for the amount of the bid.

The sheriff will start the auction by inviting your lender to make the opening bid. Your lender is in a unique position at the sale, because it can give the sheriff a copy of the court judgment and receive a credit up to the amount of the judgment.

*Example: Malik defaulted on a loan secured by an apartment building in Humbolt. Guardian Savings Bank, which holds the first deed of trust, obtained a $285,000 judgment for foreclosure. At the foreclosure sale, a representative of Guardian Savings credit bids $285,000.*

The sheriff then invites higher bids from those assembled. If no one else bids, your lender becomes the owner of the property. If the sheriff receives higher bids, each bid constitutes an irrevocable offer to purchase your property at a specific price, and each bid automatically cancels the next higher bid. (CC § 2924h(a).) When the bidding is exhausted, the highest bidder is the new owner of your property.

### c. Sheriff Finalizes Sale and Distributes Proceeds

Within a week after the foreclosure sale is completed, the sheriff will distribute the proceeds as directed by the court judgment. The costs of sale, including the sheriff's fees, will be paid first. Next, your lender will be repaid up to the amount of its judgment. If there is any surplus—and there seldom is—it will go to any junior lienholder. The remainder, if any (don't hold your breath), will be paid to you.

If your lender sought a deficiency judgment, the sheriff will give the purchaser a Certificate of Sale document. (CCP § 729.040.) The Certificate of Sale states that the property was sold subject to your right to repurchase (redeem) it by paying the foreclosure sales price. (See Section B12 below on post-sale redemption rights.)

In the event that your lender did not ask for a deficiency judgment, the sheriff will give the purchaser a Deed of Sale. (CCP § 701.660.) This document contains the title of the court in which the judgment was entered, date of the entry of judgment, name and address of the foreclosing lender, your last known address, a description of

your property and the date of sale. At this point, you can no longer redeem the property.

### d. What Happens to Liens After the Foreclosure Sale

All liens that are junior (recorded subsequent) to the foreclosing lender's deed of trust, such as a second deed of trust, mechanic's liens, abstract of judgment, writs of attachment, or similar liens, are extinguished by the foreclosure sale. (CCP §§ 701.630 and 729.080(e).) However, property tax liens will continue to encumber the property (regardless of when they were recorded) unless they are paid off at the foreclosure sale.

Although junior liens may disappear, the underlying debts remain intact. In other words, those "wiped out" junior lienholders now have the right to sue you directly to recover their debt.

Further, creditors holding mechanic's liens, tax liens, writs of attachments or judgment liens have the right to record those liens on other property you own or later buy.

## 11. Deficiency Judgment

*Not all lenders seek deficiency judgments.* If your lender did not file a Complaint seeking a deficiency judgment against you, or subsequently waived it, you can skip this section and go to Section B12 below, which covers post-sale redemption rights.

Your lender won't recover the full amount of your unpaid debt from the foreclosure sale if your property sells for less than the unpaid balance of your promissory note, plus costs and attorney fees. This shortage is called a deficiency. A court-ordered deficiency judgment entered against you for this shortage allows your lender to recoup its loss. (Of course, if your property sells for more than the amount of money you owe your lender, you won't be liable for a deficiency.)

To obtain a deficiency judgment, your lender must request it in the original Complaint and file an application for a deficiency judgment with the Superior Court (that conducted the foreclosure trial) within three months of the foreclosure sale. Your lender must mail you a copy of the application. If your lender doesn't file an application on time, it will probably lose the right to get a deficiency judgment.

---

**ANTI-DEFICIENCY LAWS: AN HISTORICAL PERSPECTIVE**

During the depression of the 1930s, California homeowners suffered foreclosures in record numbers. To make matters worse, home prices spiraled downward, which meant that foreclosure sales inevitably brought prices less than the amount of the debt. Consequently, it became routine for defaulting homeowners first to lose their homes—bad enough in any economic context—and then find themselves liable for the deficiency.

Confronted with the economic ruin of millions of homeowners, California lawmakers passed legislation that severely restricts a lender's right to collect a deficiency judgment ("anti-deficiency legislation"). Today, California is in the minority of states protecting homeowners by offering anti-deficiency legislation.

## a. "Fair Value" Hearing

*If you believe your property was sold for fair value, skip this section and proceed to Subsection b, below.*

Let's say you believe that your property sold for substantially less than its current market value. In response to your lender's application for deficiency judgment, you have the right to petition the court to conduct a hearing to determine the market value of your property. (CCP § 726(b).) This hearing is called a "fair value hearing."

The sole function of the hearing will be for the judge to determine the fair market value of your property on the date of the foreclosure sale. The judge will also determine whether your indebtedness (plus interest and costs of the levy and sale) exceeds the fair value of your property.

To prepare for this hearing, you should hire an appraiser to testify as to the market value of your property as of the date of the foreclosure sale. The appraiser will take about two weeks to appraise your property and charge anywhere from $250 to $1,000, depending on the size of the property.

The hearing will probably be conducted in front of the same judge who conducted the foreclosure trial, and should last approximately one to two hours. A representative of your lender will be present, and you should also attend, although it is unlikely that you will be required to testify. After listening to the appraisers you and your lender bring to court, the judge will decide the fair market value of your property on the date of the foreclosure sale.

After the fair market value of your property has been determined, the judge will enter its ruling. If the court determines that the fair market value of your property was greater than the price obtained at the foreclosure sale, it will adjust the deficiency judgment accordingly.

*Example: First Savings Bank forecloses Norma's apartment building in Monterey, on which she owes $290,000, plus a total of $10,000 in foreclosure costs and attorney fees. The property has a current market value of approximately $250,000 but sells for only $200,000 at the foreclosure sale. First Savings files an application with the court requesting a deficiency judgment against Norma for $100,000 ($300,000–$200,000). Norma objects and requests a fair value hearing. At the hearing, Norma presents an appraiser who testifies that the property had a value of $250,000, and First Savings presents an appraiser who testifies that the property had a value of $225,000. The judge agrees with Norma's appraiser and lowers the deficiency judgment to $50,000 ($300,000–$250,000) rather than $100,000.*

### b. Court Issues Deficiency Judgment

The deficiency judgment will consist of your unpaid debt, plus interest and costs, minus the fair value of the property (as determined at the hearing). It will also state that the amount of the deficiency—exclusive of interest and costs—may not exceed the difference between the entire amount of your indebtedness and the sale price. The deficiency judgment will be issued by the Superior Court that heard your case.

Once you receive the deficiency judgment, there is nothing more you can do—except, of course, pay the deficiency judgment if you can. If you cannot pay, your lender will be permitted to pursue all the various collection procedures allowed under California law, including wage garnishments, bank attachments and seizing and selling your valuable property. Remember, you always have the right to negotiate with your lender for a reduced lump-sum payment in full settlement or a payment schedule. In addition, there are ways to prevent a creditor from seizing your assets. (See Chapter 5 on negotiating with your lender and Chapter 9 for more on bankruptcy options.)

*For information on your rights and options as a judgment debtor, refer to Money Troubles: Legal Strategies to Cope with Your Debts, by Robin Leonard (Nolo Press). For the creditor's perspective, see Collect Your Court Judgment, by Gini Scott, Stephen Elias and Lisa Goldoftas (Nolo Press).*

## 12. Post-Sale Redemption Period

After the foreclosure sale, the sheriff will give you a Notice of the Right to Redemption. (CCP § 729.050.) The notice states that, provided your lender is seeking a deficiency judgment, you have the right to redeem your property by paying the full foreclosure sales price plus the sheriff's costs and expenses. (See the sidebar below, "How Much Will It Cost to Redeem Your Property?" for details.) Only you, the former owner of the property, may redeem your property after the foreclosure sale. Junior lienholders, guarantors, and tenants cannot redeem the property.

If you redeem your property by paying the redemption price, ownership of the property will be restored to you, with all junior liens wiped out. Ironically, even if you redeem your property, your lender may still have a deficiency judgment against you. In that event, you will find yourself in the precarious position of once again owning your property while simultaneously owing your lender.

*Example: Jaimie's lender sells his commercial property for $323,000 at a foreclosure sale and gets a deficiency judgment for $120,000 for the unpaid amount of his loan plus costs of the sale. Jaimie redeems the property for $328,000 (which includes costs incurred by the purchaser plus interest). Jaimie's lender still has a judgment against him for $120,000, and can pursue collection methods to get paid, including selling his property!*

The only way your lender can block your redemption rights is to waive its deficiency claim against you before the foreclosure judgment is ordered by the judge. (CCP § 726.)

How long you have to redeem your property depends on the selling price at the foreclosure sale or the price determined at the fair value hearing (if higher):

- If the sale did not bring in enough to satisfy the indebtedness (including interest and costs), there is a deficiency. If your lender seeks to recover this deficiency, you have one year from the date of sale to redeem. (CCP § 729.030(b).)
- If the sale proceeds satisfied your total indebtedness (including interest and costs), you have three months from the date of sale to redeem. (CCP § 729.030(a).)

*You will not receive reminders of the redemption deadlines.* You are expected to know the expiration date of your redemption period on your own.

---

### HOW MUCH WILL IT COST TO REDEEM YOUR PROPERTY?

To redeem your property, you pay the sheriff a total of the following, minus any rents and profits the purchaser received during the redemption period:

- the purchase price at the foreclosure sale (not necessarily the fair market value of your property)

- any assessments or taxes due

- reasonable amounts for fire insurance, maintenance, upkeep, repair or improvements on your property incurred by the purchaser during the redemption period

- any amounts the purchaser paid to senior lienholders during the redemption period, and

- interest on all amounts specified above from the date paid until the date you deposit the redemption price with the sheriff.

*Example: John loses his Modesto apartment building in a foreclosure sale, where a purchaser pays $250,000 for the property. A month later, John receives a hefty inheritance from his grandfather and decides to redeem the property. The sheriff gives John these figures:*

| | |
|---|---:|
| *Purchase price:* | $250,000 |
| *Property taxes paid:* | 7,633 |
| *Fire and casualty insurance:* | 2,500 |
| *Property repairs and maintenance:* | 1,745 |
| *Interest on the above amount:* | 2,182 |
| *Subtotal:* | $264,060 |
| *Minus rents purchaser received:* | - 12,000 |
| *Total:* | $252,060 |

### a. You Retain Possession of Property During the Redemption Period

It may be hard to believe, but during the redemption period, you are permitted to retain possession of your property. That means you can live there or rent it out as you wish. During this period, however, the purchaser is entitled to receive:

- the fair rental value of your use and occupancy of the property, if you live there, or
- any rents and profits from your property, if you have tenants.

If you fail to pay either of these items, the purchaser has the right to go into court and file an action to recover this lost income.

### b. Certificate of Redemption

Once you have deposited the required amount to redeem your property, the sheriff will turn over the funds to the purchaser of your property (who is not necessarily your lender). The purchaser must accept the money and give up ownership (and possession, if applicable) of your property.

The sheriff will then cancel the previously issued Certificate of Sale, issue a Certificate of Redemption, record it in the county recorder's office, and send you a certified copy by registered mail within ten days. Once this Certificate is recorded, you will once again legally own the property.

*What if the purchaser refuses to accept payment?* If the sheriff notifies you that the purchaser disputes the amount needed to redeem your property, you can file a motion asking the court to resolve the redemption price. Within 20 days of receiving your motion, the court will schedule a hearing to resolve the monetary dispute. Prior to the hearing, you'll need to deposit the undisputed portion of the redemption price with the sheriff. At the hearing, each side will be required to present evidence to the judge as to what is the redemption price. The judge will then determine the correct amount required to redeem the property.

### c.  After the Redemption Period Expires

If you don't redeem your property before the redemption period expires, the sheriff will record a Sheriff's Deed conveying title of your property to the purchaser at the foreclosure sale. The sheriff will deliver the deed directly to the purchaser. You will not receive a copy.

At this point, you (or your tenants) must vacate the property unless the purchaser allows you to stay. If you are interested in staying, you can contact the purchaser directly and negotiate an extended rental of the property. If you (or your tenants) don't leave when asked, the purchaser may serve you with a three-day Notice to Quit. If you still refuse to move voluntarily, the purchaser may file an unlawful detainer action (eviction) and evict you.

*chapter*

# 5

# NEGOTIATING WITH YOUR LENDER

**M**ost people don't realize that one of the most effective ways to stop a foreclosure is to negotiate a solution directly with the foreclosing lender. Most lenders would prefer if you simply bring your loan current. After all, they're in the business of loaning money, not owning properties. Only if you fail to work out a resolution of the default will your lender be forced to foreclose.

Your first course of action should always be to negotiate with your lender. You may be pleasantly surprised by the results. Property owners often miss this obvious starting point because they are intimidated by their lenders or embarrassed by their predicament. This chapter is designed to take the mystery and fear out of contacting and negotiating with your lender.

*If your finances are still in shambles.* Do not proceed with this chapter or negotiate with your lender unless you have your financial problems under control and have the ability to bring your loan current and resume your monthly payments. If, after a realistic look at your situation, you conclude that you cannot afford the monthly payments, consider the other strategies described in this book, introduced in Chapter 1.

## A. Negotiating Strategies

Good communication is the underlying basis of any successful negotiation. Unless you communicate directly with your lender and understand your lender's goals and priorities, you will have little chance of stopping foreclosure. To prepare for negotiations with your lender, consider the suggestions below.

### 1. Act Immediately

You may think that waiting to the last minute will buy you some extra time. You couldn't be more wrong. If you are interested in negotiating with your lender, don't wait! Lenders rarely cooperate with borrowers who contact them on the eve of a foreclosure sale.

Establish a dialogue as soon as possible. If the lender's office is local, request a face-to-face meeting with a representative of your lender at his or her earliest convenience. If the lender's office is out of town, you will have to do your negotiating by telephone and correspondence.

Either way, be prepared to discuss specific proposals for restructuring your loan or bringing the arrears current (workout). It is your responsibility—not your lender's—to propose a manageable solution. If possible, bring several different proposals in writing.

### 2. Respond to All of Your Lender's Calls and Letters

Respond to every communication you receive from your lender. Even if you have nothing to say, at least confirm in writing its calls or receipt of its letters, request a meeting as soon as possible, and reiterate your determination to resolve the loan default.

Create a log that chronicles all telephone conversations and letters. Include the date, time, who you spoke to, what was discussed, and anything else noteworthy about the call or letter. (See the Communications Chart in Chapter 1, Section A.)

*Resources on negotiating.* Several books on negotiating may be helpful in your discussions with your lender, including *Getting to Yes: Negotiating Agreements Without Giving In*, by Roger Fisher and William Ury (Penguin Books), *Getting Past No: Negotiating Your Way from Confrontation to Cooperation*, by William Ury (Bantam Books) and *You Can Negotiate Anything*, by Herb Cohen (Citadel Press).

## 3. Make Sure You Are Dealing With Your Current Lender

Although you may be receiving monthly statements, letters, and telephone calls from a certain company, it may not actually own your loan. The company may be acting merely as the loan "servicer"—a company (occasionally your former lender, if it sold the loan) that receives a fee for administering loans. A loan servicer may not be as willing to avoid a foreclosure as your current lender because the money is not theirs. They are only responsible for collecting the monthly payments. In contrast, the actual lender may be more accommodating as to how and when they will be paid back. So, it behooves you to go around the servicer and contact your current lender as soon as possible.

There are several ways to get the name of your current lender:

- call the institution that loaned you money and simply ask
- look at your billing statement and see if another name appears in addition to the name of your original lender
- contact the customer service department of a local title insurance company, or
- go to the county recorder's office and find out if an assignment of your deed of trust has been recorded, and to whom.

Once you determine the name and address of your current lender, contact its loan workout department.

## 4. Negotiate in a Spirit of Cooperation

This is no time to be belligerent. Remember, your property is in, or soon may be in, foreclosure and your lender is already dubious that you are serious about paying your loan. Express your willingness to cooperate and your commitment to curing the default.

## 5. Talk Your Lender's Language, Not Yours

Obviously, you are preoccupied with stopping the foreclosure. This is not your lender's primary concern. In a lender's view, foreclosure is an effective method to catch your undivided attention and to see that a delinquent loan is quickly brought current.

Do not demand that the foreclosure be stopped. Rather, focus on solving your lender's problem first. Your lender may eventually agree to stop the foreclosure, but only after it is assured that you have the ability and intention to bring your loan current and resume making monthly payments.

## 6. Explain Reasons for the Non-Payment

Do not shy away from this issue. Anticipate your lender's inquiry and be prepared to concisely explain why you failed to make your loan payments. Regardless of whether the reason was a divorce, illness, death in the family, loss of job, business reversal or other financial problem, be prepared to assure your lender that the cause of the default is being (or has been) resolved. Generally, a lender will need to feel comfortable that your problems are behind you before it will work out a solution to the defaulted loan.

## 7. Know the Facts

Do you know the date you took out your loan? How about the date you made your last payment? When was the Notice of Default recorded? When was the last date someone called from your lender's office regarding your loan?

All of these facts, and many more, are extremely relevant to the negotiations. Take the time to organize your documents (we give suggestions in Chapter 1, Section B), and write down the relevant facts about your property, loan, the amount of the default, the pending foreclosure and any communications with your lender. Use the Notice of Default Worksheet in Chapter 3 if yours is a nonjudicial foreclosure, or the Judicial Foreclosure Worksheet in Chapter 4 if it is a judicial foreclosure, to set up a chronology of events.

## 8. Don't Make Promises You Can't Keep

The worst thing you can do while negotiating with your lender is to make an unrealistic promise. Your credibility is already in question because you failed to make your payments as promised. As a result, your lender has gone to the trouble of starting foreclosure proceedings. Now that your lender has your undivided attention, do not offer or agree to a settlement you cannot keep. The temptation may be great and your intentions may be noble, but do not be seduced by the pressure. Only agree to what you can really afford.

You also need to appreciate the financial impact of your promises. You may end up with higher monthly payments or a balloon payment. In that event, if you temporarily stop the foreclosure, the actual dollars-and-cents impact to your pocketbook may be more disastrous in future years.

## 9. Remind Your Lender of Its Foreclosure Costs

You already know that it will cost you money if you lose your property in foreclosure. But did you realize that your lender will also lose money if it forecloses?  For example, if your lender completes the foreclosure, it stands to lose back payments, foreclosure costs, wear and tear while you occupy the property, damage to the property when you (or your tenants) leave, loss of future payments until the property is sold and marketing costs to resell the property. Don't forget to mention these costs when you talk with your lender. Your lenders may need to be frequently reminded that these costs can be avoided if it will negotiate a resolution of the default with you.

## 10. Consider Working With a Foreclosure Consultant

At some stage during the foreclosure process, you may be contacted by foreclosure consultants eager to help you resolve your foreclosure or negotiate with your lender. If you are considering working with a foreclosure consultant, read Chapter 12, Section B.

## 11. Learn About Your Lender

The approach you use to negotiate should depend on which kind of lender has instituted the foreclosure. Because different lenders have different criteria for resolving loans in foreclosure, your approach should depend on who you are dealing with. You need to read only the section of this chapter that is geared to your particular lender:
- institutional lenders (Section B)
- private lenders (Section C)
- U.S. Department of Housing and Urban Development (HUD) (Section D)
- U.S. Department of Veteran Affairs (Section E)
- California Department of Veteran Affairs (Section F)

## B. Negotiating With an Institutional Lender

Banks, savings and loans, credit unions, mortgage companies and pension funds are all "institutional lenders." An institutional lender lends its customers' deposits, not its own money. For purposes of this book, this category also includes the Resolution Trust Corporation and secondary market investment groups, including the Federal National Mortgage Association (FNMA or Fannie Mae), the Federal Home Loan Mortgage Corporation (FHLMC or Freddie Mac), and the Government National Mortgage Association (GNMA or Ginnie Mae).

## 1. Goals of an Institutional Lender

Before negotiating with an institutional lender, you should understand what it needs to achieve. The goals of an institutional lender are twofold:

- To receive a steady cash flow. If your lender can count on you and its other borrowers to make regular loan payments, cash flow is steady. When cash flow is interrupted, your lender is not getting the money it needs to pay expenses. Usually, lenders maintain a delicate balance between cash flow and expenses. When expenses exceed cash flow, the institutional lender loses money and endangers its own continuing existence.
- To avoid a loss. Your lender wants to avoid a loss on its balance sheet. A loss does not, however, come about by foreclosing. When your lender forecloses, it simply performs a book-keeping entry. Instead of a deed of trust owned as an asset, your lender's books will now show a property owned (known as "Real Estate Owned" or "REO"). In both cases, this is an asset. A loss would show up on your lender's books only if the property sells for less than the balance of your loan.

Remember that if your lender ends up taking your property back, there will be additional costs (repairs, marketing costs, legal fees, escrow charges, title insurance and the like). If your property's sale price won't cover the outstanding loan balance and these additional costs, your lender will experience a loss. This explains why a lender should be highly motivated to resolve your defaulted loan.

## 2. Contact Your Lender

Call your lender and ask to speak to an officer in charge of your loan. Politely refuse to deal with the collection department or someone who calls you to find out why you haven't made your payments. They don't have the authority to negotiate with you. You dealt with an officer when you obtained the loan—surely you deserve the same respect when you are resolving the repayment of that loan.

*How to track down a person with authority to solve your problem.* Call the main office of your lender and ask for the name of the branch manager or senior loan officer. Then hang up. Call back a while later and ask for that specific person by name. Once you are connected, request an appointment. If this person will not take your call (or does not call you back), send a letter chronicling these events and repeat your request for a meeting. Mail a copy of the letter to the president of your lender. Sooner or later, someone with authority will return your call.

Once you reach a loan officer or someone else who has the authority to negotiate with you, request an appointment if they have a local office. An actual meeting will exponentially increase the odds of reaching an agreement. During the meeting, you'll need to convey that your default is a temporary problem and emphasize that you want to avoid foreclosure. You should also update your lender on the condition of your property. If there are problems, be sure to let your lender know. On the other hand, if you have made improvements and repairs, point them out.

Ask your lender to explain the foreclosure process. Gently coach your lender into explaining what happens to REO ("real estate owned") properties your lender takes back in foreclosure. Ask if your lender has a large inventory of REOs or needs more. Initially, the loan officer may be reluctant to discuss these issues, but as he or she sees that you understand the ramifications of foreclosure (from your lender's perspective), the loan officer may be more willing to talk. The discussion may reveal how eager—or reluctant—your lender is to take your property back in foreclosure. Especially if the loan officer admits that they don't want another REO on their hands, you can proceed with concretely discussing alternatives.

Propose possible solutions, such as restructuring the promissory note, additional moratorium on payments, forbearance, or refinancing. As your lender considers various options, you will learn exactly how flexible it is towards solving your problem. Keep in mind that the options are as varied as the terms of your promissory note. For example, a restructuring of your note could involve a modification of principal, interest, term and/or payment. The variations are limited only by the creativity and negotiating skills of you and your lender.

If you're unlucky and confront a recalcitrant lender who's set on taking your property back regardless of the outcome, your job is more difficult. Be prepared to discuss aspects of the foreclosure procedures that may have been conducted improperly (see Chapter 3 or 4). This should certainly grab your lender's attention.

If all else fails, and your lender isn't budging, you may want to mention bankruptcy. Bankruptcy automatically stays (stops) all foreclosure activity, causing your property to be tied up for months or even years. During that period, your lender may not receive payments, would incur attorney fees and most importantly, lose time. Of course, your lender already knows these possibilities. What's important is that now your lender knows that you know them too.

After discussing the foreclosure procedural defects and/or bankruptcy, your lender may have a change of heart. During this stage in the meeting, it is important for you to remain calm and cordial. Don't be rude or make threats, no matter how uncooperative your lender is. Be professional and eager to find a solution. Emphasize that you don't want to file bankruptcy, but unless you can work out a amicable solution to the foreclosure, you may be left with no other alternative.

## 3. Main Issues in a Workout

If your lender is willing to consider a workout (an arrangement to bring your loan current and stop the foreclosure), there are generally two main issues that must be addressed separately:
- future payments, and
- past due payments (arrears).

Your circumstances will dictate your approach. For example, you may be able to bring your loan current, but be unable to make future payments as

they come due. On the other hand, you may be ready to resume monthly payments, but need time to bring the arrears current. Following are some guidelines on these two areas of negotiation.

### a. Workouts for Future Monthly Payments

In general, lenders are more concerned that monthly payments resume immediately than how the arrearage is going to be paid. If, however, you can't resume your monthly payments in full, there are two alternatives:
- Delay making payments for a period of months (forbearance). As part of an overall loan workout, lenders will typically allow you to skip your monthly payments for three to six months, provided you have reasonable justification. You repay this amount over a period of months in addition to your regular payments.
  *Example: George owns a four-unit apartment building in a small college town. Renters are hard to come by in the summer, and he misses several loan payments. His bank threatens foreclosure. George immediately contacts the bank, explains his financial situation and negotiates a workout. The bank agrees that George can forebear from making payments for four more months. He then must repay the total arrears over 18 months while simultaneously making his monthly payments.*
- Make reduced payments for a set time. You make partial payments for several months until you are back on your feet. Typically, lenders will accept partial payments for six months to one year, provided you have an explanation for the missed payments, a reason for the partial payments and a prognosis for when full payments can resume.
  *Example: Arthur owns a cattle ranch in Mono County. Rumors of mad cow disease at his ranch have a devastating effect on business. While Arthur is successfully countering the negative PR (started by a competitor), he doesn't have enough funds to make his regular loan payments, and Sierra Savings Bank starts foreclosure proceedings. Arthur immediately contacts Sierra. Because he cannot afford to resume payments, Arthur suggests that he make one-third payments for three months and then half payments*

*for three more months. Beginning with the seventh month, Arthur will resume the monthly payments in full. At the end of one year, Arthur will pay the balance of the arrears over 12 months. Sierra agrees to the workout and stops the foreclosure.*

### b. Workouts for the Arrears

If you can't afford to pay the arrears (past due payments) all at once, you have three basic options, with endless variations:

- Add arrears to the principal loan balance and resume regular scheduled payments. Your loan will immediately return to current status, the principal balance will increase (by the amount of your arrears) and your monthly payment will increase minimally. Unfortunately, strict banking regulations make this option exceedingly difficult for some lenders. Nevertheless, it is worth proposing because it is the most effective workout for the financially strapped borrower.
  *Example: Henry and Susan run into financial problems and miss four monthly house payments. After several meetings with an officer at their bank, they successfully negotiate a workout of their default. The bank agrees to stop the foreclosure and add the default amount ($6,000) to the loan balance ($150,000), provided Henry and Susan immediately resume making the monthly payments. Henry and Susan's monthly payments increase from $1,500 to $1,560 per month.*

- Make partial payments until arrears are paid. Financial institutions will often agree to let you resume your regular monthly payments and pay a portion of the arrears over the course of six months to a year.
  *Example: After five years of running a small bed-and-breakfast in Monterey, John and Sally decide they need a break. They take a whirlwind trip around the world and return home to a mountain of credit card bills. The weather is unusually cold and business is slow. They miss four monthly payments of $1,425 on their home loan. They work out an arrangement with their bank to make six equal monthly payments of $950 plus their regular monthly payment of $1,425 until their loan is*

*brought current. After paying $2,375 for six months, their payments will return to $1,425 per month.*

- Make a balloon payment at a later date. You may agree to pay the arrears in total in one payment on a specific date. However, do not commit to this arrangement unless you believe you will be able to pay the balloon payment when it comes due.
  *Example: Adriana owns a farm in the Sacramento Valley. Times have been rough, and she's missed five loan payments ($6,250). Now she has a new crew working for her and a bumper crop on the way. Adriana convinces her bank that although she doesn't have the full $6,250 now, she will have it within six months. Her bank reviews her financial records, checks the farmer's almanac and finally agrees to accept $6,250 within six months—provided that Adriana resumes her regular monthly payments immediately.*

## 4. Submit a Written Version of Your Workout Proposal

Once you and your lender negotiate a resolution of your defaulted loan, you should sign a written agreement, commonly known as a "workout," "standstill" or "forbearance agreement." It behooves you to take the initiative to get your agreement in writing, which can be done by letter, such as the sample below. If your lender submits an agreement, consider having an attorney review it to be sure it conforms with your understanding of the workout.

*Without a signed agreement, you don't have a deal.* Simply sending a letter to your lender doesn't count for anything unless it is signed and returned to you. Some lenders will respond by sending their own workout agreement.

### SAMPLE WORKOUT LETTER

April 17, 199X

Fourthway National Bank
2700 Fourth Street
Petaluma, California

Re: Property located at 1256 Magnolia Street,
Petaluma, California

Loan No.: 12345

Dear Mr. Plimpton:

Your bank holds a deed of trust encumbering my property as security for a promissory note in the amount of $135,000. Your bank initiated a nonjudicial foreclosure after I missed three payments ($1,200 per month). On April 16, 199X, the bank agreed to stop the pending foreclosure, provided I make payments as follows:

| DUE DATE | AMOUNT | FOR THE MONTH |
|---|---|---|
| Aug 1, 199X | $600 | 50% of Jan, 199x payment |
| Sep 1, 199X | $600 | 50% of Jan, 199x payment |
| Oct 1, 199X | $600 | 50% of Feb, 199x payment |
| Nov 1, 199X | $600 | 50% of Feb, 199x payment |
| Dec 1, 199X | $600 | 50% of Mar, 199x payment |
| Jan 1, 199X | $600 | 50% of Mar, 199x payment |
| Feb 1, 199X | $600 | 50% of Apr, 199x payment |
| Mar 1, 199X | $600 | 50% of Apr, 199x payment |
| Apr 1, 199X | $600 | 50% of May, 199x payment |
| May 1, 199X | $600 | 50% of May, 199x payment |
| Jun 1, 199X | $600 | 50% of Jun, 199x payment |
| Jul 1, 199X | $600 | 50% of Jun, 199x payment |
| Aug 1, 199X | $600 | 50% of Jul, 199x payment |
| Sep 1, 199X | $600 | 50% of Jul, 199x payment |

I understand that these payments are in addition to my monthly $1,200 payment, which will resume on August 1, 199x. Once all of the above payments are paid, the Bank has agreed to rescind the Notice of Default.

If this letter accurately reflects our agreement, please sign in the space provided below and return a copy of this letter to me.

Sincerely,


Bill Smith
AGREED AND ACCEPTED TO:

_____

Authorized Officer on behalf of Fourthway National Bank

## 5. Getting Help From Your Private Mortgage Insurer

*If you don't have private mortgage insurance.* If your loan is not insured by a private mortgage insurer (check your loan coupons or ask your lender), skip this section.

Private mortgage insurance is occasionally purchased by institutional lenders (and paid by the borrower) to insure against a lender's loss in the event of foreclosure. Because most defaults occur early on, the private mortgage insurance (PMI) typically insures only the first five years of a loan against default.

If your lender forecloses, the PMI must pay out a claim to your lender up to the limits of its coverage. To avert this potential liability, the PMI may want to participate in workout negotiations to minimize its losses. A PMI won't necessarily hear about a foreclosure until a property has been sold and the lender makes a claim. You may need to alert the PMI to the pending foreclosure and your efforts to work out a resolution with your lender.

Only get the PMI involved if negotiations with your institutional lender are stalled—but don't wait too long in the foreclosure process. If you come to an impasse with your lender, write a letter to the PMI, request its assistance and ask to meet in person as soon as possible. At the meeting, explain your financial situation and your plans for resolving your defaulted loan, and request help in dealing with your lender.

If you and your lender have reached a deadlock, the PMI may be able to jump-start stalled negotiations. The PMI may have more influence and leverage with your lender than you. If you have no success in dealing with a stubborn lender, the PMI may come to the rescue, if you ask. After all, the PMI has nothing to lose and everything to gain!

As an alternative, you may request that the PMI help you out of the foreclosure by fronting a portion of your delinquent payments for several months. You may wonder why a PMI would cover any portion of your arrearage. If your lender forecloses, the PMI will likely have to pay a claim to your lender. It may be more economical for the PMI to assist you now by covering your arrears than to pay a claim to your lender later. In return, you'll agree to reimburse the PMI.

Convincing a PMI that it make good business sense to pay some of your delinquent payments (rather then the lender's eventual claim) is not usually an easy task. You will need to show that:

- you can afford to resume monthly payments to your lender immediately, and
- you will be able to reimburse the PMI for its advances within a reasonable period of time, usually a period of months.

## C. Negotiating With a Private Lender

Private lenders are typically concerned with retirement income, taxes or ways to defer income. Spend some time talking with your lender to get a handle on her financial objectives. You cannot be creative about a financial solution that benefits both of you until you understand your lender's fears and goals.

On the other hand, if your private lender is a family member or close friend, personal relationships may be at stake and patience may have worn thin. It's your responsibility to take charge of the situation and defuse problems before they get out of hand.

Most private lenders have never confronted the prospect of foreclosing and probably won't know exactly what's involved. Some private lenders won't use an attorney, preferring to handle it themselves. You may need to explain how a foreclosure works (a copy of this book may help) and point out that it is to neither party's advantage to proceed. Start by describing or reminding your lender about the high costs of foreclosure, including lost interest income and potential losses when reselling foreclosed property.

*Private investors in real estate.* Occasionally, private lenders are as sophisticated as institutional lenders and hold large portfolios of real estate loans. If that sounds like your lender, treat her as an institutional lender and refer back to Section B, above.

Here are several options for negotiating an end to the foreclosure with a private lender:

- You resume making your scheduled loan payments and agree that the arrears will be paid back as a balloon payment at a later date.
- You "rollover" your loan into a new longer-term loan, which is also secured by your property.
- If your monthly payments were consistently late, you can volunteer a late fee (if your promissory note does not call for one) or a security deposit.
- Although not necessarily a good move, you could offer to increase the interest rate and/or the amount of the monthly payments.
- If your private lender is concerned with a large financial commitment (such as taxes or college tuition), you can propose to increase the monthly payments to cover her commitment.
- You can also utilize some of the methods described for institutional lenders in Section B3, above.

If all else fails, an emotional appeal may work. Most individuals (or their spouses) will go out of their way to spare a family from losing their home.

# D. Negotiating With HUD and the FHA

The U.S. Department of Housing and Urban Development (HUD) is a federal agency that runs various housing (predominately residential) programs for American citizens.

One of HUD's most popular programs is run by the Federal Housing Administration (FHA). The FHA insures mortgage loans that banks and other institutional lenders make for new and existing properties. The FHA funds itself by charging a one-half percent in mortgage insurance each month, which is included in your monthly payments.

When the FHA insures a loan, it agrees to reimburse the lender if the borrower defaults on payments. Because of the FHA program, lenders can make loans that they would not otherwise risk. In the past 50 years, millions of homes have been financed using FHA insurance.

When there are a lot of foreclosures, as there have been during the 1990s, the FHA is overloaded with properties. Conceivably, it could take back tens of thousands of properties, but that would drain money from its fund. Therefore, HUD looks for alternatives to foreclosure and essentially offers homeowners a "second chance" to make good on a defaulted loan.

The "HUD Home Mortgage Assignment Program" is designed to prevent FHA-insured homeowners from losing their homes in foreclosure. You must take specific steps to participate in the program; it is not automatic. Under the program, your lender assigns (turns over) your promissory note and deed of trust to HUD instead of foreclosing on your property. HUD pays off your loan and works with you to structure a plan to cure your default.

The good news is that HUD is likely to be far more flexible than an institutional lender in negotiating a workout that fits your financial needs.

---

**HUD DEED-IN-LIEU PROGRAM**

If you don't want to keep your property: HUD also has a deed in lieu program for property owners that do not want to keep their property, but nevertheless want to avoid the foreclosure. More information on this program is available through the HUD hotline (see below). Chapter 11 also covers HUD's program for deeds in lieu of foreclosure.

---

## 1. Will You Qualify for the HUD Program?

You can only take advantage of the HUD assignment program if your loan is FHA-insured. If you don't know whether or not your loan is FHA-insured, either ask your lender or check your monthly payment loan coupon; if it includes a charge for FHA insurance, yours is an FHA loan. You may also call HUD and ask if your loan is FHA-insured:

> HUD Housing Hotline
> 800-733-3238

You must meet three criteria to qualify for HUD's assignment program:

- You must be behind at least three monthly payments.
- You must have a good reason, beyond your control, for missing payments—such as being laid off from work, becoming ill or suffering an injury. The reason must be temporary—for example, permanent illness or paralysis will not qualify.
- You must have a reasonable prospect of resuming monthly payments in a specific period of time, not to exceed 36 months.

Once HUD determines that these three criteria are met, it will contact your lender and have your loan assigned to HUD.

## 2. Overview of HUD Assignment Program

Below is an overview of the steps involved in HUD's Home Mortgage Assignment Program. Follow these steps carefully, because the procedures have strict compliance deadlines.

### a. Lender Advises You of HUD Program

Your lender should send you a letter advising you of the pending foreclosure and the availability of HUD's Home Mortgage Assignment Program. Your lender's letter will probably state that you have 15 days to contact HUD before it will initiate foreclosure. If you don't receive a letter from your lender, call the HUD hotline directly and request that HUD contact your lender.

### b. Ask Your Lender to Assign Your Loan to HUD

It is up to you to request that your lender assign your loan to HUD; your lender will not do it for you. You have 15 days from the date your lender mailed you a letter about the HUD program to furnish your lender with a completed HUD-92068F form (your lender has blank copies, if you need them). Your lender will forward this form to HUD.

If your lender won't provide you with the information and paperwork you need, send HUD a letter, such as the sample below, and request HUD's immediate involvement. You can get the address of your local HUD office by calling the HUD hotline (above). Send the letter by certified mail, return receipt requested, or overnight express.

September 12, 199X

HUD Home Mortgage Assignment Program
HUD Office Address
City, State, Zip Code

To whom it may concern:

I own property located at 2560 Main Street in El Cerrito, California. General Savings Bank holds the first deed of trust encumbering my property securing a loan in the amount of $150,000. The loan is insured by the FHA.

I am currently three months behind in my payments and General Savings has threatened foreclosure. General Savings has not responded to my request that my loan be assigned to HUD under your Home Mortgage Assignment Program. The purpose of this letter is to formally request such an assignment.

Please contact me at your earliest convenience so that I may submit whatever documents you need to accept the assignment.

Sincerely,

Jonathan Dutton
2560 Main Street
El Cerrito, California

cc: General Savings Bank

### c. Complete HUD Application

The self-explanatory HUD application form (HUD-92068F) must include a statement of current income and expenses and potential sources of future income, an explanation of events causing you to fall behind in payments, an explanation of future events that will allow you to resume full monthly payments within three years and a budget of future income and expenses.

Fill out and return your application to HUD within 15 days of receipt, along with copies of relevant documents (for safety's sake keep the originals in your personal files). Send everything by certified mail, return receipt requested, or overnight express.

### d. HUD Makes Preliminary Determination

A HUD field office will review your application for assignment and send you a letter with one of four responses:

- HUD will accept your application for assignment.
- HUD has referred your application to your lender for further handling.
- HUD needs more information to determine whether you are eligible. In this case, promptly gather whatever additional documentation and supporting evidence may support your position (letters, receipts, bills and the like) and deliver copies to the HUD office.
- HUD has primarily rejected your application.

### e. What to Do If Application Is Rejected

If HUD initially rejects your application, don't be disheartened. It is only a preliminary decision. You have 15 days from the date the rejection was issued to appeal. HUD will typically explain exactly why you do not appear to be eligible for assignment. Fortunately, HUD will also tell what additional information would change its preliminary determination.

Immediately telephone your local HUD office and request:

- a reconsideration conference, which will be scheduled within 25 days of HUD's initial decision letter, and
- copies of all documents in your file at HUD.

*If you do not appeal within 15 days.* HUD will send a letter to your lender authorizing foreclosure. At that point, there is nothing else HUD can do to assist you.

Your task is to prepare a written response (with documentation, if possible) to each of the requirements HUD contends you did not meet. Prepare a current detailed budget of your income and expenses as well as a projected budget for the next three years. In addition, explain in writing how

you'll be able to resume your loan payments within three years.

At the conference, you should discuss why your loan qualifies for assignment to HUD. Be prepared to present all of your documents and respond to each of HUD's reasons why your loan may not qualify for assignment. You may bring an attorney or financial advisor to this conference, but it is not required.

### f. HUD Makes a Final Decision

Within 30 to 90 days from the date you first requested an assignment, HUD will notify you and your lender of its decision. During this period, your lender is required to hold off starting foreclosure and you are not required to make the monthly payments.

If HUD accepts the assignment, HUD will set up a meeting to discuss the terms of a workout plan. In the interim, HUD will work directly with your lender to handle the actual assignment documents. HUD will also advise your lender not to report your loan as a foreclosure to the credit reporting agencies—but check your credit report to make sure. After the assignment, only HUD (not your old lender) will be involved in your loan.

If HUD rejects the assignment of your loan, your only recourse is to appeal HUD's decision directly to the Federal Court. This is beyond the scope of this book and you will probably need a lawyer.

### g. Meet With HUD to Finalize Workout

To finalize the assignment, you and a HUD representative will discuss and sign a loan workout agreement—really a loan extension. Workouts are customized and will depend on your individual situation. They typically involve a payment of the arrears within a maximum of three years, as well as lower monthly payments and an extension of the loan. Once you sign the HUD agreement, you will make all future payments directly to HUD.

HUD may also refer you to a HUD-approved financial counseling agency, which provides advice and counseling to help you understanding the responsibilities of home ownership and financing.

# E. Negotiating With the U.S. Department of Veteran Affairs

If you are a veteran, your loan may be guaranteed by the United States Department of Veteran Affairs ("VA"). The VA helps veterans obtain loans for owner-occupied single family residences by providing loan guarantees (insurance) to lenders. The cost of the insurance is added to your monthly loan payment.

VA loan guarantees are a benefit program bestowed upon U.S. veterans to repay them for serving our country. As an extension of those benefits, the VA "Foreclosure Avoidance Program" assists financially distressed veterans in foreclosure keep their homes.

To check whether your loan is VA-guaranteed and whether you qualify for their Foreclosure Avoidance Program, call the VA office nearest you or:

Veterans Affairs Hotlines
Oakland ........................................... 510-637-1325
Los Angeles .................................... 310-827-1000
San Diego ........................................ 619-297-8220

## 1. VA Servicing Procedures

Lenders must carefully follow proscribed VA guidelines, summarized below, before foreclosing or they risk losing their VA insurance. At the heart of the VA guidelines is an expectation that your lender will communicate with you and try to work out a mutually acceptable solution.

If your lender does not follow VA procedures or is uncooperative, immediately let the VA know. You can telephone your VA office, but it is more effective to write a letter or personally visit your local VA office. If the VA office is unresponsive to your lender's indifference, you may want to write your local congressional representative or senator, with a copy to your VA office.

### a. Telephone Calls

The VA expects lenders to telephone veterans who have missed monthly payments. Telephone calls are intended to establish personal communication and encourage a discussion of potential solutions.

VA guidelines prohibit your lender from insinuating that nothing can be done to stop your foreclosure. Your lender is required to explain the various VA programs that are available to avoid foreclosure and encourage you to contact your local VA office. Be sure to make a note of your lender's approach using the Communications Chart, Chapter 1, Section A.

### b. Letters

Your lender must send you a personalized letter within 20 days from the date your monthly payment is late. The VA requires that the letter:
- advise you that your payment is late
- request immediate payment
- request a personal interview
- if you made only a partial payment, explain that your check is being returned because it's not the full amount
- confirm any agreements with you, your lender and/or the VA regarding the default

- remind you that you must keep your payments current, and
- address any issues that are relevant to your particular circumstances.

As always, keep copies of all letters you receive.

### c. Field Visits

If your lender can't reach you by telephone or you don't respond to its letters, a representative must meet with you and inspect your property, called a "field visit." A field visit will normally occur in the evening, when you are likely to be home, and will not necessarily be announced. As the VA Servicing Guidelines states:

"...before the foreclosure decision is made, it is imperative that there be a meaningful, detailed interview with the borrower. The purpose of the analysis is to gain a thorough understanding of the nature and reasons for the default, the prospects of curing the default, both short-term and long-term, and to determine what action might avoid foreclosure. The pre-foreclosure analysis provides an opportunity to look at the borrower's attitude, willingness to cooperate, and motivation."

Although you may not appreciate having your lender show up unexpectedly at home to interview you, use the field visit as an opportunity to demonstrate your commitment to resolving your defaulted loan. It is also an excellent time to show the representative any physical conditions on the property that may be creating a problem (foundation, plumbing, electrical, roof, heating). Physical problems frequently contribute to a lender's newly discovered willingness to negotiate a workout plan rather than taking a troubled property back in foreclosure.

*Keep a log of the field visit.* On your Communications Chart (Chapter 1, Section A), write down the date and time of the visit, the name of the representative, what was inspected during the visit, what was dis-

cussed, and the representative's attitude. Keeping good records helps to pressure sloppy lenders to follow VA procedures.

After the visit, the representative must write a report and submit copies to your lender and the VA. If the report is positive, your lender is likely to forestall the foreclosure and be more willing to negotiate a workout with you than to proceed with the foreclosure. Obviously, your goal should be for your lender to write a good report.

If you miss payments for at least three months, your lender must give the VA notice of its intention to foreclose at least 30 days before commencing foreclosure. The VA will then send you a letter advising you of your lender's intention to foreclose.

## 2. VA In-House Financial Counseling

You don't have to wait for your lender to contact you; you may contact the VA and ask for financial counseling to help resolve your financial difficulties before you lose your home in foreclosure. The VA can provide in-house counseling or can refer you to non-VA, federal, state, local or private organizations that provide low-cost or free financial counseling.

Keep in mind that financial counseling requires a face-to-face meeting with an interviewer to discuss your financial situation in detail. You should be prepared to talk about the following:

- *Reasons for the default.* Acceptable reasons for missing payments include illness, accident, unemployment, death or injury of family member and business reversals. An unwillingness or refusal to make the payments is not acceptable.
- *Your domestic situation.* Because divorce or separation often prompts a foreclosure, the VA interviewer must find out if you are single, married, separated or divorced. Are there marital problems that will affect your ability to repay the loan? Who is responsible for repaying the loan? Who has the ability to pay? Who lives in the property?

- *Employment.* Unemployment is also a frequent reason for foreclosure, so the interviewer will ask if you're employed, the name and address of your employer and your weekly income. She will also question you if you are self-employed. Is your income based upon a salary or commission? If your income has decreased, will it increase again soon? If unemployed, will you be able to get a new job in the near future?
- *Your financial situation.* The interviewer will ask questions about your regular income, expenditures, assets and liabilities. She will use this data when determining whether you can accomplish a workout of your defaulted loan.

## 3. Delinquency Classifications

After analyzing your situation, the VA will classify you in one of the following two categories:
- *Distressed delinquent.* This means you have reasonable excuses for the default, along with the ability and desire to cure it. The VA will request that your lender work out a repayment plan with you and see that you get financial counseling. It is to your advantage to be classified as a distressed delinquent.
- *Chronic delinquent.* If you're in this category, the VA believes you have no justified reason for missing loan payments and are habitually late. You cannot appeal this designation. The VA refers these cases back to the lenders, who may proceed with foreclosure.

## 4. Overview of VA Foreclosure Avoidance Program

The VA requires a series of procedural steps to help a borrower who's defaulted on a VA-guaranteed loan:

### a. Your Lender Issues a VA Notice of Default

Once your lender files a Notice of Default, your lender must send the VA a Form 26-6850a (VA Notice of Default) between 60 to 105 days of your first uncured default.

### b. Get Help From Your Lender or Seek Supplemental Servicing

Immediately contact your lender and ask for help. If your lender is uncooperative, contact the local VA office and request "supplemental servicing." With supplemental servicing, a VA representative is assigned to work directly with you to assure that you have every opportunity to avoid foreclosure. There is no cost for this service.

### c. VA Intervenes

Your VA servicing representative will contact your lender and try to work out a solution to your foreclosure. He or she will try to resolve the default, work out a repayment plan, and minimize the VA's risk of paying a claim. Once the VA intervenes, your lender is required to stop, or at least delay, the foreclosure until an adequate resolution can be achieved. If you have any evidence that your lenders didn't follow VA procedures, bring it to the VA representative's attention.

### d. Agree on a Workout Plan

If the VA determines that you can bring the default current within a reasonable period of time, the VA representative will negotiate a workout plan with your lender. There are several ways your delinquency may be resolved with your lender with the assistance of the VA:
- *Loan forbearance.* Your lender may agree to accept less than your regular monthly payment over a longer period than the term of your promissory note. Within 12 months of the date of the workout agreement, however, the delinquency must be cured by increased payments, payment of a lump sum or a sale of your property. Although VA-assisted, this type of relief does not need formal VA approval.

### PARTIAL PAYMENTS

VA servicing guidelines encourage lenders to accept partial payments whenever possible rather than insisting on the full arrearage. Nevertheless, there are several circumstances in which VA-insured lenders are authorized to refuse partial payments:

- You are keeping rental income from your property instead of turning it over to your lender.

- Your partial payment is less than one full month's payment.

- Your payment is less than $100 or less than 50% of the total amount due, whichever is less.

- Your payment is made by personal check instead of cash or cashier's check, if previously requested by your lender.

- Any part of your payment is more than six months past due.

- A Notice of Default has been recorded.

- *Loan modification.* Your lender may agree to change the terms of your promissory note. For example, monthly payments can be reduced or increased by adjusting the interest rate, extending the loan term or re-amortizing the loan. The VA does not need to formally approve this type of relief.

- *Compromise sale agreement.* Typically, this occurs in a down market when you have no equity in your property and no foreseeable way to cure your loan. You will be allowed to sell your property at its current market value, presumably less than the amount of your loan. The VA will reimburse the lender for its loss. Although you may be required to sign a promissory note in the amount of the VA's loss, the VA rarely chases veterans in this predicament. Because of the VA's direct involvement, this type of agreement requires VA approval. The VA will only approve a compromise sale agreement if the loss will be no greater than the VA guaranty, unless your lender agrees to waive the difference.

- *VA "Refunding" program.* Under this program, you request that the VA purchase your loan from your lender. This process is called "refunding." The VA will purchase your loan only if it believes the VA has a reasonable chance of saving your property from foreclosure. The VA will agree to refunding if it is the only alternative to stopping foreclosure.

- *Deed in lieu program.* Under the VA's deed in lieu program, you deed your property to the VA to avoid the foreclosure. Although you end up losing your property, you keep a foreclosure sale off your credit report. For more on the VA's deed in lieu program, see Chapter 11.

## F. Negotiating With the California Department of Veteran Affairs

The California Department of Veterans Affairs ("Cal-Vet") offers home ownership programs (single family owner-occupied) to veterans wanting to live in California. Veterans who purchased property under a Cal-Vet home loan program may work directly with the agency to resolve the delinquency and keep their property.

Let's refresh your memory about how Cal-Vet's home loan programs work. When you bought your home, you entered into a land contract with Cal-Vet. You agreed that if you stopped making your payments, Cal-Vet could cancel the contract and repossess your property without following any formal foreclosure procedures.

At the end of this procedure, which takes about six to eight weeks, your land contract is terminated and you lose all interest and rights in your property. Cal-Vet may contract with another qualified California veteran to purchase the property or sell it in the open market.

**WHY DOES CAL-VET USE LAND CONTRACTS?**

Under its California charter, Cal-Vet cannot lend money (like institutional lenders) or insure loans (like FHA and VA). So Cal-Vet purchases the home directly, then turns around and contracts with the veteran to acquire the property through monthly payments over a period of years—called a land contract.

The veteran has the benefits of home ownership and can earn any equity that may build up in the residence over the years. When the veteran finishes paying for the property, Cal-Vet deeds the property to the veteran.

*Example: John, a Desert Storm veteran, locates a beautiful home in Ventura. Cal-Vet purchases the residence and enters into a land contract with John. John agrees on a purchase price of $125,000 for the residence by paying $1,200 a month for 20 years. Title to the home will transfer to John after he successfully completes the 20-year payment schedule.*

Although Cal-Vet's land contract procedures are strict, don't assume the worst. Because Cal-Vet is a veteran's service organization, it is dedicated to helping veterans acquire and keep their homes. Cal-Vet is extremely flexible in negotiating workouts and eager to avoid taking back the property. Your first step should be to telephone the Cal-Vet foreclosure hotline and ask for assistance:

Cal-Vet Foreclosure Hotline ............ 800-952-5626

## 1. Overview of the First Three Months of Delinquency

Cal-Vet will bend over backwards to help you keep your property. Cal-Vet has devised procedures to help you bring your loan current, based upon the length of your delinquency and your current financial position. During this entire process, you may implement other strategies covered in this book to bring your contract current and avoid losing your home.

### a. First Month of Delinquency

Cal-Vet will contact you by telephone or letter to find out why you haven't paid. In this initial contact, Cal-Vet may offer several workouts or other options, including:

- pay the arrearage over four months
- add arrears to the principal balance of your contract, which will be paid at the end of the term
- defer payments for a specific period of months, or
- have your veterans disability insurance kick in and pay your monthly payments to Cal-Vet if your default was due to injuries.

### b. Two Months of Delinquency

Cal-Vet will issue a 30-day written Notice of Intent to Cancel. The notice must be delivered to you by registered or certified mail (return receipt requested) and by first-class mail, or by personal service. The Notice of Intent to Cancel explains that you have 30 days to bring your contract current or your land contract will be canceled and you'll lose your equitable interest in your property. Cal-Vet will also request its local field office to contact you.

The notice will also encourage you to contact your local Cal-Vet office. You should immediately schedule an appointment. Be prepared to explain why you've fallen behind, how you propose to pay the arrears and when you will resume the monthly payments. Cal-Vet will discuss a workout of your loan and may propose the alternatives mentioned in Section F1a, just above.

### c. Three Months of Delinquency

If your loan falls three months behind and you are unable to enter into some type of repayment plan, Cal-Vet will issue a pre-cancellation letter. The letter will state that unless you cure the default within 30 days, your land contract will be subject to cancellation.

## 2. Cancellation of Land Contract (Title 12 Action)

If all workout attempts fail and the loan is still delinquent by the end of the fourth month, Cal-Vet will initiate a Title 12 Action. This is a nonjudicial procedure that cancels your land contract with Cal-Vet. A Title 12 Action follows these general steps:

- *Cal-Vet orders a litigation report.* The local Cal-Vet office will order a litigation report from a local title company. The report, which describes your property, lists any lienholders and provides a history of the land contract, is sent to Cal-Vet's Foreclosure/REO (real estate owed) unit in Sacramento, with a request to begin an action to clear title and cancel the land contract.

- *Cal-Vet gives notice to junior lienholders.* If you have junior lienholders (lenders holding deeds of trust recorded after Cal-Vet's land contract), Cal-Vet will notify them of its intention to terminate your land contract, thereby eliminating their liens. Junior lienholders will have the opportunity to cure the delinquency and conduct their own foreclosure.

- *Cal-Vet issues Notice of Cancellation of Land Contract.* If the 30-day notice period to junior lienholders expires and the delinquent amount is still not cured, the Cal-Vet's Foreclosure/REO unit will issue a Notice of Cancellation of Land Contract. Copies will be sent to you and the local Cal-Vet office, and it will be recorded in the recorder's office of the county in which your property is situated.

- *You lose all ownership rights.* Once the Notice of Cancellation has been recorded, your interest in the property (as well as the liens of any junior lienholders) are eliminated. It will take another day or two for title to clear. At this point, you must vacate the property. Cal-Vet is free to sell the property to other veterans or in the open market.

## 3. Cal-Vet's Procedures Protect the Servicemember

As you can see by these lengthy procedures, Cal-Vet attempts to do everything possible to help service members overcome their financial difficulties and avoid losing their properties.

# 6

# REFINANCING OUT OF FORECLOSURE

Refinancing consists of obtaining a loan from a new lender to pay your existing lender. In a foreclosure context, you'll want a loan to either pay off your foreclosing lender entirely or bring your foreclosing loan current.

The thought of refinancing property that is already in foreclosure may at first seem a formidable task. Granted, foreclosure may make it more difficult to obtain a loan and may require you to aggressively shop around. It should be possible to refinance your property as long as either your credit is in reasonably good shape or you have some equity in your property. In fact, an entire industry of lenders caters to property owners in foreclosure. This chapter explores when and how refinancing can be a viable option to stop foreclosure.

*Message to readers.* If you have bad credit (two or more derogatory marks on your credit report) and no equity in your property, this chapter probably won't help you and you should skip ahead.

*If you've already received a Notice of Sale (or Notice of Trustee's Sale), you have limited time to refinance. In fact, you have less than 20 days to get a loan before your property will be sold. Because of the time constraints, you should limit your loan options to home equity lenders (See Section E2), hard money lenders (See Section E3), or family and friends (See Section E4).*

# A. Deciding Whether to Refinance

Before you pursue refinancing, compare it to the other strategies described in this book.

## 1. Other Ways to Raise Money

Assuming that refinancing still looks like the best strategy, you should consider one more option (especially if you're only behind a couple of thousand dollars) consider borrowing or raising the money to bring your loan current (reinstate the loan). You might seek an unsecured loan or sell some of your assets. For example, you could:

- borrow against the cash value in your insurance policy
- sell a major asset, such as a car, furniture or stocks
- sell your jewelry, electronic equipment or musical instruments at a pawnshop
- have a large yard or garage sale
- cash in an IRA, 401(k) plan or tax-deferred account (and pay the resulting penalties)
- use a savings account earmarked for something else
- borrow from a finance company (such as Household International, Beneficial Corporation or ITT) and pledge an asset other than your real estate as collateral, or try for an unsecured consolidation loan
- contact the IRS's Problem Resolution Program and ask to get your tax refund early
- get a short-term, unsecured loan from a friend, or
- take a cash advance from your credit cards.

Although each of these resources can provide cash in a hurry, you may face high interest rates and another monthly payment that stretches you beyond your means.

## 2. Refinancing Considerations

If you pursue refinancing, keep these thoughts in mind:

- *Be clear about how much you need to borrow.* You need enough money to cover the costs of the new loan and pay off the foreclosing lender, including the foreclosure costs and accrued interest on the loan. (See Section G for more on the specific costs to refinance.)

- *Make sure you can afford ongoing payments.* Don't burden yourself unnecessarily; if refinancing isn't a long-term solution to your problem, it probably isn't worthwhile. Only agree to a loan if the lender's total cost for the loan (including points and additional fees) is affordable on an ongoing basis. Be especially wary of loans with balloon payments, such as interest-only loans ending with a large balloon payment that you may not be able to make.

- *Shop around.* Lenders have different criteria for granting loans, and vary in their abilities to approve loans quickly. Because of the pressing foreclosure, you don't want to put all your eggs in one basket. You'll want to compare the different loan terms offered and get the best deal in the limited time available. You can even fill out several loan applications (with very small application fees, if any) and then take the first loan that comes in.

- *Seek a loan with the lowest possible interest rate.* Among the many terms and conditions you will negotiate in a loan, interest is probably the most important because of its cost over time. If you are confused about the variety of interest rates and points, don't be afraid to ask potential lenders to explain their charges. Then compare them to what other lenders charge.

- *Find out how long it will take to get the loan.* It may take your lender days, weeks or months to process your loan application, depending on the type of lender you deal with. Ask the lender pointedly when you can expect approval and how long it will be until your loan is "funded" (you receive your money). Most lenders will charge you extra if you want a commitment in writing. But, above all, don't risk losing your property by agreeing to a funding date that occurs too close to the foreclosure sale. If something goes wrong, you may not receive the new loan in time to stop the foreclosure.

- *Interest payments may be tax-deductible.* The loans discussed in this chapter are tax-deductible, which means that you can deduct the interest portion of your monthly or periodic payment from your income on your tax returns.

- *Be on the lookout for restructuring opportunities.* Refinancing should not be viewed as a final solution that must remain unchanged once you have completed the refinance. For example, you may have taken out a high-interest-rate loan to get through this temporary difficultly. The important concept to remember is that this isn't the end of the line; there will always be new opportunities to refinance or restructure your loan in the future to obtain better terms, either with your existing lender or some new lending source.

## B. Should You Use a Mortgage Broker?

A mortgage broker is an individual (or company) that, for a fee, will help locate and obtain loans from lenders to refinance your property. Mortgage brokers connect qualified borrowers with lenders, such as obscure banks and mortgage companies flush with cash to lend. A good mortgage broker can get a loan for just about anybody, including someone in foreclosure! In contrast, a bad mortgage broker is a waste of your precious time.

The advantage of a good mortgage broker is that he or she will have a pulse on the financial markets and know which lenders are giving loans and on what terms. A mortgage broker can comparison shop among many lenders—and a lot more quickly than you ever could. Good mortgage brokers do business with at least five to ten lenders. They can quickly tell you whether you qualify for a particular loan and help you fill out the necessary paperwork. They are usually very flexible, offering various refinancing packages depending on your individual circumstances.

On the other hand, some mortgage brokers tend to become too cozy with a handful of favorite lenders with whom they regularly do business. There is always a temptation for the broker to choose the loan that's best for his or her business, instead of the loan that's best for you. A mortgage broker can be costly too. He or she will receive a commission of approximately 1%, which you must pay out of your loan proceeds.

---

**DIFFICULTY IN GETTING A GOOD DEAL UNDER FORECLOSURE CIRCUMSTANCES**

Depending on the time remaining in your foreclosure and your ability to find a lender, a mortgage broker may be a welcome addition to your team. You can use the broker alone or in connection with your own efforts to track down a willing lender. Just check all loan terms carefully and don't be pressured into accepting a bad deal. Nevertheless, appreciate that your property is in foreclosure and that the deals offered to you may not be as favorable as you would receive under normal refinancing circumstances.

---

To locate a mortgage broker, look in your local yellow pages under "mortgage brokers" or "real estate loans." Mortgage brokers also frequently run advertisements in the classified real estate section of the Sunday newspaper.

## C. Will You Qualify for Refinancing?

Although refinancing is decided on a case-by-case basis, lenders will normally consider two overriding issues: the extent of your equity and the weight of your credit.

### 1. Do You Have Sufficient Equity (Loan-to-Value Ratio)?

Equity is the surplus of value in property after deducting the outstanding balances of all deeds of trust and liens that are recorded against it. For example, if your property has a value of $100,000 and there are two deeds of trust recorded against it with balances totaling $65,000, you have $35,000 of equity in your property. Lenders will only loan money against property (regardless of whether it is

in foreclosure) when there is sufficient equity to support the amount of the loan.

Also, lenders will only loan on a portion of the equity in your property. Lenders always leave an "equity cushion" to offset potential unforeseen costs in the event your property loses value (depreciates) or they need to foreclose. The loan-to-value ratio (LTV) is the percentage of a property's appraised market value on which a lender will loan minus the balances of any outstanding loans and liens.

Every lender has its own LTV standards. LTVs can range from 95% on government-insured loans to as low as 65% for high-risk loans. Accordingly, it is advisable to ask a prospective lender about its LTV policy before submitting a loan application.

*Example 1: A lender with an 80% LTV standard is considering making a loan on a $150,000 house. The lender calculates the amount it is willing to loan, provided there are no liens or other claims against the property:*

| | |
|---|---|
| *Property value:* | $150,000 |
| *80% LTV:* | x    80% |
| *Lender will loan:* | $ 120,000 |

*Example 2: Let's use the same figures, but this time the borrower has a first deed of trust encumbering the property. Here's is the result:*

| | |
|---|---|
| *Property value:* | $150,000 |
| *80% LTV:* | x    80% |
| | 120,000 |
| *Amount due on first deed of trust:* | - 80,000 |
| *Lender will loan:* | $ 40,000 |

As you can see, the amount a lender will loan changes dramatically if there are already underlying loans on your property. But remember, all lenders have their own LTV standards, which vary according to the type of lender, its internal policies, the type of loans it gives and financial conditions in the marketplace.

To figure out your property's equity, the lender will hire a licensed real estate appraiser to determine the property's current market value. Lenders charge the borrower for the appraisal, which can run from $500 to $1,000 depending on the size of the property. Some lenders will add this cost to the amount of your loan, while others will demand you pay the appraisal fee up front.

## 2. Are You a Good Credit Risk?

Although not all lenders place as much value on credit as equity, credit is still a significant criterion. The issue of credit really breaks down into two questions:

- Do you have the financial resources to repay the loan? You typically need to submit complete financial statements to demonstrate that notwithstanding the foreclosure, you will be able to make loan payments on the refinanced loan. You must include all income sources, including investments, non-job-related sources, assets and liabilities, including child support and alimony, dividends and royalties).
- What is your credit history? The lender will check out your creditworthiness by ordering your credit report from at least two of the three major credit reporting agencies (Experian [formerly TRW], Trans Union and Equifax). Most lenders aren't fazed by one or two negative marks on your credit report. However, if you have a bad credit report with several negative marks, you will need to explain your problems to your new lender. (For more on credit reports and how lenders interpret them, read *Money Troubles: Legal Strategies to Cope with Your Debts*, by Robin Leonard [Nolo Press].)

*Check out your credit if you're planning to refinance.* You should anticipate the credit issue and obtain a copy of your credit report from each of the three major credit bureaus:

Experian: ......................................... 800-682-7654
Trans Union: ................................... 800-851-2674
Equifax: ............................................ 800-685-1111

Experian will supply a free credit report if you were denied credit within the past 30 days.

## D. Overview of Refinancing

To refinance your property in time to stop the foreclosure, you'll generally follow the steps set out below.

### Step 1. Decide What Type of Refinancing to Seek

There are four different options for refinancing your property: conventional refinancing, home equity loans, hard money loans and loans from family and friends. Guidelines for selecting the best kind of loan in your circumstances are described in Section F below.

### Step 2. Compare Different Lenders

Every lender provides different kinds of loans, terms and services. To ensure that you make a wise consumer decision, check out and compare several different lenders.

### Step 3. Apply for Loans

Most banks and lending institutions will require that you meet and fill out their loan applications. In contrast, a hard money lender (who specializes in high-risk loans with correspondingly high interest rates) has an "application" that consists of a series of questions asked over the telephone. And of course, family and friends are unlikely to require any kind of application.

*Avoid the anxiety and aggravation of a delay in getting the loan approved.* Before signing your application, ask for a commitment, in writing, that addresses specifics about the kind of loan, term, interest rate, prepayment penalties, points and other costs. Make a condition of your application that the lender will approve or reject your application by a specific date. If you can't get such a written commitment, you have no choice but to go elsewhere.

### Step 4. Lender May Check Your Credit

A conventional or home equity lender will check your credit report to be assured that you have a history of paying your bills on time. On the other hand, a hard money lender will probably ignore your credit report, and a friend or relative probably wouldn't think of it.

### Step 5. Lender Checks Title and Has Property Appraised

Your lender will contact a title insurance company and request a title report. The title insurance company checks the county recorder's office and confirms that you hold title to (own) your property and the number of deeds of trust and liens recorded against it.

Your lender will have your property appraised to determine its current market value. The lender will then subtract the outstanding balances of the deeds of trust and liens from the current market value to determine the amount of equity in your property and whether it is within its LTV ratio. If it is, your loan can be approved. Otherwise, the lender will deny your loan.

### Step 6. Sign the Loan Agreement

Assuming your loan goes through, you will receive a telephone call, and shortly thereafter, a letter announcing that your loan has been approved. The letter will include a form confirming that you agree to the terms of the loan and your formal request that the lender prepare the loan documents. If possible, to keep the ball rolling, deliver the letter in person rather than mailing it back to your lender.

When you deliver the form, your lender will schedule an appointment to sign the loan documents, assuming the lender is local. Request that the meeting be as soon as possible. (Whatever date the lender proposes, request a date sooner! You have a foreclosure swirling over your head and need these funds immediately.) If your lender is out of town, request that the documents be sent by overnight mail. Similarly, make sure you return all of the loan documents by overnight mail.

Most lenders will simply have you sign a promissory note and deed of trust (see Chapter 2). However, depending on the size of the loan and its complexity, some lenders may also ask that you sign a separate loan agreement that spells out in detail (in contract form) the terms and conditions of your loan. Either way, read these documents closely before signing. In addition, make absolutely sure that any promises or representations that your lender is making, such as the initial interest rate or the term of the loan, are included in the loan documents.

### Step 7. Three-Day Rescission Period Begins

After you sign the loan documents, a commercial lender must tell you (under the requirements of the federal Truth-in-Lending Act) that you are entitled to withdraw from the loan agreement any time during the next three days. This provision in the law originated to protect consumers against fast talking door-to-door salespeople who signed people up at their front doors for short-term consumer loans before borrowers realized they were mortgaging their homes at exorbitant interest rates. Since then, these laws have been expanded to cover practically all real estate financing transactions.

Even though it is unlikely that you will cancel after all the trouble you went through to obtain a loan, this option is nevertheless available to you.

## E. Kinds of Loans

As mentioned earlier, there are several alternative ways to refinance your property:
- conventional loans
- home equity loans
- hard money loans, and
- loans from friends or family.
  Let's explore each category of loans separately.

## 1. Conventional Loans

*Conventional refinancing takes approximately six to eight weeks to process.* If you've already received a Notice of Sale (or Notice of Trustee's Sale), don't waste your time on a conventional loan; they take to long to obtain. Instead, pursue the other refinance options described in this chapter.

A conventional loan is a single loan that you use to pay off and replace all of your underlying loans, including the foreclosing lender's. A conventional loan will typically be for 15 to 30 years and be fully amortized (paid off during the term of the loan). A conventional loan will be from a new lender, not the lender that is foreclosing.

A conventional loan is the hardest loan to qualify for. You must have a good credit rating and demonstrate an ability to make monthly payments. You will need to supply your tax returns for at least the last three years, as well as an income verification from your employer. If you are already in foreclosure, or have fallen behind in your payment schedule, there's a good chance that you won't qualify.

### a. How Much Can You Refinance With a Conventional Loan?

The average loan-to-value ratio on a new conventional loan is between 70% to 80%. In other words, if your property has a current market value of approximately $100,000, most conventional lenders will not loan you more than $70,000 to $80,000. If you owe your foreclosing lender more than an amount equal to 70% of your property's value (in principal, interest, late fees and foreclosure costs), a conventional loan is probably not a viable option.

### b. Costs of a Conventional Loan

The typical costs associated with a new conventional loan will average approximately 4% to 5% of the amount borrowed, and will include points, title search, title insurance, escrow fees, credit reports, attorney fees, processing fees and other related costs. (We cover costs in detail in Section G below.)

You already paid loan fees to your original lender when you first took out your loan. Now you are borrowing a similar amount from another lender to pay off your first lender, and paying loan fees a second time.

Whether it is to your advantage to obtain a new conventional loan (rather than a home equity loan or hard money loan) will depend on your particular situation. Assuming all other criteria are equal, you need to do the math. Ask yourself whether the cost of a conventional refinance will be less than the combined payments of your existing first loan and a new second. If it is cheaper, and you qualify, it is to your advantage to seek a conventional loan.

### c. Interest Rates on a Conventional Loan

The interest rate on a conventional loan will be lower than the combined average interest rates of several loans. This is because your lender will be in senior position to be paid with a first deed of trust. In contrast, a lender with a deed of trust in second or junior position is in a risker position if there is a foreclosure. This is because there may not be sufficient sale proceeds from a foreclosure sale to pay a lender in a junior position. As a result, a lender in a junior position traditionally charges a higher interest rate because it is taking more risk.

Conventional lenders will charge either a fixed rate or a variable rate, depending upon which type of loan you prefer. With a new loan you may be able to lower your interest rate if rates have come down. You may also obtain this advantage if you switch to an adjustable rate mortgage ("ARM") or similar type of loan, rather than a fixed rate. A lower interest rate will allow you to make lower payments, at least for a while, which should also help your financial situation. (Note, however, that the interest rate will be somewhat higher if you don't live in the property.)

*For more information on the distinctions between fixed rate versus adjustable interest rate loans*, read *How to Buy a House in California*, by Ralph Warner, Ira Serkes and George Devine (Nolo Press).

## 2. Home Equity Loans

A home equity loan is nothing more than an old-fashioned second mortgage (or second deed of trust) with a fancy new marketing name. The loan is based on the available equity in your property after deducting the balances of any underlying deeds of trust and liens. The new loan will be secured by a junior deed of trust encumbering your property. Assuming you already have a first deed of trust on your property, your home equity loan will be in second position. If you already have first and second deeds of trust recorded against your property, the home equity loan will be in a third position.

A home equity loan application can be taken over the telephone in a matter of minutes, or you can fill out a relatively short application at your lender's office. Usually, you will receive an answer within 24 to 48 hours. Most lenders can then process a home equity loan and fund it within two to three weeks.

A home equity loan typically lasts for one year, five years or ten years, depending on what you negotiate with your lender. If you miss the payments on your home equity loan, the home equity lender will have the right to initiate foreclosure proceedings.

### a. Kinds of Home Equity Loans

There are two kinds of home equity loans, both of which are secured by a junior deed of trust recorded against your property:

• *Closed-ended home equity loan*. This is a one-time loan that closes—or ends—once the loan is paid off. You pay a fixed rate of interest on the amount you borrow (a higher rate than you would initially pay on an open-ended home equity loan).

• *Open-ended home equity loan*. This is nothing more than a revolving line of credit that is secured by a deed of trust recorded against your property. Although your loan is for a specific amount, you are not required to borrow (or repay) the entire amount all at once.

The promissory note for your open-ended home equity loan will be for the total amount the lender approves, even if you don't actually borrow the full amount. For example, if you are approved for $25,000 and you borrow only $10,000, your lender will still have you sign a promissory note for $25,000 and record a deed of trust for $25,000. Of course, you can always borrow the balance if and when you need it. In addition, you can pay off the amount you borrowed without canceling the right to re-borrow on the credit line later.

The interest rate on an open-ended home equity loan is usually variable, and you are charged interest only on the amount you actually borrow. For example, if you have a $12,000 open-ended home equity loan, you might use $4,500 to bring your foreclosing lender current, but not borrow the rest. You will be charged interest only on the $4,500.

At first glance, an open-ended loan may seem more attractive than a closed-ended loan. If interest rates decrease, an open-ended loan will be to your advantage. But if interest rates rise, the closed-end loan payments will not change, while the open-ended loan payments will increase.

### b. Eligibility for a Home Equity Loan

A home equity loan is difficult, but not impossible, to come by in a foreclosure situation. If you have missed only a few payments, you have some equity in your property and your credit is otherwise in good shape, you may qualify for a home equity loan. If, on the other hand, you have already received a Notice of Sale and don't have good credit, your refinance opportunities are better with a hard money loan (covered in Section E3, below).

In contrast to a conventional loan, sufficient equity in your property is the most important criterion for a home equity loan, although credit is also important to the lender. To qualify, you must provide evidence that you'll be able to afford monthly payments on a home equity loan as well as resuming payments to your foreclosing lender. Most home equity loans are based upon a loan-to-value ratio (LTV) of between 70% to 80%, minus any existing loans encumbering your property.

*Example: Alice owns a home in Clovis that has a current market value of approximately $150,000. First National Bank holds a first deed of trust securing the loan, with an outstanding balance of $100,000. When her property goes into foreclosure, Alice approaches Second Street Bank about a home equity loan. Second Street has an LTV of 80% on home equity loans. In Alice's situation, 80% of $150,000 would be $120,000. However, because the balance of the first deed of trust with First National is $100,000, Second Street Bank will lend Alice only $20,000.*

### c. Interest Rates on a Home Equity Loan

Lenders that stand second in line to recover their money in a foreclosure are taking a higher risk of loss than conventional lenders. To protect themselves, home equity lenders charge higher interest than conventional lenders. Nevertheless, the lending business is highly competitive, so lenders charge interest rates that will attract business. Because of this, you need to spend time comparison shopping among various lenders for the best rates.

---

**INTEREST RATES ON OPEN-ENDED HOME EQUITY LOANS**

Open-ended home equity loans almost always have variable interest rates. The variation is based on one of the many publicly advertised interest rate indexes (such as the Federal Reserve's prime rate, the U.S. treasury bill rate or 11th District Cost of Funds rate). These interest rate indexes increase or decrease as the financial marketplace fluctuates.

Once your lender selects an appropriate index, it will add a fixed percentage, or "spread," ranging anywhere from 2% to 4% over the index. This spread is your lender's profit margin in giving you the loan. For example, if your lender charges a spread of 4% over the prime rate and the prime rate increases to 7%, your variable interest rate will increase to 11% per year. On the other hand, if several months later the prime rate falls to 5%, your interest rate will likewise fall to 9%. Although a variable rate may benefit you in a falling market, it can cause problems in a rising market.

Most lenders will agree to put a ceiling ("cap") on the interest rate they can charge. This cap can range from 10% to 15% per year, depending on what you negotiate with your lender. For instance, although your interest rate may be 3% over the rate on six-month jumbo certificates of deposit, your rate may be capped at 12% per year regardless of how high the interest rate on certificates of deposit rise.

---

### d. Costs of a Home Equity Loan

Because of intense competition in the financial marketplace, most home equity lenders will not require any money up front for processing your loan. Home equity lenders typically front the necessary processing costs, including appraisal costs, points, title fees and escrow fees, and add them to the loan balance. If yours is an open-ended equity loan, your lender may also charge a maintenance fee (anywhere from $100 to $300, depending on the size of the loan) per year.

## 3. Hard Money Loans

A hard money loan can best be described as a loan to a borrower who is in foreclosure and has bad credit, but has some equity in his or her property. Hard money loans come from private investors, who (because of the risks involved) expect high yields on their investments. With a hard money loan, you usually make interest-only payments for a term of one to five years. At the end of the loan term, you make a balloon payment of the entire principal and any accrued interest.

A hard money loan is probably the easiest to get, but it comes with the highest interest rate (usually 5% higher than a home equity loan). Nevertheless, when all else fails, it may be your only option if you are determined to refinance.

*Example: Henry runs into financial problems and defaults on his home payments. Because of his poor credit and a pending foreclosure, Henry borrows $10,000 from Fast Cash, Inc., a hard money lender. Fast Cash charges 15 points ($1,500) plus closing costs of 2% ($200). The interest rate is 15% per year and payments are interest-only ($125) per month. At the end of three years, Henry will have paid $4,500 in interest, $200 in closing costs and $1,500 in points— and he'll still owe a balloon payment of $10,000. In all, he'll pay a total of $6,200 to borrow $10,000.*

Applications for hard money loans are typically taken over the telephone and can be processed within one to two weeks. (If it takes longer, there is a problem with the lender and you should move on.)

The danger of a hard money loan is that although you receive the money to bring your defaulted loan current and stop the pending foreclosure, you may end up in a more precarious financial position than you started in. You'll still have your previous loan(s) to pay, so your overall monthly loan payments will be substantially larger than before. At the end of the term of the hard money loan (just a few short years), you will be faced with a balloon payment that may be extremely difficult to pay. Because of this potential problem, it should come as no surprise that a larger portion of hard money loans go into default and cause foreclosure then all other types of loan combined.

### a. Eligibility for a Hard Money Loan

If you have equity in your property, you can obtain a hard money loan. You do not need good credit and you usually do not even need to provide tax returns or income verifications.

The loan-to-value ratio of a hard money lender is usually much narrower than a conventional or equity loan. A hard money lender will not loan in excess of 60% to 65% of your property's value, less amounts already owed against your property.

*Example:*

| | |
|---|---:|
| *Market value of property:* | $150,000 |
| *Hard money lender's LTV:* | x    65% |
| | 97,500 |
| *Existing loans and liens:* | -   90,000 |
| *Available equity for hard money loan:* | $   7,500 |

### b. Costs of a Hard Money Loan

As mentioned earlier, the costs of a hard money loan are much higher than conventional or home equity loans, especially the "points" charged by the lender. Points are nothing more than pre-paid interest—another way for your lender to make an extra buck at your expense! You may be charged anywhere from 10% to 15% of the principal loan amount as "points."

Similar to conventional loans and home equity loans, you will be charged regular closing costs (including title search, title insurance and escrow fees), which will equal roughly 2% of the principal loan amount. These costs will be deducted from the loan before you receive any money.

### c. Watch Out for Unscrupulous Hard Money Lenders

Although the majority of hard money lenders are honest and reputable, some unscrupulous lenders spoil the pot with unethical and questionable business practices.

Hard money lenders have been known to wait until the last days before a foreclosure sale and then suddenly say that you don't qualify for a loan. They then advise you that they can give you an emergency loan with less appealing terms than previously offered—for example, 20 points rather than

15 points, or 18% interest instead of 15%. Unfortunately, although these lending practices are unethical, they are not necessarily illegal. Besides, you don't have the time nor money to sue these lenders for breach of contract; you are in foreclosure and need new financing by a certain date.

The best methods to safeguard yourself against these tactics are:

• Negotiate with more than one hard money lender. Because most lenders will not require an up-front fee when they take your application, you can apply to several lenders and pick the first one that gives you a loan or the one that comes through with the best terms.

• Insist that the lender make a written commitment about the interest rate and points during negotiations.

• Do not sign loan documents that state "subject to lender's approval," which would allow the lender to switch to a more expensive loan at the last minute.

When all is said and done, steer clear of hard money lenders that charge outrageous rates, fully expecting (and wanting) you to default so they can foreclose and take over your property. There is no point digging deeper into trouble with a hard money lender that will eventually cause a foreclosure anyway.

### 4. Loans From Friends or Family

Many people believe this is the most expensive loan of all. Asking for money from a friend or family member almost always comes with unexpected baggage. But this may be your only viable financing option, particularly if your LTV and credit are insufficient for normal lenders. If you go this route, it is your responsibility to make the business arrangement work out. In other words, don't borrow from your friends or family if you don't truthfully believe you can pay them back.

If you approach a friend or relative to request a loan to stop the foreclosure, offer them interest on their money. Make an offer they can't refuse and one you can afford. Knowing what you now know about the range of lenders, you can offer a rate of

interest that, while lower than what you would have been charged in the marketplace, would still be higher then what they would receive from a certificate of deposit or money market fund.

Finally, formalize your agreement by writing a promissory note, which contains all of the terms of the loan, and recording a deed of trust. (For more information on promissory notes and deeds of trust, see *Simple Contracts for Personal Use*, by Stephen Elias and Marcia Stewart and *The Deeds Book*, by Mary Randolph [Nolo Press].)

## F. How to Find a Lender to Refinance Your Property

There are at least eight different categories of available lenders to consider for refinancing out of foreclosure:

• commercial banks
• savings banks (formerly savings and loan associations)
• mortgage companies
• credit unions
• life insurance companies
• stock brokerage houses
• hard money lenders, and
• individuals.

Lenders offer a wide variety of interest rates, terms, costs, conveniences and services. Unfortunately, most borrowers don't spend the time necessary to shop different lenders. The tendency is to borrow from an institution that is conveniently located, recommended by someone you know or that solicits your business. Knowing that other lenders are available will hopefully encourage you to shop around, even if it is only by telephone. The more lenders you talk to, the better equipped you will be to decide which lender suits your particular needs.

*Check with a reputable real estate agent.* A local real estate agent can be an excellent resource if you want to find the names of banks, mortgage companies and other institutions that give conventional and home equity loans. Remember to pump them, politely, for the names of several lenders, not just one.

## 1. Commercial Banks

Increasingly, commercial banks have become large consumer lenders and substantial real estate–based lenders. More recently, they have activity encouraged home equity loans.

The range of a bank's consumer loan services will vary. With the exception of hard money loans, large metropolitan banks usually have all the loan products you will need: home equity loans and conventional loans. Smaller banks, on the other hand, may not write conventional loans.

Commercial banks are more interested in home equity loans than conventional loans, and will actively compete to get home equity loan business. A home equity loan is profitable to a commercial bank because of its low service costs—there is little for the bank to do after it sets up an equity loan. Banks eager to give home equity loans advertise their rates in the Sunday newspapers. You can also shop around by telephoning major banks in your area (check the yellow pages) and ask for their current interest rates, points, application fees and other charges for conventional and home equity loans.

## 2. Savings Banks

Because of the 1980s debacle in the savings and loan industry (S&Ls were permitted to expand into many unrelated activities, and many of them met financial disaster), the vast majority of savings and loan associations have distanced themselves from this notoriety. They've achieved this by changing their names to "savings banks," the new buzzword for the nineties. While you should be very concerned about the financial strength of an institution when you are a saver, you personally need not worry as a borrower. After all, you have their money; they don't have yours.

Savings banks continue to write over 50% of Americans' conventional loans, so it is only natural that borrowers would also turn to these institutions when seeking home equity loans. The positive result is that savings banks process loans faster than commercial banks, regardless of whether it is a conventional loan or a home equity loan. Savings banks, being real estate specialists, tend to be more aggressive in going after home equity loans than commercial banks. Similar to commercial banks, savings banks do not provide hard money loans.

In this period of deregulation, it has become virtually impossible to distinguish savings banks from commercial banks. So the decision really comes down to investigating which institution offers you the best rates and terms. Shop around before you decide.

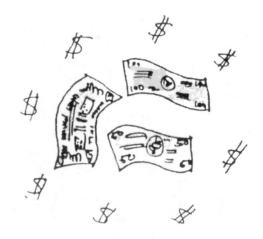

## 3. Credit Unions

Credit unions are the sleepers among real property lending possibilities because few people think of them as potential lending sources. Credit unions are financial institutions established for the benefit of their members, who open accounts and borrow money. In effect, the members borrow from each other. Being non-profit cooperative institutions, credit unions' interest rates are one to two points below rates charged by commercial banks and savings banks. However, their services are available to members only. They generally don't advertise, which helps keep their costs down.

Credit unions are authorized to grant loans secured by real property. In fact, the conventional real estate loan business is one of credit unions' largest activities. Credit unions have also expanded into home equity loans in recent years.

If you do not belong to a credit union, don't despair. There may still be time if the foreclosure clock has not ticked too long. Check out whether you are eligible to join the credit union of some group with which you are already associated. Ask your employer, government bureau, educational institution or cooperative association whether they are affiliated with a credit union. You can find a list of credit unions in your local yellow pages under "credit unions" and check with them directly about eligibility requirements.

## 4. Mortgage Companies

Mortgage companies are "money merchants" that borrow money wholesale and lend it out retail. The spread in this procedure is their profit. After they have loaned you money, they sell off the loan in the secondary market and recycle the funds.

Mortgage companies can provide conventional as well as home equity loans. However, they typically make smaller loans and charge higher rates than banks, savings banks and credit unions. Nevertheless, mortgage companies provide a needed service because they tend to be more liberal in their credit allowances and LTV ratios and are willing to take more risks. They often lend to people whom banks do not consider eligible.

One advantage of using a mortgage company is that it can process loans faster than a commercial or savings bank. Keep this in mind if the foreclosure clock is running out of time.

The largest mortgage companies are national companies that are listed in ads in your local yellow pages: Beneficial Finance Corporation, Household International, Commercial Credit and ITT. Smaller regional or local companies also advertise in the yellow pages.

## 5. Life Insurance Companies

Life insurance companies invest heavily in commercial real estate financing. If you own commercial property in foreclosure, you should check with life insurance companies. A list of insurance companies is easy to locate in your local yellow pages under "life insurance."

In contrast, if you own residential property, either a single family residence or apartment building, contacting a life insurance company is probably a waste of your precious time. Life insurance companies rarely deal directly with homeowners.

## 6. Brokerage Firms

Deregulation has opened the "financial services" floodgates to stock brokerage firms to participate in real estate loans. Most commonly, they invest in home equity loans. Although they are still small players in the refinancing field, there are currently several major brokerage firms in the United States (with local offices throughout California) as well as many small brokerage houses in your city that offer real estate loans. Look in your local yellow pages under "stockbrokers."

### 7. Hard Money Lenders

Hard money lenders tend to be individuals or small companies that loan only on local properties that they can keep a close eye on. The easiest way to find hard money lenders is the yellow pages under "Real Estate Loans" or the Sunday classified real estate section of your local newspaper. Hard money lenders' advertisements will scream out at you: "no qualifying," "easy cash," "no credit required," "cash within days."

Then again, you may not need to find hard money lenders—they may find you! Hard money lenders typically subscribe to special court publications that give them a weekly list of properties in foreclosure. The lenders may send you a letter or promotional mailer advertising their loan services. If you have already received a Notice of Default, you have probably been flooded with these advertisements. Hint: proceed with caution, for reasons discussed in Section E3, above.

### 8. Individuals and Real Estate Investors

The problem with individuals who loan money as a living (not family and friends) is that they tend to charge a higher rate of interest than banks or mortgage companies. Nevertheless, individuals may be an excellent sources of home equity loans, provided the interest rates and fees are acceptable to you.

It may be difficult to distinguish between an individual investor and a hard money lender, especially if the proposed interest rate is incredibly high. If you are confronted with this situation, you can assume you are dealing with a hard money lender, regardless of whether it is an individual or a company.

## G. Closing Costs

If you go forward with a refinance, significant closing costs will be paid out of your loan proceeds. These costs are set out here so that you can not only

anticipate them, but perhaps negotiate with your lender on how costs can be waived or reduced:

- *Application fee.* Some lenders charge a fee when you apply for the loan. The justification is that the lender needs to cover the cost of processing your application. Application fees may be a flat amount, such as $250, or they may be set as a percentage of the loan amount, such as 1% or 2%. Some lenders will refund the application fee if you don't qualify, while others will apply the fee towards your closing costs if your loan is funded. If, however, you qualify for a loan and choose not to take it, you often forfeit the application fee. Check a potential lender's policy before you plunk down any money.
- *Appraisal fee.* Because a lender must make sure that your property is worth enough to provide adequate collateral for a loan, it will hire a state-licensed appraiser to calculate your property's current market value. You pay the cost of the appraisal, which often ranges from $500 to $1,000, depending on the size of your property.
- *Title search.* Before your lender will consider giving you a loan secured by your property, it will have a title insurance company conduct a search of the county recorder's office to determine the chain of title and what claims are recorded against your property, such as deeds of trust, mechanic's liens, attachments, easements, liens and judgments. The fee is typically several hundred dollars. Once again, you will pay this fee out of your loan proceeds. You will not pay this fee if your loan is not funded.
- *Title insurance.* Your lender wants to be assured that you have clear and unimpeded title to your property and that its deed of trust is recorded in the correct priority position. To avoid the possibility that someone else may claim title to your property or a lien senior to your lender's, your lender obtains insurance from a title insurance company. The cost is based on the value of your property, and can run anywhere from $250 to $1,000. Like everything else in a refinance, this one-time insurance premium is deducted from your loan proceeds.
- *Credit report fees.* The cost of credit reports comes to about $25 to $50 per report. Some

lenders will charge this expense when you apply for the loan, while others will deduct the expense out of your loan when it is funded. If the loan is not funded, you are not responsible for the cost.

- *Impound account.* Most lenders giving a conventional loan will set up a special account (called an impound account), out of which they will pay your property taxes, mortgage insurance premiums and property insurance premiums. Lenders prefer to be responsible for these payments so they can verify that payments are made (and your property's value is protected). When the loan is funded, the lender will require that the escrow company withhold enough funds in an impound account to fund several months of payments.

- *Loan origination fee ("points").* This is a fee you pay to your lender for the "privilege" of getting a loan. The loan origination fee is often expressed in terms of "points," where each point represents 1% of the loan amount. Sometimes the loan origination fee is a flat fee, in addition to any points you may pay. Points are likely to be one of your biggest closing costs, and unfortunately they are rarely negotiable. Points are charged only if the loan is granted. They are deducted from the loan proceeds when funded.

- *Lock-in fee.* Some lenders charge a lock-in fee of 1% to 2% of the loan amount if you want your lender to guarantee in writing the interest rate the lender happens to be charging at the time you applied for the loan, regardless of whether interest rates subsequently go up (or down!).

- *Private mortgage insurance (PMI).* This insurance should really be called "loan default insurance" because it protects your lender if you default on your scheduled payments. Although it would seem logical that a lender should pay for PMI, no such luck. This cost is also pushed onto you. The good news is that lenders do not usually require mortgage insurance unless you are refinancing more than 80% of the value of your property. The cost is usually .03% to 1% of the loan amount.

- *Notary fee.* This fee covers the services of a notary public, a person licensed by the state to verify that people's signatures on legal documents are genuine. This is a one of the smallest fees you will pay, often $50 or less.

- *Recording fee.* All sales of property are recorded in the recorder's office of the counties where the property is located. The cost to record, anywhere between $25 to $100, is charged to you.

*chapter*

# 7

# USING YOUR MILITARY STATUS TO STOP FORECLOSURE

*If you don't have a military connection.* Skip this entire chapter if you are not in the military and are not the dependent of someone in the military, or did not co-sign a loan with someone in the military.

One of the primary benefits of the Soldiers' and Sailors' Civil Relief Act (SSCRA) is the protection of active military personnel and their families (and anyone who co-signed a loan with them) from foreclosure. Although the SSCRA will not relieve you of your obligation to repay your loan, it will allow for temporary suspension of collection actions—including foreclosure—while you are on active duty. The SSCRA has far-reaching effects and may be used to:

• *stop a foreclosure.* If you are on active duty, you may get immediate relief from a pending foreclosure. (See Sections C and D.)
• *invalidate a foreclosure sale.* If your property was sold while you were on active duty, you may be able get your property back. (See Sections C and D), and
• *reduce your loan interest rate to 6% per year.* While you're on active military duty, you may be entitled to a 6% interest rate on your property loan—whether or not you're in foreclosure. This may significantly reduce your monthly payments. (See Section B, below.)

This chapter helps you assess whether or not you are eligible for protection under the SSCRA. You'll also find a helpful overview of how you can use the SSCRA to stop your foreclosure. This chapter does not, however, go into depth on the court documents and procedures you might need. At some point, you may need to consult with an attorney or your military commander.

## A. Are You Covered by the SSCRA?

To use the SSCRA as a shield to stop the foreclosure, you must be able to show a court that all of the following apply:
• You are on active duty, or you are the dependent or co-signer of a servicemember on active military duty.
• The debt is secured by a deed of trust (or mortgage) against your property.
• You incurred the debt prior to your active duty in the military.
• You, or your dependents, still own the property.
• Your lender has started foreclosure proceedings.
• Your ability to meet your financial obligations has been "materially affected" by your military service (see Section A5, below). For example, your in-service income is substantially below your pre-service income or you're stationed overseas.

Courts have broad discretion in interpreting and applying the SSCRA to foreclosure situations. Most courts are sympathetic with a servicemember unable to keep current on his or her loan payments. Courts are almost always compassionate to servicemembers (and their co-signers and dependents) attempting to stop foreclosures of their property.

## 1. Are You on Active Duty?

If you are on active duty in the armed forces, you are entitled to special protection under the Soldiers' and Sailors' Civil Relief Act (SSCRA). Section 532 of the SSCRA helps active military personnel by temporarily suspending all foreclosure proceedings (both nonjudicial and judicial, covered in Chapters 3 and 4, respectively).

---

### DEVELOPMENT OF THE SOLDIERS' AND SAILORS CIVIL RELIEF ACT (SSCRA)

In 1918, Congress formally recognized that servicemembers couldn't reasonably attend to their financial and legal commitments while serving during wartime. Finding it unfair for lawsuits to proceed to the detriment of someone who had volunteered in the armed forces or was drafted in time of war, Congress passed the Soldiers' and Sailors Civil Relief Act of 1918. The SSCRA was intended to boost morale and allow U.S. troops to devote their attention exclusively to the war effort, without concern for their financial obligations back home.

The present SSCRA statute was passed in 1940 during World War II and has subsequently gone through only minor changes. For foreclosure purposes, you'll be primarily interested in Chapter 4, Section 532 of the SSCRA, which deals with promissory notes, deeds of trust and other liens.

## 2. Are You a Servicemember Covered by the SSCRA?

The SSCRA protects members of the U.S. armed forces (army, navy, air force, marine corps and coast guard), including reservists, who are on active duty. The U.S. armed forces defines "active duty" as full-time presence on a military base due to military assignment or full-time training prior to induction. The SSCRA also protects officers of the Public Health Service who are detailed for duty with any branch of the military.

*Not all military personnel are covered.* The SSCRA does not protect servicemembers who are not on active duty, are on unauthorized absence (AWOL) or are in a military prison.

## 3. Are You a Co-Signer for or a Dependent of a Servicemember on Active Duty?

Frequently, a spouse, friend or family member may have signed loan documents along with a service member. When a lender discovers that it cannot legally pursue the servicemember because of his or her active duty status in the military, it may attempt to collect from a co-signer on the loan. In these circumstances, the SSCRA extends to everyone who co-signed an active servicemember's loan.

The SSCRA also covers a service member's dependents who didn't sign the loan, such as children or a spouse. In other words, a lender can't proceed against a servicemember's dependents while he or she is on active duty.

**PERIOD OF COVERAGE**

If you are in the military, the Act protects you the day you begin active duty. The coverage also extends for 90 days after the date your active military service is completed. This protection extends to co-signers and family members.

## 4. Was the Debt Incurred Before Active Duty Began?

The SSCRA applies only to debts incurred before you began active duty in the military.

*Example: Five years ago, George purchased a farm in Modesto. He later enlisted in the U.S. Navy and was assigned to the Long Beach Naval Shipyard. Several months after George went on active duty, he defaulted on his loan payments and his lender started foreclosure proceedings. Because George purchased his property before going on active duty, he can invoke the SSCRA and demand that his lender temporarily stop the foreclosure.*

The SSCRA does not, however, apply to loans entered into after beginning active military duty. If you borrowed money to purchase property while you were on active military duty (or after you'd left the military), the Act will not stop your foreclosure.

*Example: Henry, a buddy of George's, is also stationed at the Long Beach Naval Shipyard. After being on duty for several months, Henry purchases a house in Long Beach. Almost immediately, he begins missing payments and his lender initiates foreclosure proceedings. Unfortunately for Henry, the SSCRA, and its protection against foreclosure, does not apply to him because he purchased his property after he was already on active duty.*

## 5. Was the Servicemember "Materially Affected"?

To understand your rights under the Act, you'll need to learn a bit of legal jargon. The SSCRA only covers servicemembers who are "materially affected." A servicemember who cannot protect his or her legal rights or fulfill his or her financial obligations because of being on active duty is "materially affected." Let's look more closely at these issues.

### a. Inability to Protect Your Legal Rights

If a servicemember is sued for judicial foreclosure in court, and that servicemember cannot participate in the lawsuit because of active duty in another city, state or country, that servicemember may petition the court for a stay (postponement) until he or she can personally appear and participate. In that event, the court must determine whether military service materially affects the servicemember's ability to protect his or her rights.

*Example: June purchases a triplex in Santa Clara and takes out a loan with Scarlet Pension Fund. The next year, June volunteers for the Army and is assigned to a military base in Germany. When Scarlet starts a foreclosure, June disputes its legal right to foreclose. Because June's ability to protect her legal rights in California is materially affected by her military status in Germany, the SSCRA will apply and Scarlet will be prohibited from foreclosing at least until June returns from active duty in Germany.*

### b. Servicemember's Inability to Meet Financial Obligations

If a servicemember defaults on a loan obligation because he or she can no longer afford the payments due to being on active duty, that servicemember can contend that the military's lower wages has "materially affected" his or her financial ability to pay debts as previously agreed. This issue arises because servicemembers typically receive substantially less income in the military than they received in private life, or they are in combat and unavailable to make loan payments.

In either circumstance, the servicemember (or a co-signer or dependent) must file papers with a court asking it to stop the foreclosure until the servicemember is off active duty.

*Example: John borrows $250,000 from Ace Financial Corporation to purchase a house in Salinas. Several years later, John volunteers for the U.S. Navy and is assigned to San Diego, where he's paid $1,500 per month. When John defaults on his monthly payments, Ace starts foreclosure proceedings. Because John's active duty in San Diego materially affects his ability to meet his financial obligations to Ace, John may invoke the SSCRA to stop the foreclosure until he returns home.*

You will be pleased to learn that in determining the meaning of "materially affects," courts have traditionally favored the servicemember. In fact, the Supreme Court has declared that the Act must be read with "an eye friendly to those who drop their affairs to answer their country's call." (*LeMaistre v. Leffers*, 333 U.S. 1, 6 (1943).)

## B. How to Use the SSCRA to Reduce Your Interest Rate and Payments

Regardless of the interest rate stated in your promissory note, your lender must reduce your interest rate to 6% per year while you are on active duty, assuming that you qualify under the "materially affected" test. Your lender's obligation to lower your interest rate is not affected by whether you are in default or there is a pending foreclosure. (50 U.S.C. § 526.)

Your only obligation is to give your lender a written request to lower the interest rate. Your lender is not required to lower the interest rate automatically if you are on active duty.

Of course, if your interest rate is lowered, your monthly payments will be correspondingly lower.

*Example: Sally borrowed $120,000 from Hightop Financial Services to purchase a home in Brawley. The promissory note provided for an annual interest rate of 11%, payable at $1,143 per month. Several months later, Sally was called up for active duty in the Air Force and stationed in Seattle. Sally, aware of the SSCRA, notified Hightop of her active duty in the Air Force and asked that her interest rate be reduced to 6% while she remained on active duty. Hightop reluctantly agreed, and her monthly payments dropped to $719.*

### 1. Send Your Lender a Letter

To reduce your interest rate on a loan you obtained before entering active military duty, you'll need to send your lender a letter. Include a copy of your military orders. Mail the letter certified mail, return receipt requested, or by overnight mail, return receipt requested. You can use the accompanying sample letter below as a guide.

**SAMPLE LETTER ASKING LENDER TO REDUCE INTEREST RATE**

June 3, 199X

Mr. Peter London
Vice President
Baltor Insurance Corporation
2343 Baltor Court
San Rafael, California

Re: Account No. 65-3421

Dear Mr. London:

I own the property located at 467 Briar Street, San Rafael, California. In 199X, I borrowed $155,000 from Baltor to purchase this property, which was secured by a deed of trust against my property. The purpose of this letter is to advise you that I am on active duty with the United States Army.

Because of my call-up, and for the duration of my active duty status, I will lose my civilian employment income. As a result, my ability to repay my loan as previously agreed has been materially affected by the temporary reduction in my income. I estimate that my period of active service will end in approximately July of 199X. I will notify you in writing upon my return.

I understand that the Soldiers' and Sailors' Civil Relief Act ("Act") limits the annual rate of interest on this debt to 6% while I am on active duty (50 U.S.C. § 526). As used in the Act, the term "interest" includes service charges, carrying charges, renewal charges, fees and any other charge (except bona fide insurance) added to my loan. I understand that my dependents and co-signers are also provided protection under the Act.

Upon receipt of this request, please adjust my account to reflect the statutory 6% rate and notify me of the revised payment schedule. Thank you for your understanding and cooperation in this matter.

Sincerely,

Thomas Eagle
Private First Class
U.S. Army

Enclosure: Copy of military orders

## 2.  What to Expect From Your Lender

If your lender ignores the SSCRA and proceeds with the foreclosure, you have the right to bring a lawsuit to enforce the SSCRA (See Chapter 8). In that event, your lender can be sanctioned by the Court for ignoring the SSCRA after you advised the lender of your active duty. Because of this potential liability, most lenders will promptly respond to your request by lowering your interest rate to 6% per year. The 6% interest rate will continue until your tour of active duty is completed.

Occasionally, a lender may prefer to go to court and demonstrate that your financial condition is not "materially affected" by active duty and that you can still afford the regular interest rate. (We discuss the meaning of "materially affected" in Section A above.) In that unlikely event, you must demonstrate to the court that you are making substantially less money during your active duty then you did in your previous civilian employment. Needless to say, this should be fairly easy, given the low wages paid by the military.

When you are discharged from the military, your lender has the right to automatically increase the interest rate to the rate provided in your promissory note. Fortunately for you, your lender can't retroactively charge you the interest it "lost" during your period of active duty.

*Example:  George borrowed $100,000 from Pismo Beach Savings Bank, with an interest rate of 9% adjustable. When George was called to active duty in Navy, George notified the Bank and requested that the interest rate on his loan be reduced to 6% pursuant to the SSCRA. When George completed his active duty, the Bank automatically increased his interest rate to 9%. Even better, George was not liable for the 3% spread (9% in the promissory note versus the 6% while on active duty) that the Bank lost during his tour of active duty.*

## C. How to Use the SSCRA to Stop a Nonjudicial Foreclosure

*If your lender filed a judicial foreclosure only, you can skip this section and read Section D, below.* For a review of the nonjudicial foreclosure process, read Chapter 3. Judicial foreclosures are covered in Chapter 4.

A lender cannot foreclose nonjudicially without court permission, once you inform it that you are on active duty and are seeking protection under the SSCRA. You can do this by simply advising your lender of your active military status. Either contact your lender before you leave or after you arrive at the military base where you are stationed. Once you notify your lender that you are away from home on a military assignment, your lender has two choices:

- Your lender may stop the nonjudicial foreclosure and wait for you to return from active duty.
- Your lender may file an action in court, asking permission to proceed with the nonjudicial foreclosure.

Because most judges understand the significance of your military duty, they are unlikely to allow foreclosure. Thus, you are likely to be protected for as long as you are on active duty in the military.

### 1. Send a Letter to Your Lender

Write your lender a letter as soon as you are called to active duty and mail it certified mail, return receipt requested. Your letter should advise your lender that you have been called into the military. Request that your lender stop the foreclosure (or hold off initiating a foreclosure) and lower the interest rate to 6% during your active duty. You can use the following sample letter as a guide.

---

**SAMPLE LETTER TO LENDER (NONJUDICIAL FORECLOSURE)**

December 22, 199X

Ms. Karen Johnston
Vice President
Sanctity Savings Bank
25 Main Street
Eureka, California

Re: Loan No. 976555

Dear Ms. Johnston:

In199X, I borrowed $125,000 from Sanctity Savings Bank to purchase property located at 6701 Third Avenue, Eureka, California. I signed a promissory note and a deed of trust, which was recorded against my property. On July 6, 199X, I received notice from Sanctity that it was initiating a nonjudicial foreclosure of my property.

I understand that the Soldiers' and Sailors' Civil Relief Act prohibits the sale, foreclosure or seizure of my property for non-payment of any sum due under the loan, or for any other breach of the terms of my promissory note and deed of trust, prior to or during the period of my military service and for 90 days thereafter (50 U.S.C. § 532).

The purpose of this letter is to advise you that I am on active duty with the United States Coast Guard. Because of my call-up, and for the duration of my active duty status, I will lose my civilian employment income. As a result, my ability to repay my loan according to the terms I previously agreed has been materially affected by the temporary reduction in my income.

Accordingly, I request that you stop the pending foreclosure until I return from active duty. I estimate that my period of active service will end in approximately July of 199X. I will notify you in writing upon my return.

I also understand that the Act limits the rate of interest on this debt to six percent (6%) per year while I am on active duty (50 U.S.C. § 526). As used in the Act, the term "interest" includes service charges, carrying charges, renewal charges, fees and any other charge (except bona fide insurance) related to the liability. I understand that my co-signers and dependents are also provided protection under the Act.

Upon receipt of this letter, please adjust my account to reflect the statutory 6% rate and notify me in writing of the revised schedule.

Thank you for your understanding and cooperation in this matter.

Sincerely,

John Overton
Seaman
U.S. Coast Guard Reserve

## 2. What to Expect From Your Lender

Because the SSCRA allows the courts to sanction lenders who pursue foreclosure knowing that the borrower is in the military, most lenders will stop the foreclosure and lower your interest rate to 6% per year during your active military duty without further question.

Your lender may comply with your request and stop the foreclosure. In this case, your lender will advise you that upon the termination of your active duty, the foreclosure will resume unless you cure the default.

If your lender ignores your request and proceeds with a nonjudicial foreclosure, you have the right to file an action in court to enjoin the foreclosure based upon the SSCRA. (See Chapter 8 on how to file a lawsuit to enjoin a nonjudicial foreclosure.) If the court finds that you have been materially affected by your active duty, it may take any or all of the following actions:

- stay (stop) the nonjudicial foreclosure until you return from active duty
- lower your monthly payments until you return from active duty
- if a trustee's sale has already occurred, set aside (invalidate) the sale and stay the foreclosure until you return from active duty, and
- sanction your lender if it knew you were in the military and proceeded with a foreclosure anyhow.

If your lender wants to go to court to prove that you will not be adversely affected by a foreclosure, it will file a judicial foreclosure. Guidelines on how to deal with a judicial foreclosure are in Section D, below.

## D. How to Use the SSCRA to Stop a Judicial Foreclosure

*If your lender filed a nonjudicial foreclosure, you can skip this section and read Section C, above.* For a review of the judicial foreclosure process, read Chapter 4. Nonjudicial foreclosures are covered in Chapter 3.

If your lender files a judicial foreclosure, you need to advise the court immediately that you are on active duty. This will allow the Court to determine whether you have the ability to defend the action or it should be stayed until you return from active duty.

## 1. File Affidavit With the Court

Write an affidavit (sworn statement under penalty of perjury) on lined legal paper and file it with the Superior Court that is handling the foreclosure. You will need to include on your affidavit the court's name and address, the case number and other important information which you will find in the Summons and Complaint you received. There is no fee for filing an affidavit. A sample affidavit, in a form recommended by the military, follows. A blank piece of lined legal paper is provided in the Appendix.

SAMPLE AFFIDAVIT REQUESTING STAY OF FORECLOSURE PROCEEDING

1

William Thurston
234 Hilltop Drive
Fremont, California
510-666-5656

2

3

4

Defendant
In Pro Per

5

6

7

8

THE STATE OF CALIFORNIA SUPERIOR COURT

9

FOR THE COUNTY OF ALAMEDA

10

11

Donkey Pension Fund,                    )        Case No. 67-45445

12                                       )

        Plaintiff,                       )

13                                       )        DECLARATION OF WILLIAM THURSTON

v.                                       )        RE ACTIVE DUTY IN MILITARY SERVICE

14                                       )

15

William Thurston, and                    )

DOES 1 to 5, Inclusive,                  )

16                                       )

17

        Defendants.                      )

18 ──────────────────────────────        )

19

I, WILLIAM THURSTON, declare as follows:

20

        1. I am a private, presently on active duty in the United States Navy and assigned to the

21

San Diego Naval Station. I am the owner of the property located at 234 Hilltop Drive, Fremont,
California.

22

        2. I know each of the following facts to be true of my own personal knowledge and if

23

called as a witness, I could and would competently testify with respect thereto.

24

        3. I am the defendant in civil action No. 67-45445, Donkey Pension Fund vs. William

25

Thurston, et al., currently pending before this Court.

26

        4. I am not represented by an attorney.

27

        5. My ability to appear and protect my interests in this action are materially affected by

28

reason of my active military service in San Diego at the Naval Shipyard. Due to my commitments
of my military unit, I am unable to presently obtain leave to attend these proceedings.

1       6. I estimate that my active duty in the U.S. Armed Forces will continue to approximately

2  December of 199__.

3       7. In reliance upon the Soldiers' and Sailors' Civil Relief Act of 1940, as amended (50

U.S.C. 501 et seq.), I hereby respectfully request that the Court, on its own motion, stay these

4  proceedings against me until such time as my ability to present a defense is no longer materially

5  affected by my military service.

6       8. In the alternative, if the Court will not stay these proceedings, I respectfully request that

7  the Court appoint an attorney to represent me (50 U.S.C. 520).

8       9. I agree to notify the Court and the plaintiff of my return to Fremont upon my release by

the Navy from active duty.

9       10. This request is in no manner intended, and should not be construed, to constitute an

10  appearance in this case and does not submit me to the jurisdiction of this Court.

11       I declare under penalty of perjury of the laws of the State of California that the foregoing

is true and correct.  Executed on <u>July 1</u>, <u>199X</u>, in San Diego, California.

12

13

14                                 _____

                               William Thurston

15                                 Declarant

16

17

18

19

20

21

22

23

24

25

26

27

28

## 2. What Your Lender Will Do

Once you file an affidavit with the court, the court will order that your lender stop the judicial foreclosure until you return from active duty. Because your lender can be sanctioned by the court for pursuing a foreclosure in violation of the SSCRA, it will probably comply with the court order and wait until you return from active duty before proceeding with the lawsuit. It will also lower your interest rate to 6% per year during your active military duty. You should also not be surprised if your lender suddenly wants to negotiate new loan terms with you.

Occasionally, a lender will try to convince the court that you will not be adversely affected if it is allowed to proceed with the judicial foreclosure. For example, that you are making more money in the military or that your military activity is a rouse.

## 3. If You Don't Respond to the Lawsuit

Let's say you didn't get notice of the lawsuit or you didn't file a formal affidavit or answer to your lender's Complaint. To prevent a lender from getting a judgment against you while you're on active duty, your lender must file a statement, under penalty of perjury, that you are not in the military. In the statement, your lender must specify that it took reasonable steps to ascertain that you are not in the military. If there is any doubt of your military status, the court may order your lender to post a security deposit to protect you in the event you need to later set aside the default judgment. The security deposit will be used for damages you may have suffered as a result of a default judgment incorrectly entered against you.

If a default judgment for foreclosure was entered by the court while you were on active duty, you have powerful rights under the SSCRA. Within 90 days from the date of your discharge, you must file an application with the court and mail a copy to your lender. Your application should request that the court set aside (invalidate) the default judgment, based upon the following:

- you were on active duty in the military when the default judgment was entered by the court
- you have suffered damages (you lost your property or a blemish was put on your credit) or your case is prejudiced because you could not properly present your side of the case, and
- you have a valid, legal defense you wish to present to the court.

In the unlikely event your lender obtains a default judgment of foreclosure by falsely stating on the court form that you were not in the military, you may ask the court to sanction your lender and nullify the default judgment.

*If your lender gets a default judgment against you.* If you find yourself in this predicament, you will probably need to hire an attorney to file an application with the court. For more on finding an attorney, turn to Chapter 12.

# 8

# USING THE COURTS TO STOP
# A NONJUDICIAL FORECLOSURE

*If your lender filed a judicial foreclosure.* A judicial foreclosure uses the court system to conduct foreclosure proceedings. You will know that a judicial foreclosure has been filed because you will have been served with an official Summons and Complaint. You may present arguments against the foreclosure as part of your answer or by way of a Cross-Complaint. We cover judicial foreclosures in Chapter 4.

As you probably know by now, a nonjudicial foreclosure is ordinarily conducted without any court involvement. (We cover the step-by-step nonjudicial foreclosure procedures in Chapter 3.) Fortunately, you can use the court system to stop a nonjudicial foreclosure if you believe that either:

• your lender did not follow the correct foreclosure procedures, or

• your lender didn't have legal grounds to foreclose in the first place.

To use the court system you must file a lawsuit—in legal jargon, an "action to enjoin the trustee's sale"—that asks a judge to temporarily enjoin (prevent) the trustee's sale until your objections are resolved. If the judge rules in your favor, he or she will grant an injunction—a court order that staves off the foreclosure. Injunctions can last anywhere from several weeks to several years, depending upon the validity of your objections and the type of injunction issued.

This chapter gives an overview of how to use the courts to stop a nonjudicial foreclosure. You'll examine whether or not you have grounds for going to court and what an action to enjoin the trustee's sale will accomplish. You'll also find instructions on how to file your lawsuit and get a type of injunction known as a temporary restraining order (TRO). Most lenders will be anxious to negotiate if you succeed in getting a TRO. If, however, you need to proceed further with the lawsuit, you'll need to go beyond this book. We summarize the legal proceedings and give suggestions on where to go for help.

## A. Do You Have Grounds to Go to Court?

Before you make up your mind to file a lawsuit, be sure you have a valid legal basis for stopping the foreclosure. Don't consider going to court if you simply missed payments and now are desperately searching for a way to delay the foreclosure. Personal problems such as illness, divorce or job loss, while crucial to you, are not relevant to the basic legal issue of whether your lender has the right to foreclose.

The legal grounds for filing a lawsuit to enjoin (stop) the trustee's sale fall into two general categories:
- disputes over the foreclosure procedures, and
- disputes with your lender over the terms of your promissory note or deed of trust.

Below, we examine these two categories in detail. If you find you have legal grounds to file a

lawsuit, first read the rest of this chapter to get a sense of what is involved in an action to enjoin the trustee's sale.

### 1. Disputes With Trustee Over Foreclosure Procedures

Let's say your lender has the legal right to foreclose. That is, you are in default because you haven't made your payments. But, in the process, the trustee violates the procedural requirements of a nonjudicial foreclosure. For example, there may be defects in the Notice of Default or Notice of Trustee's Sale or an irregularity in how the trustee mails the notices. (CC §§ 2924–2924i.) A judge may order that the foreclosure be enjoined (stopped) until the trustee corrects the procedural mistake. If the trustee made a minor mistake, a judge is not likely to enjoin the trustee's sale for very long. More likely, the judge will order that the process start over at the point the trustee went astray. Nevertheless, even a minor delay may provide the additional time you need to utilize other strategies described in this book.

In the event a trustee makes several procedural mistakes, the judge will probably order the trustee to start the foreclosure process over again from the beginning. If this should occur, you may suddenly find a plethora of possibilities, not the least of which may be your lender's sudden willingness to negotiate.

In Chapter 3, we examined each of the nonjudicial foreclosure steps in detail. Below, we help you assess whether or not the trustee handled all these procedures correctly. The bottom line is, if the nonjudicial foreclosure process wasn't conducted properly, you have grounds to file a lawsuit.

### a. Notice of Default

In Chapter 3, Section B, we provide a worksheet to help you spot errors in the Notice of Default. If you haven't already completed the Notice of Default Worksheet, and compared the information in the Notice of Default to your promissory note and deed of trust, turn to Chapter 3, Section B, and do so now. Specifically make sure the following are accurate in the Notice of Default:

- name of trustor (you)
- name of beneficiary (your lender)
- name of trustee
- legal description of your property
- amount of original indebtedness
- date deed of trust was recorded, and
- document number of the deed of trust.

Also double-check that the trustee followed the correct requirements for mailing, publishing, posting and recording the Notice of Default. Again, refer to the Notice of Default Worksheet. If you don't have all of the information, you have the right to ask the trustee to provide evidence (typically an affidavit) that it mailed, published, recorded and posted the Notice of Default.

## b. Reinstatement Period

As you may recall, the reinstatement period is the time period that runs from the date the Notice of Default is issued to five calendar days before the trustee's sale. If, during the reinstatement period, any of the following occurred, you have grounds to stop the foreclosure:

- The trustee or your lender failed to respond to your written request for a beneficiary statement within two months after the Notice of Default was filed or within 21 days of your written request, whichever occurs later. (We show you how to request a beneficiary statement in Chapter 3, Section B4.)
- The trustee or your lender sent you a beneficiary statement, but the statement did not fulfill the legal requirements because it didn't include a breakdown of your unpaid balance, the total arrears, the amount of your monthly payment, the date your loan is due, the amounts of any liens paid by your lender, the date through which taxes have been paid, the amount of insurance (if any), the amounts in any impound accounts or a statement of whether your loan is assumable.
- If your loan was assigned to another lender, your lender failed to send you a notice of the

assignment by mail, which included the name and address of your new lender (or servicer), the date of the transfer and the due date for your next payment.

- You offered to pay the total arrears and trustee's fees during the reinstatement period, but the trustee or your lender refused to accept it. (For more on the reinstatement period, see Chapter 3, Section C.)

## c. Notice of Trustee's Sale

The Notice of Trustee's Sale must be consistent with the information in your promissory note, deed of trust and Notice of Default. Carefully scrutinize these documents for errors. If the information is inconsistent, you may have grounds to stop the foreclosure. We provide a Notice of Trustee's Sale Worksheet in Chapter 3, Section D3 to help you with this process. We also review some of the common errors trustees make in Chapter 3, Section D4. Cross-check the following:

- name of trustor (you)
- name of beneficiary (your lender). If the name of the beneficiary is different, ask the trustee or a title insurance company whether the new lender has recorded a Notice of Assignment of Beneficial Interest.
- name of trustee. If the trustee is different that the trustee named on your deed of trust, ask a title insurance company to determine whether a Substitution of trustee was recorded in the county recorder's office prior to the Notice of Default being recorded.
- legal description of your property
- amount of original indebtedness
- date deed of trust was recorded
- document number of the deed of trust
- were the mailing requirements properly followed? (See worksheet in Chapter 3, Section D3 for this and succeeding questions.)
- were the publishing requirements properly followed?
- were the posting requirements properly followed?
- were the recording requirements properly followed?

- was the Notice of Sale recorded more than three months after the date the Notice of Default was recorded?
- does the Notice of Sale state the date, time, location and terms of the trustee's sale?
- if an IRS or Franchise Tax Board lien has been recorded, did the trustee send a copy of the Notice of Sale to the taxing agency at least 25 days before the scheduled sale date? (If the trustee doesn't have or won't disclose this information, contact the customer service department of a local title insurance company to determine whether any tax liens are recorded against your property. Then, armed with this information, contact the particular taxing agency and inquire whether they received a copy of the Notice of Sale.)
- is the trustee's sale scheduled more than 20 days after the date of the Notice of Sale?

### d. Redemption Period

The last five calendar days before the trustee's sale are called the redemption period. During the redemption period, the trustee may have mishandled the foreclosure procedures. For example, if your lender refused to accept your payment even though you offered full payment of the amount you owed

(including principal, unpaid interest, costs, penalties, late fees and foreclosure costs).

---

**IF THE TRUSTEE'S SALE HAS ALREADY HAPPENED**

If your property was already sold at a trustee's sale, it's obviously too late to file a lawsuit to enjoin the trustee's sale. Nevertheless, if the trustee conducted the foreclosure procedures improperly, you may still have some recourse.

If your lender purchased the property, you may ask a court to invalidate the trustee's sale and return the property to you, known as a lawsuit to set aside the trustee's sale. This lawsuit will be somewhat complicated by the fact that you must justify why you waited until after the trustee's sale before filing the lawsuit.

If your property was sold at the trustee's sale to a third party (rather than your lender), you cannot set aside the sale or get back your property. Instead, you're limited to filing a lawsuit for money damages against your lender or trustee.

Because filing a lawsuit after the fact is quite complex, you should see a lawyer if you want to proceed.

## 2. Disputes With Lender Over Amount Due or the Terms of Promissory Note or Deed of Trust

You have the right to challenge your lender's right to foreclose if:

- you dispute the amount your lender claims you owe
- Regulation Z requirements (federal disclosure laws designed to protect borrowers) were not followed
- there was fraud in the original transaction, or
- the promissory note or deed of trust is defective.

Let's explore each of these categories separately, starting with the most common problem and progressing to the least likely.

### a. Disagreements Over the Amount Owed

Disputes frequently arise over the amount that is in default or whether a payment was (or wasn't) made. If this should occur and you believe your lender is overcharging you to reinstate or redeem your property, you have the right to file a lawsuit to stop the foreclosure. If you can convince a judge that there is a legitimate dispute over the amount in default, he or she may stop the pending foreclosure until the correct amount owed can be determined. There tend to be more disputes over adjustable-rate-mortgage (ARM) notes than fixed-interest-rate notes, primarily because ARMs are complex and are more likely to contain mathematical errors.

At first glance, you may think that the chances of your loan being improperly calculated by your lender are improbable at best. Well, think again. According to John Geddes, a certified public accountant and former banking regulator (who addressed a U.S. House of Representatives Task Force on this very issue), adjustable rate (ARM) real estate loans are frequently overcharged so that lenders can sell loan portfolios in the secondary market for higher prices.

Geddes found a 47.5% error rate in the 9,000 ARM loans that were audited. Overcharges averaging $1,588 per loan occurred in 37% of the audited loans. Why are errors so prevalent? More than 75% of the errors were caused by lenders using the wrong index value in determining the interest rate. Personnel who manage thousands of promissory notes on a daily basis usually are overworked and inadequately trained. They often input incorrect dates or rates. Outmoded computer systems and the sheer number and variety of loans also contribute to the problem.

Geddes identified six separate warning signs of loan errors:

- *Your original lender sold your loan.* When loan data are transferred from one lender to another lender or servicer, there is a chance that processing systems are incompatible or data was interpreted incorrectly.
- *Your loan is based on an uncommon index.* The one-year treasury bill is a common index. Less common indices, such as the 11th District Cost of Funds, require ongoing research to ensure that current statistical information from the index is used to adjust the interest rate. If your lender is using an unusual index, its calculations are likely to be wrong.
- *Your promissory note contained blank spaces.* If any spaces were left blank, your lender could have added terms you didn't agree to.
- *Your ARM was issued before 1990.* These loans have a higher error rate because the software and hardware used then was often inadequate.
- *Your loan has complex or unusual terms.* Loans with short terms (three years or less), bi-weekly payments, or an unusual term or condition (such as graduated payments depending on irregular principal reductions), leave more room for error because the figures cannot be plugged into a standard computer program.
- *Your lender can't answer your questions.* If you aren't satisfied with your lender's explanation about a problem, there's a good chance your lender is confused about it as well.

## GETTING HELP

Companies that specialize in calculating the correct interest rates, payments, arrears and outstanding balances on loans spring up and disappear quicker than you can say "My lender is cheating me!" Such companies can typically be found in your local yellow pages . Nevertheless, the better approach, if you can afford it, is to hire a certified public accountant who has experience in auditing loans.

If even one warning sign applies, immediately write a letter to the lender and demand to have your CPA audit your loan, at your expense, before the lender proceeds further with the foreclosure. Refer to the sample letter below as a guide.

Don't be surprised if your lender is extremely responsive and temporarily postpones the foreclosure sale until your CPA can audit the loan. If your lender is not willing to cooperate, go ahead and file your lawsuit to enjoin the foreclosure. You are still in a better position than if you had not written the letter, as you now have additional "ammunition" to use in your lawsuit to demonstrate your lender's bad faith. Based on this evidence, a court would certainly order an audit before allowing your lender to proceed with a foreclosure. The only caution here is to avoid waiting too long for your lender to respond.

*If you're running out of time.* If a Notice of Trustee's Sale has already been issued, file a lawsuit and request that the court enjoin the foreclosure until an audit can occur.

August 12, 199X

Mr. Edgar Williams
Vice President
Toucan Mortgage Company
6666 Main Street
Richmond, CA

Re: Loan No. 3423464

Dear Mr. Williams:

In September of 199X, I borrowed $160,000 from Toucan Mortgage Company. This loan was secured by a deed of trust recorded against my property located at 234 Bird Street, San Mateo, California.

Last month, Toucan's trustee initiated a nonjudicial foreclosure by recording a Notice of Default in the county recorder's office. Upon close inspection of the Notice of Default, I saw that it states I owe $5,245 to reinstate my loan. This amount is incorrect. I believe I owe less than $2,930. I believe this mistake is caused by your incorrect calculation of the interest rate.

Under the circumstances, I request that my certified public accountant audit your books and records with respect to my loan. I will follow up this letter by telephoning your office on Wednesday morning to schedule an appointment for my CPA to conduct the audit. If you will not be available to accept my call, please designate someone to discuss the audit arrangements with me. In the interim, I request that the foreclosure be postponed until we can determine the correct amount owed.

Thank you in advance for your anticipated cooperation in this matter.

Sincerely,

Peter Berger

### b. Failure to Comply With Truth-in-Lending (Regulation Z) Disclosures

The federal Truth-in-Lending Act provides a series of laws to protect consumers who are borrowing money. For purposes of foreclosure, the most important section of the Act is called "Regulation Z."

Regulation Z applies to all lenders who loan money more than 25 times a year (or more than five times a year if the loans are secured by owner-occupied residences). Private lenders who are not in the business of loaning money, such as the previous property owner who accepted a deed of trust as a portion of the purchase price, ordinarily are not required to comply with Regulation Z.

Under Regulation Z, lenders must disclose the following information, in writing, to each borrower:

- total amount financed
- annual percentage interest rate charged (APR)
- amount of each payment
- total interest to be paid
- time schedule for payments
- total finance charge
- total of all payments during the term of loan
- any transaction or service charges
- loan fees
- premiums for private mortgage insurance, if applicable, and
- premiums for property insurance, if applicable.

If your lender didn't comply with Regulation Z, you may have the right to stop the foreclosure until your lender gives you all of the required disclosures, even if you took out the loan years ago. Even minor errors in the disclosures or calculations, especially in the interest rate, may be sufficient grounds to have a judge enjoin the foreclosure. Regulation Z also slaps penalties on lenders that make errors or fail to properly disclose financial information. Penalties may include a loss of interest due the lender and punitive damages up to three times the amount of the loan.

Most lenders provide a Regulation Z form that contains all required information at the top of the document in a series of easy-to-understand boxes and a Notice of Right to Cancel. A good lender will also have you sign or initial the forms so it has physical evidence that you reviewed the required information. If, however, your lender never gave you a Regulation Z form and a Notice of Right to Cancel, neglected to disclose all financial terms in writing or incorrectly calculated the financial information on the form, you may have legitimate grounds for filing a lawsuit.

Start by locating your Regulation Z form and Notice of Right to Cancel (if you have it) and carefully checking the accuracy of the financial information. If you have any problems analyzing the calculations, consider hiring a bookkeeper or an accountant to determine whether your Regulation Z form is correct.

---

**IF YOU CAN'T FIND YOUR REGULATION Z FORM**

If you can't find a copy of your Regulation Z form and Notice of Right to Cancel, call the escrow company that handled your loan and ask if there's a copy in its closed file. If you can't get a copy from the escrow company, call your lender and ask for the name of the President, Vice President, branch manager or loan officer. Then write a letter to that person and request a copy of your Regulation Z form and Notice of Right to Cancel. Because the foreclosure clock is ticking, you can't afford to lose any more time, so arrange to pick up the copy at their office. A sample letter requesting a Regulation Z form appears below.

July 10, 199X

Mr. John Smith
Vice President
Ocean Savings Bank
2525 Ocean Avenue
Oceanside, California

Re: Loan No. 67-45654

Dear Mr. Smith:

My wife, Susan, and I obtained a loan with Ocean Savings Bank in August of 199X for $150,000. The loan was secured by a deed of trust encumbering our property located at 234 Oak Street, Oceanside, California.

As you may know, last month, Ocean initiated a nonjudicial foreclosure. While preparing to resolve the foreclosure, we looked for a copy of our Regulation Z form but were unable to locate it. In fact, I do not recall ever receiving a Regulation Z form.

If you have a copy of the Regulation Z form we received, please photocopy it for me. I will telephone you in the morning on Monday, July 15 to arrange to pick up the copy. Thank you for your prompt attention to my request.

Very truly yours,

John Sousa

If your lender doesn't comply within several days, immediately send a second letter. At the bottom, indicate that you're sending a copy to the United States Office of Thrift Supervision ("OTS"). The OTS is the department of the United States government responsible for regulating lending institutions. The California office of the OTS is located at 1 Montgomery Street, San Francisco, CA, 94120. You will be amazed at how quickly your lender may now respond when it sees that you sent a copy to the OTS.

*If your lender won't give you a copy of your Regulation Z form and Notice of Right to Cancel.* It's probably because your lender didn't provide the forms in the first place, cannot find them or doesn't want you to see your forms because there are errors in them. Your lender's recalcitrance in turning over a copy (if one even exists) will exemplify its bad faith and provide evidence that it failed to comply with Regulation Z. Proceed with your lawsuit to enjoin the foreclosure and attach your two letters, and any written response you receive from your lender, as exhibits.

### c. Fraud in the Original Transaction

This category of disputes is a catch-all for any situation in which your lender may have acted improperly when it lent you money. If nothing comes to mind, it probably does not apply to you. On the other hand, if the words "fraud" and "misrepresentation" set off alarm bells in your head, and remind you that there was something dishonest in the way your lender dealt with you, you may have grounds to ask a court to stop the foreclosure.

Following are some examples of fraud:
- When you signed the loan documents, your lender promised in writing (forget it if the promises were only oral) that you could extend the loan when it came due, or that it would gladly refinance your loan if you ever needed to.

Now suddenly, that same lender is foreclosing and won't even return your telephone calls.
- You signed a promissory note and deed of trust that contained onerous conditions, such as an extremely high (usurious) interest rate.
- After foreclosing on property you owned, your lender required that you sign a deed of trust on another property.
- The party foreclosing is a foreclosure consultant you previously hired to help you with another foreclosure, who (improperly) took back a deed of trust as part of his or her compensation.

*If any of these scenarios sound familiar to you.* Consult an attorney immediately. This very technical area is beyond the scope of this book. A lawyer can assist in filing a lawsuit based upon your lender's fraud in the original transaction.

### d. Defects in the Promissory Note or Deed of Trust

Although rare, there are occasionally defects in a promissory note, such as incorrect or inconsistent terms. Likewise, sometimes deeds of trust are not signed, never recorded, recorded against the wrong property, or contain incorrect or inconsistent terms. If you believe that your loan documents are invalid for any reason, you should contact a lawyer for assistance in preparing a lawsuit. (See Chapter 2 for explanations of promissory notes and deeds of trust.)

---

**MONITOR TRUSTEE'S ACTIVITIES**

Even if you have an agreement with your lender to temporarily postpone the foreclosure sale, you should still monitor the trustee's activities. If the trustee schedules a sale anyway, immediately advise the trustee and lender in writing. In most cases, your letter will stop the sale. If it doesn't, you need to file a lawsuit to enjoin the foreclosure based upon your lender's breach of your agreement. (See Section B below.)

# B. Overview of a Lawsuit to Enjoin Foreclosure

If you file a lawsuit, you will ask the court for an injunction (court order) stopping the foreclosure until the issues you've raised can be resolved. Different injunctions apply at various stages of your lawsuit. First you get a temporary restraining order (TRO), then a preliminary injunction, and finally, if the dispute is still going on, a permanent injunction.

## 1. Temporary Restraining Order (TRO)

In the foreclosure context, a temporary restraining order (TRO) is an emergency interim court order that immediately stops all foreclosure activity. A judge can grant a TRO within a very short period of time, typically within 24 hours, and with a brief hearing in the courtroom. A TRO will last approximately 14 days, or until the judge can schedule a formal hearing on the matter.

A TRO won't be granted automatically. In a foreclosure situation, you must present evidence (your Declaration and supporting documents) at a hearing and convince a judge of these three points:

1. *You will be "irreparably harmed" if the TRO is not granted.* If you are trying to protect your home, you are in an excellent position to argue that you will be "irreparably harmed" unless the TRO is granted. A single-family, owner-occupied residence is presumed "unique" because there is no real substitute. (CC § 3387.) Because your home is unique and has special sentimental value to you, losing it in foreclosure would be unquestionably harmful. On the other hand, if your property is not your personal residence, you have a more difficult burden. Multi-residential or commercial property is presumed to be an investment, the value of which can be recovered in a regular lawsuit. If the property being foreclosed is not in fact your residence, be prepared to argue that your property is nevertheless unique (because of its architectural attributes, historical significance or some other special feature)

and that you will be irreparably harmed if you lose it through foreclosure.

2. *Money damages are not adequate.* This test is easy to demonstrate. If you lose your residence through foreclosure, and then win your lawsuit, you would be entitled only to monetary damages. Judges understand and sympathize that money damages would not make up for the loss of your family residence. If, however, your property is non-residential, money damages normally are presumed adequate unless you can prove otherwise.

3. *You are likely to win the case.* A judge will grant a TRO only if it appears from the papers you submit that (1) there is a real question as to how much you owe, (2) your lender acted improperly, or (3) the trustee committed a procedural error while conducting the foreclosure. But, until all of the evidence and testimony have been presented—which won't happen until your case goes to trial in two to three years—the judge can't know for sure whether you will win. As a result, judges treat this requirement with less significance than the previous two, as long as your case looks good on paper.

If a judge decides the three issues in your favor, he or she will grant the TRO to stop the foreclosure. Otherwise, the judge will deny the TRO and allow the trustee to proceed with the foreclosure. Either way, the judge will schedule a hearing for a preliminary injunction within 15 days, and usually request that you and your lender prepare additional memoranda (legal briefs on the relevant legal issues) and present further evidence to support your respective positions.

When granting a TRO, judges sometimes require that you tender (pay) any arrears that you admittedly owe your lender. However, you may convince a judge to waive this requirement in situations where:

- the promissory note or deed of trust is defective
- there was fraud in the original transaction
- the amount you owe is in dispute and an audit must be conducted determine how much you owe
- payment might be construed as relinquishing your right to rescind (as in a Regulation Z violation. Where the lender has violated Regulation Z, if the borrower continues to make the

payments, she is deemed to have waived the violation), or

• you can prove that nothing is due, or you have a claim against your lender, such as a setoff for an amount that exceeds the amount you owe your lender.

---

### BOND MAY BE REQUIRED

Depending on the facts of your case, don't be surprised if a judge grants a TRO on the condition that you post a bond to protect your lender should the TRO turn out to be unwarranted. (CCP § 529.) A bond is a written contract you enter into with a bonding company. Similar to insurance, you pay the bonding company a fee (typically 10% of the amount of the bond) and the bonding company agrees to reimburse your lender for its actual damages (such as lost interest and legal fees) in the event the TRO is subsequently terminated.

The amount of the bond is frequently the most contentious issue at a TRO hearing. Your lender will try to convince the judge to set the bond as high as possible, so you won't be able to pay for it. Be prepared to argue that if there is adequate equity in the property (pre-lien equity), the lender is protected because the deed of trust already protects your lender against defaults. The bond should protect your lender only against losses caused by delays in the foreclosure. You'll want to point out that if a bond is required at all, it should cover less than one month's payment, because the TRO will delay the foreclosure for only two weeks.

---

## 2. Preliminary Injunction

Approximately two weeks after the TRO hearing, you will attend another hearing and ask the judge for a preliminary injunction—an order enjoining (stopping) the foreclosure until the trial. (CCP § 527.) Because the trial may not take place for two to three years, a preliminary injunction is a powerful weapon. Of course, if the TRO was denied and the trustee's sale occurred, you will no longer need a preliminary injunction. However, even without a preliminary injunction, your lawsuit against your lender may still proceed. In that event, you will be limited to recovering monetary damages against your lender rather than an injunction of the foreclosure.

The same three issues the judge considered at the TRO hearing will apply at the preliminary hearing: you will be irreparably harmed if the injunction isn't granted, monetary damages are inadequate and there is a reasonable likelihood that you will win at trial. The only difference now is that the judge will have heard your lender's version of the story and reviewed most of the evidence. The trustee typically will not attend these hearings unless there is a dispute over the trustee's handling of the foreclosure procedures.

If the judge grants a preliminary injunction, that order will replace the TRO. (CCP § 527.) You will be allowed to keep the property while your case is wending its way to trial and the bond will stay in effect. At this point, don't be surprised if your lender is suddenly eager to negotiate with you.

If the judge denies the preliminary injunction, the TRO will be extinguished and the foreclosure will resume. You'll still have the right to try your case. However, you may decide against doing so because by the time your case goes to trial, you will no longer be the owner of your property. Further, you'll be limited to seeking monetary damages rather than your right to keep the property.

## 3. Permanent Injunction

As you can see above, most cases are settled early and never go to trial. If you get the TRO and preliminary injunction, lenders typically negotiate a settlement with you. On the other hand, if you lose the injunction and the property is lost in foreclosure, you probably won't have the impetus to pursue the lawsuit.

Nevertheless, if your case does go to trial, a judge will make a final ruling on the foreclosure dispute. If the judge rules in your favor, she will issue an injunction that permanently stops the foreclosure (and supersedes the preliminary injunction). If the judge rules in favor of your lender, the preliminary injunction will be terminated and your lender will resume its foreclosure.

Although legally possible, it is rare for either side to appeal to a higher court. An appeal would require a lawyer's help.

## C. How to File a Lawsuit and Get a Temporary Restraining Order

Filing a lawsuit to enjoin a nonjudicial foreclosure is not an easy task. The lawsuit must be filed in the California Superior Court—the state court with the trickiest rules and the least help for someone appearing without a lawyer. If you have the funds, or qualify for legal aid, a lawyer can be valuable asset during the proceedings.

*If you hire a lawyer.* This chapter will help you understand the procedures involved in a lawsuit to enjoin the foreclosure. You'll be better equipped to help your lawyer fight the foreclosure in court.

That being said, you may have difficulty finding an affordable lawyer or you may choose to forge ahead on your own. This section shows you how to file a lawsuit yourself (in pro per, in legalese) and get a temporary restraining order.

---

**RESOURCES FOR GOING TO COURT**

If you file your own lawsuit, you may be interested in the following resources, available in most law libraries:

• *California Mortgage & Deed of Trust Practice,* by Roger Bernhardt (California Continuing Education of the Bar).

• *CEB Action Guides* on foreclosure and handling a trial (California Continuing Education of the Bar).

• *California Forms of Pleading and Practice* (West Publishing), particularly the volume on handling a trial.

• *Represent Yourself in Court,* by Paul Bergman and Sara J. Berman-Barrett. (Nolo Press; see order information at back of this book.)

Chapter 12 also provides a number of helpful legal references.

---

### 1. Decide When to File the Lawsuit

Here's your dilemma. If you file your lawsuit too soon after the Notice of Default is recorded, your lender (or the trustee) has plenty of opportunity to correct its errors and proceed with the foreclosure, or start the foreclosure over from the beginning. On the other hand, if you file your lawsuit just days before the scheduled trustee's sale, a judge may interpret your timing as a bad-faith stall tactic and deny your request for a TRO.

We suggest you follow these guidelines, based on your reasons for going to court:

• If you dispute the foreclosure procedures, file your Complaint as soon as you receive a copy of the Notice of Trustee's Sale, and know the actual date and time of the trustee's sale. (Section A1, above, discusses disputes over foreclosure procedures.)

- If your dispute is over how much is owed or concerns the terms of the promissory note or deed of trust, file your Complaint within 30 days after the Notice of Default is recorded (if possible). (Section A2, above, discusses these kinds of disputes.)

## 2. Decide Where to File the Lawsuit

A lawsuit to enjoin a trustee's sale must be filed in the Superior Court of the county in which your property is located. Look in the phone book or call directory assistance to locate the court. If there are two or more branches of the Superior Court in your county, use the one that is closest to your property. If you are unsure, ask the first Superior Court clerk you encounter which Court is appropriate for enjoining a foreclosure of property located at your address.

## 3. Check Court Rules

Every court has slightly different rules governing how to file a lawsuit and seek a temporary restraining order (TRO). There is nothing terribly difficult about the rules, but you may have to do a little digging to make sure you understand and follow them. Call or visit the court and ask if you must follow special rules to file a lawsuit to enjoin a non-judicial foreclosure and obtain a TRO. In legal jargon, you will be bringing an Ex Parte Application for a TRO—meaning you won't give formal advance written notice to the other side. The clerk should refer you to:

- the court's local rules, available from the court or your local law, or
- the statewide Rules of Court, available in law libraries and some large public libraries, or
- both.

Next, get answers to the following questions by reviewing the rules—and checking with the court clerk if you get stuck:

- When are Ex Parte Applications heard? Usually, they are heard either in the morning (at 8:30

a.m.) or in the afternoon (at 1:30 p.m.), before regularly scheduled hearings. You may need to contact the court directly to find out the correct times.
- How much does it cost to file a Complaint and Ex Parte Application? The filing fees vary among counties, and range around $185. (These may be waived if you qualify as indigent.)
- How many copies of the documents are required?
- Do the documents have to be submitted in a particular form? For example, some courts may require that documents be on recycled paper, be two-hole punched at the top, or have blue paper stapled to the back of the documents.

## 4. Prepare Court Documents

If you think you have already seen a lot of paperwork, you'll need to steel yourself for a great deal more. Your lawsuit must be typed or word processed, double-spaced, on 8½" x 11" paper that is numbered and lined. A piece of numbered lined paper is provided in the Appendix. Either photocopy it in abundance or buy numbered lined paper from an office supply store.

On the first page of every document, fill in your name, address and telephone number at the top left corner. Starting on line 8, center the title of the court in capital letters. Place the caption (the name of plaintiff(s), defendant(s), case number and name of the document) several lines below. Fill in the title of the document. (See example on page 8/15.)

To file a lawsuit and get a TRO, you must prepare nine documents:

1. Complaint for Declaratory Relief and Injunctive Relief
2. Ex Parte Application for Temporary Restraining Order and Preliminary Injunction
3. Memorandum of Points and Authorities
4. Declaration in Support of the Application
5. Proposed Temporary Restraining Order
6. Notice of Lis Pendens
7. Summons
8. Civil Case Cover Sheet, and
9. Proof of Service.

Below, we describe these documents and, except for the Summons and the Civil Case Cover Sheet, provide samples you can use as templates to compose your own versions. (If you need more help preparing your court documents, check the resources described above in Section B or those described in Chapter 12.)

Also know that the idea of these papers is to tell what happened and ask for relief, not to use a bunch of jargon that you don't understand. If you have trouble with some of the language in the samples, and the book's glossary doesn't help, just do the best you can—in your own words.

*Don't use our samples blindly.* The samples in this chapter are intended as suggestions and guides, but should not be copied verbatim. You will need to substitute your own information that is unique to your case into the documents and delete material that doesn't apply in your case.

### a. Complaint to Enjoin the Trustee' Sale

A Complaint is a document that states the facts of your case, the legal theories that you believe apply (called "causes of action"), and the relief you want from the court (for instance, a TRO). Depending on your circumstances, your complaint may request:

- Declaratory relief. (A request that the court decide whether your position or your lender's position is legally correct.)
- Injunctive relief. (A request that the court enjoin the scheduled trustee's sale until the court can determine if your allegations are correct.)
- An accounting. (A request that your lender make the relevant books and records available to your accountant, so he or she can audit your loan and determine the correct amount owed.)
- A finding that fraud and misrepresentation occurred. (A request that, based upon your lender's misrepresentations or misconduct, the court rule that there was fraud in the loan transaction causing the foreclosure to be improper.)

A sample Complaint, with several different causes of action begins on page 8/15. Use only the causes of action that specifically apply to your situation.

### b. Ex Parte Application for Temporary Restraining Order

This document asks a judge to issue a court order temporarily enjoining (stopping) the pending trustee's sale. It is generally one or two pages and summarizes in a couple of sentences why the foreclosure should be enjoined.

The application is referred to as "ex parte" (without formal advance written notice to the other side) because the court will hear it within 18 to 24 hours, even if the defendants (your lender and the trustee) do not attend the hearing. You will need to justify why your application must be heard on less than the regular notice (usually 21 days). As shown in the sample beginning on page 8/19, you may simply state that the trustee's sale is scheduled to occur on a specific date that doesn't allow for the regular advance notice (which is less than 21 days away).

### c. Memorandum of Points and Authorities

This document states the facts of your case, the issues you want the judge to consider in your favor ("points"), the applicable law on those points ("authorities"), and how the law applies to your facts. If the judge grants the TRO, it will be based upon the arguments in your memorandum.

Your most important job is to present the relevant facts correctly, preferably in chronological order. Refer to the specific documents that support the facts and, if possible, attach copies of those documents as exhibits to your declaration. (See subsection d, below for guidance on how to prepare exhibits.) In the sample beginning on page 8/21, we provide some model language and give legal citations to use in your memorandum.

### d. Declaration in Support of the Application (With Documentary Evidence)

This declaration is your written statement, under penalty of perjury, that substitutes for your live testimony (a judge rarely will want live testimony at the hearing). The declaration should mirror the facts presented in your Memorandum of Points and Authorities.

All documents that confirm the facts of your case should be attached as exhibits to your declaration, to serve as documentary evidence. You should include copies of these documents as exhibits to your declaration (remember to keep the originals):

- deed to the property
- promissory note
- deed of trust
- relevant monthly statements
- relevant canceled checks
- Notice of Default
- Notice of Trustee's Sale
- letters and notices received from your lender and trustee, and
- letters you sent to your lender and trustee.

Organize copies of the documents in chronological order and label them as exhibits on the bottom of the first page of each document ("Exhibit A," "Exhibit B," and so on). Then staple them to your declaration. Make sure your declaration refers to each exhibit by document name and exhibit number—for example, "See Notice of Default, attached to this declaration as Exhibit A and incorporated herein by this reference." A sample declaration begins on page 8/24.

### e. Proposed Court Order

If a judge grants your request for a TRO, she will sign a temporary restraining order, which puts the judge's decision into effect. But, the judge doesn't write the order; you will need to supply a proposed order to the judge for her signature. Follow the sample beginning on page 8/26, modifying it to fit your situation. If the judge wants to make any modifications, she will handwrite the changes directly on the proposed order.

### f. Lis Pendens

A Notice of Pending Action ("Lis Pendens") document states that you have filed a lawsuit contesting your lender's right to foreclose your property. You don't file the Lis Pendens with the court; instead, you record it in the county recorder's office where your property is located. It should be recorded immediately after you file your Complaint in the Superior Court. (We give instructions on how to record the Lis Pendens in Section C5, below).

Once you file your lawsuit, you have the automatic right to record a Lis Pendens; you don't need court approval. The recorded Lis Pendens gives notice to everyone investigating the title of your property that a lawsuit about ownership is pending. When title companies run a title search or a purchaser obtains a preliminary title report, the Lis Pendens will appear as a cloud (defect) on title to your property.

A Lis Pendens provides great incentive for your lender to settle the lawsuit. Until your lawsuit is resolved, or the Lis Pendens is removed by the court (called expunged), any purchaser acquires your property subject to the Lis Pendens. In other words, if someone buys your property at a trustee's sale with a Lis Pendens recorded against it and you eventually win your lawsuit, the buyer will be forced to give the property back to you. This alone may scare off potential buyers and title insurance companies (which will refuse to give insurance because of your Lis Pendens). See the sample Lis Pendens beginning on page 8/28.

COMPLAINT BASED UPON DISPUTE WITH YOUR LENDER
AND/OR TRUSTEE'S IMPROPER PROCEDURE

1   Herbert Shellford
2   453 Rialto Avenue
   Sacramento, California
3   916-555-5555

4   Plaintiff In Pro Per

5

6

7            SUPERIOR COURT OF THE STATE OF CALIFORNIA

8               FOR THE COUNTY OF SACRAMENTO

9

10   HERBERT SHELLFORD,           )

11                         )   Case No: SC-734423

12      Plaintiff,             )

    v.                          )   Complaint for:

13                         )   1. Declaratory Relief

14   GOLDEN STATE SAVINGS BANK;   )   2. Injunctive Relief

   TRUSTEE SERVICE CORPORATION;   )   3. Accounting

15   and DOES 1 to 5, inclusive,     )

16                         )

     Defendants.          )

17                         )

18

19      Plaintiff HERBERT SHELLFORD ("Plaintiff") alleges:

20                FIRST CAUSE OF ACTION

                 (Declaratory Relief)

21       1. Plaintiff is a resident of the County of Sacramento, State of California. Plaintiff is the

22   owner of the real property located at 453 Rialto Avenue, Sacramento, California (the "Property").

23       2. Defendant, Golden Savings Bank ("Golden State"), a federally chartered savings bank,

24   is engaged in the banking business in California.

25       3. Defendant, Trustee Service Corporation ("TSC"), a California corporation, is a trustee

26   in the business of conducting non-judicial foreclosures of real property.

27       4. Plaintiff is unaware of the true names and capacities of the Defendants sued as Does 1

28   through 10 inclusive, and therefore sues these Defendants as Does. Plaintiff is informed and

1    believes that each of these Doe Defendants is responsible in some manner for the acts alleged in

2    this Complaint and is responsible for the damages suffered by Plaintiff described in this Complaint.

3    The Plaintiff will advise the Court of the true names and capacities of these Doe Defendants as soon

4    as their identities are ascertained.

5          5. Plaintiff is informed and believes that some of the defendants are the agents, servants,

     and/or employees of the remaining Defendants, and in doing the things described in this Com-

6    plaint were acting within the scope of their agency and/or employment.

7          6. On or about August 15, 199X, Plaintiff borrowed $160,000.00 from Defendant

8    Golden State to purchase the Property. As evidence of the loan transaction, Plaintiff signed and

9    delivered to Defendant Golden State a written promissory note. A copy of the promissory note is

10   attached to this Complaint as Exhibit "All" and incorporated by this reference.

11         7. To secure payment of the promissory note, Plaintiff signed and delivered to Defendant

12   Golden State a deed of trust dated August 15, 199X, in which Plaintiff (as trustor) conveyed to

     Defendant TSC (as trustee) an interest in the Property as security for payment of the promissory note

13   to Defendant Golden State (as beneficiary).

14         8. On or about August 16, 199X, the deed of trust was recorded in the Official Records

15   of Sacramento County, California. A copy of the deed of trust is attached to this Complaint as

16   Exhibit "B" and incorporated by reference.

17         9. On or about February 10, 199X, Defendant TSC recorded a Notice of Default and

18   Election to Sell in the Official Records of Sacramento County, California, alleging a default of the

19   promissory note and deed of trust. A copy of the Notice of Default is attached to this Complaint as

     Exhibit "C" and incorporated by reference.

20         10. On or about May 6, 199X, Defendant TSC recorded a Notice of Trustee's Sale in the

21   Official Records of Sacramento County, California, announcing that TSC will conduct a trustee's

22   sale of the Property on May 29, 199X, at the hour of 10:00 a.m., in front of the County court-

23   house, located at 10 Elm Street, Sacramento, California. A copy of the Notice of Trustee's Sale is

24   attached to this Complaint as Exhibit "D" and incorporated by reference.

25         11. However, Defendant TSC has failed to comply with the publishing and posting

26   requirements of Civil Code Section 2924f in that TSC, as trustee, failed to wait three full months

27   after issuing the Notice of Default before issuing the Notice of Trustee's Sale. As a result, an actual

     controversy exists between Plaintiff and Defendants as to their respective rights and duties with

28   respect to the pending non-judicial foreclosure. Plaintiff contends that the trustee has failed to

comply with Civil Code Section 2924f and Defendants TSC and Golden State dispute this contention and contend that the trustee acted in compliance with Section 2924 of the Civil Code.

12. The amount Defendant Golden State contends in the Notice of Default and Notice of Trustee's Sale that is in default is incorrect. Accordingly, the Plaintiff is not in default under the terms of the promissory note and deed of trust. However, Defendant Golden State refuses to accept a partial payment until the amount in dispute is resolved. As a result, an actual controversy exists between Plaintiff and Defendant Golden State concerning their rights and duties with respect to the pending nonjudicial foreclosure in that Defendant Golden State contends that $6,432 is owed and Plaintiff contends that less than $1,000 is owed.

13. Plaintiff desires a judicial determination and declaration of Plaintiff's and Defendants' respective rights and duties; specifically that Plaintiff did not breach the terms of the promissory note and deed of trust. Such a judicial determination is appropriate at this time so that Plaintiff may determine his rights and duties before the Property is sold at a trustee's sale.

14. Plaintiff has incurred attorney fees in prosecuting this action in an amount that is not yet fully ascertained. The Plaintiff will provide the total amount of attorney fees as soon as they are determined.

SECOND CAUSE OF ACTION

(Injunctive Relief)

15. Plaintiff realleges and incorporates by reference the allegations contained in paragraphs 1 through 14 of the First Cause of Action.

16. Defendant TSC intends to sell, and unless restrained, will sell the Property on May 29, 199X, at 10:00 a.m., at the County Courthouse, located at 10 Elm Street, Sacramento, California, causing great and irreparable injury to the Plaintiff in that if the trustee's sale takes place as scheduled, Plaintiff, having no right to redeem the Property after the sale, will forfeit it.

17. The trustee's sale is wrongful and should be enjoined. Plaintiff has no other plain, speedy, or adequate remedy, and the injunctive relief requested for in this Complaint is necessary and appropriate at this time to prevent irreparable injury and loss of Plaintiff's Property.

THIRD CAUSE OF ACTION

(Accounting)

18. Plaintiff realleges and incorporates by reference the allegations contained in paragraphs 1 through 17 of the First and Second Causes of Action.

19. A controversy exists between Plaintiff and Defendant Golden State with respect to the correct amount of money that is actually owed by Plaintiff to Defendant Golden State. However, Defendant Golden State refuses to provide an accurate accounting or allow Plaintiff's representatives to audit Golden State's books and records as they relate to Plaintiff's loan.

20. As a result, the correct amount of money due and owing from Plaintiff to Defendant Golden State remains in dispute and cannot be determined without an accounting.

21. Plaintiff requires that Defendant Golden State make available its books and records (only as they relate to the Plaintiff's loan) in order that Plaintiff may have a certified public accountant, or similarly qualified representative, audit the books and records.

WHEREFORE, Plaintiff demands judgment as follows:

1. That the Court issue a declaration of the rights and duties of the parties; specifically that Defendant TSC has no right to conduct the trustee's sale because the trustee failed to properly follow the foreclosure procedures described in Civil Code Section 2924, and that the amount necessary to bring the loan current is in dispute.

2. That the court issue a temporary restraining order, preliminary injunction, and permanent injunction restraining the Defendants, their agents, attorneys and representatives, and all persons acting in concert or participation with them, from selling, attempting to sell, or causing to be sold the Property either under the power of sale clause contained in the deed of trust or by a judicial foreclosure action.

3. That the court order an accounting between Plaintiff and Defendant Golden State, determining the amount, if any, actually due and owing from Plaintiff to Defendant Golden State.

4. That Plaintiff recover his attorney fees and costs incurred in this action.

5. For the costs of suit incurred by the Plaintiff; and

6. For such other and further relief as the Court may deem just and proper.

Dated: May 10, 199X

_____

HERBERT SHELLFORD
Plaintiff in pro per

1 | Herbert Shellford
2 | 453 Rialto Avenue
   | Sacramento, California
3 | 916-555-5555

4 | Plaintiff In Pro Per

5 |

6 |

7 |

8 | SUPERIOR COURT OF THE STATE OF CALIFORNIA

9 | FOR THE COUNTY OF SACRAMENTO

10 |

11 | HERBERT SHELLFORD,                          )
   |                                            )        Case No: SC-734423
12 |         Plaintiff,                         )
   |                                            )
13 | v.                                         )        EX PARTE APPLICATION FOR
   |                                            )        TEMPORARY RESTRAINING ORDER
14 | GOLDEN STATE SAVINGS BANK;                  )        AND PRELIMINARY INJUNCTION
15 | TRUSTEE SERVICE CORPORATION;                )
   | and DOES 1 to 5, inclusive,                 )
16 |                                            )
17 |         Defendants.                        )
   | _____    )
18 |

19 |         PLEASE TAKE NOTICE that Plaintiff, Herbert Shellford ("Plaintiff" or "Shellford"), hereby

20 | applies for a temporary restraining order, restraining Defendants, Golden State Savings Bank, a

21 | California corporation ("Golden State"); and Trustee Services Corporation, a California corpora-

   | tion ("TSC"), and their agents, servants, and employees:

22 |         a. From conducting a foreclosure sale of Plaintiff's interest in the property located at 453

23 |            Rialto Avenue, Sacramento, California, California (the "Property"), on May 29, 199X,

24 |            as presently noticed;

25 |         b. From performing any act in furtherance of conducting the sale of Plaintiff's interest in

26 |            the Property on May 29, 199X, or on any other day, to enforce Defendant Golden

27 |            State's deed of trust against the Property resulting from the recording of a Notice of

   |            Trustee's Sale by said Defendants on May 6, 199X, in the office of the Recorder of the

28 |            County of Sacramento, California.

1
2
3

PLEASE TAKE FURTHER NOTICE that Plaintiff hereby also applies for an Order to Show Cause why a preliminary injunction should not be granted enjoining the Defendants, Golden State, TSC, and their agents, servants, and employees, during the pendency of this action from:

4
5

    a.  Conducting the sale of Plaintiff's interest in the Property located at 453 Rialto, Sacramento, California, on May 29, 199X, as presently noticed;

6
7
8
9

    b.  Performing any act in furtherance of conducting the sale of Plaintiff's interest in the Property on May 29, 199X, or on any other day, to enforce Golden State's deed of trust against the property located at 453 Rialto, Sacramento, California resulting from the recording of a Notice of Trustee's Sale by said Defendants on May 6, 199X, in the Office of the Recorder of the County of Sacramento.

10
11
12
13
14

This Application is made on the grounds that the scheduled trustee's sale of the Property is based on an improper nonjudicial foreclosure and as such would cause Plaintiff great and irreparable injury in that if the sale was allowed to go forward as scheduled, it would deprive Plaintiff of his interest in the Property, and that there is insufficient time to declare the sale invalid in the ordinary course of the lawsuit.

15
16
17

This Application is based upon the verified Complaint on file with the Court, the attached declaration of Herbert Shellford, the attached memorandum of points and authorities, and upon such other evidence as may be presented at the hearing on this Application.

18

Dated: May 10, 199X

RESPECTFULLY SUBMITTED,

19
20

_____

HERBERT SHELLFORD
Plaintiff in pro per

21
22
23
24
25
26
27
28

1

MEMORANDUM OF POINTS AND AUTHORITIES

2

IN SUPPORT OF PLAINTIFF'S EX PARTE APPLICATION

3

FOR A TEMPORARY RESTRAINING ORDER AND PRELIMINARY INJUNCTION

4

I

5

STATEMENT OF FACTS

6

Plaintiff, Herbert Shellford ("Plaintiff" or "Shellford"), is the owner of a single family residence located at 453 Rialto Avenue, in Sacramento, California (the "Property").

7

In August of 199X, as part of a purchase of the Property, Shellford borrowed $160,000

8

from Golden State Savings Bank ("Golden State"). The loan was evidenced by a promissory note

9

and secured by a deed of trust encumbering the Property. The deed of trust was recorded in Sacramento County on August 19, 199X. Pursuant to the deed of trust, Trustee Services Corpora-

10

tion ("TSC") was designated as the trustee.

11

The loan called for a variable interest rate of prime plus 4% with a cap of 13%. The

12

monthly payments were initially $1,100 for the first twelve months of the loan and then varied according to the interest rate. The term of the loan was for 20 years.

13

On February 10, 199X, Golden State caused TSC to initiate a nonjudicial foreclosure by

14

recording a Notice of Default and Election to Sell in the Sacramento County Recorder's Office on

15

February 10, 199X.

16

On March 1, 199X, Shellford wrote a letter to Golden State requesting, pursuant to California Civil Code Section 2943, that Golden State provide a beneficiary statement with respect

17

to Shellford's loan. Golden State ignored Shellford's request.

18

On May 6, 199X, TSC recorded a Notice of Trustee's Sale in the Sacramento County

19

Recorder's office. However, under Civil Code Section 2924f, the trustee is required to wait a full

20

three months before filing a Notice of Trustee's Sale. Therefore, the Notice of Trustee's Sale is defective because it was recorded less than three months after the issuance of the Notice of Default

21

and is in violation of Section 2924f.

22

As advised in the Notice of Trustee's Sale, the sale is now scheduled for May 29, 199X.

23

Unless the trustee's sale is enjoined by this Court, Shellford will be irreparably harmed.

24

II

25

JUDICIAL REVIEW OF THE TRUSTEE'S NONJUDICIAL FORECLOSURE PROCEDURES IS PERMITTED

26

WHEN A PARTY IN INTEREST FILES AN ACTION ATTACKING THE TRUSTEE'S SALE

27

Although a nonjudicial foreclosure does not have judicial supervision, when a party in

28

interest (including the trustor) files a lawsuit in the county's superior court, the Court can review the

1    trustee's foreclosure procedures. See <u>Smith vs. Allen</u> (1968), 68 C2d 93, 65 CR 153; <u>Meadows</u>

2    <u>vs. Bakerfield</u> (1967) 250 CA2d 749, 59 CR 34; <u>Py vs. Pleitner</u> (1945) 70 CA2d 576, 161 P2d

3    393. In this case, the Court should review the action of Golden State (beneficiary) and TSC (trustee)

     because it is the trustor, Shellford, that has filed a lawsuit seeking judicial review of the nonjudicial

4    foreclosure procedures.

5

                   III

6

       <u>THE FORECLOSURE MUST BE ENJOINED WHERE THERE IS</u>

7            <u>A DISCREPANCY IN THE AMOUNT OF THE DEFAULT</u>

8        When there is a discrepancy in the amount of the default or there is other irregularity in

     the loan transaction, the Court should enjoin the foreclosure until the issues can be resolved. See

9    <u>Salot vs. Wershow</u> (1958) 157 CA2d 352, 320 P2d 926; and <u>Rice vs. Union Trust Co.</u> (1920) 50

10   CA 643, 195 P 720. In this case, the Court should enjoin the nonjudicial foreclosure until the

     discrepancy and irregularities can be resolved.

11

12                   IV

     <u>THE FORECLOSURE MUST BE ENJOINED WHERE THE BENEFICIARY</u>

13       <u>DOES NOT HAVE A VALID LIEN AGAINST THE PROPERTY</u>

14        Where the beneficiary does not have a valid deed of trust or the deed of trust is not

     property recorded against the property, the Court should enjoin the foreclosure. See <u>U.S. Hertz,</u>

15    <u>Inc. vs. Niobrara Farms</u> (1974) 41 CA3d 68, 116 CR 44; and <u>Saterstrom vs. Glick Brothers</u>

16    (1931) 118 CA 379, 5 P2d 21. In this case, the Court should enjoin TSC from foreclosing because

17    Golden State does not have a valid deed of trust encumbering the Plaintiff's Property.

18                   V

19       <u>THE FORECLOSURE MUST BE ENJOINED WHERE THERE WAS</u>

            <u>FRAUD IN THE ORIGINAL TRANSACTION</u>

20

21        If there was fraud in the original loan transaction, the foreclosure should be enjoined until

     the issues of fraud and misrepresentation can be resolved by the Court. See <u>Stockton vs. Newman</u>

22    (1957) 148 CA2d 558, 307 P2d 56; and <u>Daniels vs. Williams</u> (1954) 125 CA2d 310, 270 P2d

23    556. In this case, the foreclosure should be enjoined because Golden State committed fraud in the

     original loan transaction.

24

                  VI

25

       <u>THE FORECLOSURE MUST BE ENJOINED UNTIL THE COURT</u>

26           <u>CAN DECIDE WHAT AMOUNT IS PROPERLY DUE</u>

27        When there is a dispute as to the correct amount owed, if any, by the trustor to the benefi-

28    ciary, it is appropriate for the Court to enjoin the foreclosure until the Court can determine

with certainty what amount, if any, is due. See <u>More vs. Catkins</u> (1890) 85 C 177, 24 P 729; <u>Baypoint vs. Crest</u> (1985) 168 CA3d 818, 214 CR 531; and <u>Lockwood vs. Sheedy</u> (1958) 157 CA2d 741, 321 P2d 862. In this case, the Court should enjoin the pending foreclosure because the Court must first determine what the correct amount, if any, is due from Shellford to Golden State. Until that amount is determined by an audit of Golden State's books and records with respect to Shellford's loan, the foreclosure cannot proceed.

VII

<u>THE FORECLOSURE MUST BE ENJOINED BECAUSE THE TRUSTEE HAS VIOLATED</u>

<u>THE PROCEDURAL REQUIREMENTS OF CIVIL CODE SECTION 2924f</u>

If the trustee violates the procedural requirements of Civil Code Section 2924 with respect to the conduct of the non-judicial foreclosure, the Court can enjoin the trustee's sale until the trustee corrects the error, or order that the trustee start the entire procedure from the beginning. See <u>Crummer v. Whitehead</u> (1964) 230 CA2d 264, 40 CR 826; <u>Systems Inv. vs. Union Bank</u> (1971) 21 CA3d 137, 98 CR 735; and <u>Lockwood vs. Sheedy</u> (1958) 157 CA2d 741, 321 P2d 862. In this case, TSC has clearly violated the procedural requirements of California Civil Code Section 2924. As such, the foreclosure should be enjoined until TSC starts the foreclosure over from the beginning.

VIII

<u>INJUNCTIVE RELIEF IS PROPER WHERE THE FORECLOSURE</u>

<u>WILL CAUSE IRREPARABLE HARM TO PLAINTIFF'S UNIQUE PROPERTY</u>

A single-family residence is presumed unique and a foreclosure of that residence would cause "irreparable harm" to the trustor. As such, injunctive relief to enjoin the foreclosure until the underlying issues of the case can be resolved by the Court is proper. See <u>United Savings vs. Reeder</u> (1976) 57 CA3d 282, 129 CR 113; and <u>Wright vs. Rodgers</u> (1976) 57 CA3d 282, 243 P 866. In this case, Shellford's Property is a single-family residence in which he resides with his family. Therefore, the Plaintiff's Property must be presumed "unique" by this Court and the loss of his Property would cause "irreparable harm" to the Plaintiff. As such, the foreclosure should be enjoined until the issues in this case can be resolved.

IX

<u>CONCLUSION</u>

Based upon the foregoing points and authorities, the Plaintiff respectfully requests that the Court grant Plaintiff's Ex Parte Application and enjoin the pending trustee's sale until the Court can resolve these various issues.

Dated: May 10, 199X                          Respectfully submitted,

_____

Herbert Shellford

Plaintiff In Pro Per

DECLARATION OF HERBERT SHELLFORD

I, HERBERT SHELLFORD, declare as follows:

1. I am the Plaintiff in this action and the owner of the single-family residence located at 453 Rialto Avenue, in Sacramento, California (the "Property"). I know each of the following facts to be true of my own personal knowledge and if called as a witness, I could and would competently testify with respect thereto.

2. This Declaration is submitted in support of the Plaintiff's Ex Parte Application for a Temporary Restraining Order and Preliminary Injunction.

3. In August of 199X, as part of a purchase of the Property, I borrowed $160,000 from Golden State Savings Bank. The loan was evidenced by a promissory note and secured by a deed of trust encumbering the Property. The deed of trust was recorded in Sacramento County on August 19, 199X. Pursuant to the deed of trust, Trustee Services Corporation ("TSC") was designated as the trustee. A copy of the deed of trust is attached to the Complaint as Exhibit "A" and incorporated into this declaration by this reference.

4. The loan called for a variable interest rate of prime plus 4% with a cap of 13%. The monthly payments were initially $1,100 for the first twelve months of the loan and then varied according to the interest rate. The term of the loan was for 20 years.

5. On February 10, 199X, Golden State caused TSC to initiate a nonjudicial foreclosure by recording a Notice of Default and Election to Sell in the Sacramento County Recorder's Office. A copy of the Notice of Default is attached to the Complaint as Exhibit "B" and incorporated into this declaration by this reference.

6. On March 1, 199X, I wrote a letter to Golden State requesting, pursuant to Civil Code Section 2943, that Golden State provide a beneficiary statement with respect to my loan. Golden State ignored my request. A copy of my March 1, 199X letter is attached to the Complaint as Exhibit "C" and incorporated into this declaration by this reference.

7. On May 6, 199X, TSC recorded a Notice of Trustee's Sale in the Sacramento County Recorder's office. A copy of the Notice of Trustee's Sale is attached to the Complaint as Exhibit "D" and incorporated in this declaration by this reference.

8. Under California Civil Code Section 2924f, after issuing a Notice of Default, the trustee is required to wait three months before issuing a Notice of Trustee's Sale. However, in this case, the Notice of Trustee's Sale is defective because it was recorded on May 6, 199X, less than three

months after the issuance of the Notice of Default (February 10, 199X) and is in violation of Section 2924f.

9. A controversy exists with Golden State with respect to the correct amount of money that is actually owed by me to Golden State. However, Golden State refuses to provide an accurate accounting or allow Plaintiff's representatives to audit Golden State's books and records as they relate to Plaintiff's loan.

10. As advised in the Notice of Trustee's Sale, the sale is now scheduled for May 29, 199X. Unless the trustee's sale is enjoined by this Court, I will be irreparably harmed.

I declare under penalty of perjury under the laws of the State of California that the foregoing is true and correct. Executed on May 10, 199X, in Sacramento, California.

_____
HERBERT SHELLFORD
Declarant

1   Herbert Shellford
     453 Rialto Avenue
2   Sacramento, California
     916-555-5555
3

4   Plaintiff In Pro Per

5

6

7

8                 SUPERIOR COURT OF THE STATE OF CALIFORNIA

9                      FOR THE COUNTY OF SACRAMENTO

10

11   HERBERT SHELLFORD,              )           Case No: SC-734423

12        Plaintiff,                  )

13   v.                                 )           TEMPORARY RESTRAINING ORDER
                                     )           AND ORDER TO SHOW CAUSE RE:

14   GOLDEN STATE SAVINGS BANK;    )          A PRELIMINARY INJUNCTION
     TRUSTEE SERVICE CORPORATION;    )

15   and DOES 1 to 5, inclusive,        )

16                                        )

17        Defendants.               )
    _____ )

18        On reading the verified Complaint of Plaintiff on file in the above-entitled action, the

19 Declarations, and the Memorandum of Points and Authorities submitted therewith, it appears to the

20 satisfaction of the Court that this is a proper case for granting a temporary restraining order, and

21 an order to show cause for a preliminary injunction, and that unless the temporary restraining order

22 prayed for is granted, great and irreparable injury will result to Plaintiff before the matter can be

23 heard on regular notice.

24        IT IS HEREBY ORDERED that the above-named Defendants, and each of them, appear in

25 Department A of this Court, located at 10 Elm Street, Sacramento, California on

26 _____, 199X at _____ a.m., or as soon thereafter as the matter may be

27 heard then and there to show cause, if any they have, why they and their agents, servants,

28

1  employees, and representatives should not be enjoined and restrained during the pendency of this

2  lawsuit from engaging in, committing, or performing, directly or indirectly, any and all of the

3  following acts:

4     a. From conducting the trustee's sale of Plaintiffs' interest in the Property on May 29,

      199X, as presently noticed;

5

6     b. From performing any act in furtherance of conducting the trustee's sale of Plaintiffs'

7        interest in the Property on May 29, 199X, or on any other day to enforce the aforemen-

      tioned deed of trust against the Property resulting from the recording of a Notice of

8        Trustee's Sale by said Defendants on May 10, 199X, in the Office of the Recorder of

9        the County of Sacramento.

10      IT IS FURTHER ORDERED that, pending the hearing and determination of the foregoing

11  order to show cause, the above-named Defendants, and each of them, shall be and hereby are

required and ordered forthwith:

12

13     a. From conducting the trustee's sale of Plaintiffs' interest in the Property on May 29,

      199X, as presently noticed;

14

15     b. From performing any act in furtherance of conducting the trustee's sale of Plaintiffs'

16        interest in the Property on May 29, 199X, or on any other day, to enforce the afore-

      mentioned lien against the Property resulting from the recording of a Notice of Trustee's

17        Sale by said Defendants on May 10, 199X, in the Office of the Recorder of the County

18        of Sacramento.

19      IT IS FURTHER ORDERED that copies of the Complaint, Declarations, the Memorandums of

20  Points and Authorities, and this Order to Show Cause and Temporary Restraining Order be served

on Defendants, and each of them, no later than _____, 199X.

21

22      IT IS FURTHER ORDERED that the Defendants are to have until, _____, 199X, in which to

file a written response to the Order to Show Cause.

23  Dated:  May _, 199X

24

25  _____
      Judge, Superior Court

26

27

28

1　Recording requested by and mailed to:

2　Herbert Shellford
　453 Rialto Avenue
3　Sacramento, California
　916-555-5555

4

5　Plaintiff In Pro Per

6

7　　　　　　　　SUPERIOR COURT OF THE STATE OF CALIFORNIA

8

9　　　　　　　　　　FOR THE COUNTY OF SACRAMENTO

10　HERBERT SHELLFORD,　　　　　　　　　　)

11　　　　　　　　　　　　　　　　　　　　　)　　　Case No: SC-734423

　　　　　　Plaintiff,　　　　　　　　　　)
12　v.　　　　　　　　　　　　　　　　　　　)　　　NOTICE OF PENDING ACTION

13　　　　　　　　　　　　　　　　　　　　　)　　　CCP § 409
　　　　　　　　　　　　　　　　　　　　　　)　　　Lis Pendens
14　GOLDEN STATE SAVINGS BANK;　　　　　　)
　　TRUSTEE SERVICE CORPORATION;　　　　　)
15　and DOES 1 to 5, inclusive,　　　　　　)

16　　　　　　　　　　　　　　　　　　　　　)
　　　　　　Defendants.　　　　　　　　　　)
17　_____)

18　　　　　NOTICE IS HEREBY GIVEN that the above-entitled action concerning and affecting real

19　property as described herein was commenced on May 10, 199X, in the above-named Court by the

20　Plaintiff herein, Herbert Shellford, against the Defendants Golden State, TSC, and Does 1 to 5,

　　inclusive. The action is now pending in the Sacramento County Superior Court, State of California.
21
　　　　　　The action affects title to real property situated in Sacramento County, State of California,
22
　　and is legally described in Exhibit "A" attached hereto and incorporated herein by this reference.
23
　　　　　　The object of Plaintiff's action is to enjoin the Defendants' trustee's sale because the
24
　　foreclosure sale procedures are improper.
25
　　Dated: May 10, 199X
26

27　　　　　　　　　　　　　　　　　　　　_____
　　　　　　　　　　　　　　　　　　　　HERBERT SHELLFORD
28　　　　　　　　　　　　　　　　　　　　Plaintiff in Pro Per

## 5. Complete Summons and Civil Case Cover Sheet

There are two additional documents you will need to prepare—the Summons and the Civil Case Cover Sheet. Tear-out copies are in the Appendix.

### 1. The Summons

To complete the summons:
a. Enter the names of the lender and the trustee (the parties you named in the Complaint as the defendants).
b. Enter the name and address of the Court (the Superior Court you put on the Complaint).
c. Enter your address and telephone number in the indicated space (assuming you are representing yourself).
d. Leave the rest of the form blank for now.

### 2. The Civil Case Cover Sheet

To complete the Civil Case Cover Sheet:
a. Enter the same information on the top of the form that you put in your Complaint.
b. In the box following "1" enter the number 17 [for Injunctive Relief]
c. In item 2, check the box for Nonmonetary.
d. In item 3, enter the number corresponding to the number of causes of action you used from the sample Complaint. For most people this should be two (injunctive relief and declaratory relief). If an accounting is requested, then the number is three.
e. In item 4, check the box for No.
f. Print or type your name and sign the form.

## 6. Photocopy and File Documents With Court

Make at least three photocopies of all your documents (or more, if your local rules require it). At least one day before the day you scheduled the hearing (with the clerk's office), take all the documents, together with a check for filing fees, to the Superior Court. The court clerk will file or lodge

(temporarily place the documents in the court file pending the hearing) the original, and file stamp your copies. The clerk will give the judge the original documents and perhaps one set of copies. (If your court doesn't require the documents be filed in advance, you can simply bring them to the hearing.) The clerk will give you back the original Summons after signing it. Later, if necessary, you will fill out the bottom portion and the reverse side (Proof of Service) and then file it with the court. After receiving the original Summons back from the clerk, make two copies and staple two copies to the front of two copies of the Complaint.

### CHECKLIST OF DOCUMENTS

You should be filing the following documents:

- Complaint for Declaratory Relief and Injunctive Relief
- Ex-Parte Application for Temporary Restraining Order and Preliminary Injunction
- Memorandum of Points and Authorities
- Declaration in Support of the Application
- Proposed Temporary Restraining Order
- Notice of Lis Pendens
- Summons
- Civil Case Cover Sheet

*If you can't afford the filing fee.* Most Superior Courts in California have fee waiver programs where you can pay the filing fee over a period of months. If you are below the poverty line, you may not have to pay at all. If you need this service, ask the clerk for the fee waiver form to fill out when you file your documents.

## 7. Record Lis Pendens

After you file your lawsuit, you should immediately record a Notice of Pending Action (Lis Pendens) in the county recorder's office. You must record the lis pendens in the county where your property is located. You should take several copies of the Lis Pendens for recording. (The county recorder's Office will charge a small fee for recording the lis pendens, approximately $10 to $20). As we pointed out earlier, if you eventually win the lawsuit, the foreclosure will be invalidated and you will be entitled to your property.

*Don't neglect to record the Lis Pendens.* If you don't record the Lis Pendens and for some reason the sale goes through before you can get a court order preventing it, you may lose your property, even if you win in court. Unless the buyer is your lender or someone closely associated with your lender, it will be presumed that the buyer at the trustee's sale had no notice of your pending lawsuit and thus will receive good title to your property. Even if you ultimately win your lawsuit, you will not be able to get your property back (although you may get money damages from your lender).

## 8. Provide Notice and Prepare Declaration

At least 18 to 24 hours before the scheduled hearing date, you must give both your lender and the trustee notice of the hearing on your Ex Parte Application (called "ex parte notice"). You may provide oral (verbal) notice by a polite telephone call telling them that an ex parte hearing will be held, and advising them of the date, time, and location of the hearing. It is a good idea to write a script with the pertinent information and stick to it. In that way, you can repeat the exact words in your Declaration of Telephonic Notice (see below). Be sure to write down the name of each person you spoke to.

*If the lender or trustee requests copies of the application.* If the lender or trustee demands copies of the papers you have filed, politely explain that copies will be waiting for them at the entrance to the courtroom before the hearing. If they ask the basis of your application, state it in very general terms: "It involves a dispute over the actual amount I owe you," or "It involves a dispute over the trustee's procedures." Don't elaborate or try to justify your reasons for suing. You'll only get yourself in trouble, and may see your comments used by the other side during the hearing.

After making your phone calls, draft a Declaration of Ex Parte Telephonic Notice. Indicate the name of each person you spoke to, his or her telephone number, the date and time of the call, and the actual words you used regarding notice of the hearing on your ex parte application.

This document is extremely important. If you don't show up at the hearing with a Declaration of Telephonic Notice, signed under penalty of perjury, the judge probably will not consider your application unless the defendants also attend. A sample Declaration of Ex Parte Telephonic Notice appears below.

<u>DECLARATION OF TELEPHONIC NOTICE</u>

I, HERBERT SHELLFORD, declare as follows:

1. I know the facts stated herein from my own personal knowledge except those facts stated to be based upon information and belief, and as to those facts, I believe them to be true, and if called as a witness I could and would competently testify thereto.

2. On May 10, 199X, at 10:30 a.m., I called (916) 889-1158, the telephone number of Golden State Savings Bank. I spoke to a woman who identified herself as Rochelle. She indicated that she was the administrative assistant for the foreclosure department.

3. On May 10, 199X, at 10:35 a.m., I telephoned the offices of Trustee Services Corporation, at (916) 207-2027, the trustee scheduled to conduct the Trustee's Sale. The telephone was answered by a voicemail system, and I left a message on the voicemail system.

4. In each of these conversations, I gave the following information:

> "My name is Herbert Shellford. I am the owner of the home at 453 Rialto Avenue, Sacramento, California. Trustee Services Corporation is the trustee of a sale scheduled on May 29, 199X, attempting to sell by private sale the Property. I will be appearing at 8:30 a.m. on Tuesday, May 11, 199X in department "W" of the Superior Court located at 11 Elm Street, Sacramento, California seeking a Temporary Restraining Order and an Order to Show Cause Re: Temporary Injunction seeking to enjoin the forthcoming trustee's sale."

5. At 1:20 p.m. on May 10, 199X, I received a return telephone call from the secretary for Mr. Ober at TSC, and I gave her the same information. She acknowledged that a representative from her office would be appearing at the hearing.

I declare under penalty of perjury, according to the laws of the State of California, that the foregoing is true and correct. Executed on May 10, 199X, at Sacramento, California.

_____
HERBERT SHELLFORD
Declarant

## 9.  Attend the TRO Hearing

On the day of the hearing, arrive at the courthouse early and bring at least three copies of all your documents. Give yourself plenty of time to find the room where your ex parte application will be heard. Check in with the courtroom clerk or bailiff. (If the court doesn't have a clerk or bailiff, just sit quietly until your case is called.) Ask the clerk if your lender or foreclosure trustee or their attorneys have checked in. If not, request that the bailiff advise you when they arrive. Once the attorney for the lender or trustee checks in, introduce yourself and give him or her copies of all the documents you filed with the clerk. Ask for copies of any pleadings the attorney brought in opposition to your ex parte application. If you have time, review these documents carefully, because you will need to counter the arguments during the hearing.

While you wait for your case to be called, you'll want to observe your judge handling other cases, to the extent they're handled in open court.

Many judges prefer handling ex parte matters informally in their chambers rather than in open court. The judge will first read the motion and responding briefs (if any) and then call the parties into her chambers to discuss the case. Occasionally, a judge might read all of the papers and then give her ruling from the bench without any oral arguments from either side, although this is rare.

When your case is called, if it is being handled in open court, step forward and introduce yourself as the plaintiff. Remember to always address the judge as "Your Honor," and to address all of your arguments directly to the judge, not to the lender's lawyer.

Some judges prefer to ask questions, while others will ask you to make a brief opening statement explaining why the foreclosure should be enjoined. If so, succinctly explain your request in your own words. Your lender's attorney, if one shows up, will be given an opportunity to respond. Never interrupt or speak directly to the other attorney.

During the hearing, the judge will probably ask you questions. Be sure to listen carefully to the judge's questions and answer them directly. What-ever you do, don't avoid or ignore the judge's question. If possible, "turn into the skid" by incorporating your answer to the judge's question into your argument for enjoining the foreclosure. For example, if the judge asks why you waited until the last minute to file the lawsuit, explain that (if true) you wrote letters to your lender and tried to negotiate, but your letters were ignored or the negotiations were going nowhere.

## 10. Judge Rules on the TRO

After the judge has heard arguments from you and your lender's attorney, she must make a ruling. The judge may make a decision on the spot or take the matter under submission, which means she will decide later and send written notice of the decision to all parties.

If the judge agrees with your ex parte application, she will issue a TRO enjoining the trustee from proceeding with the foreclosure for approximately 14 days and schedule a preliminary hearing. The judge will sign your proposed order, possibly with changes.

If the judge denies the TRO, the trustee will proceed with the foreclosure. Your lender may also recover money damages for defending against your ex parte application, including attorney fees and costs.

## 11. Make Sure All Service Requirements Are Met

Assuming that the lender or the trustee (or their lawyer) shows up for the hearing, you don't have to worry about serving the order or the other papers you filed. The fact that you handed them the papers when they arrived in court is good enough. Similarly, if the lender or trustee (or their attorney) is in court when the judge signs the order, they will receive a copy then and there, and service is unnecessary.

But what if nobody for the other side shows up? In that case, you will have to serve both the Order and the other papers on the lender and the trustee. How to do this? Because time is usually very important in these situations, and because you'll want to be able to prove that the lender and trustee received the order before the sale, your best approach is to have the order personally served. And because you'll have to have the other papers you filed personally served to continue with your lawsuit, you can kill two birds with one stone by including in the package to be served all your papers, both those you filed and the order signed by the judge.

Papers can be personally served by anyone over the age of 18 who is not a plaintiff. That is, parties can't serve their own papers, and you'll have to get someone to do it for you. We strongly recommend that you find a private process server to serve the papers. Although the sheriff's office will do it for less money, many of them are so overworked that there may be a significant delay. If you do decide to have the papers served by a friend or relative, make sure they understand that the papers must be personally delivered to a person who is authorized to accept service on behalf of the party being served. They should also understand that personal delivery means handing the papers to the person or, if the person refuses to take them, dropping them on the person's desk or at the person's feet.

Whoever serves the papers must then fill in and file one proof of service for each party served. So, assuming personal service is made on the lender and on the trustee, separate proofs of service must be filled out. One proof of service should be filled out on the original Summons issued by the court. Any additional proof of service can be filled out on the separate Proof of Service form contained in the Appendix.

If you are using a private process server or the sheriff, all you need to do is deliver the original summons to them. They will handle the rest. If, however, you are having a friend or relative carry out the service, you will need to have that person fill in the bottom part and back of the original summons and, if a second party is served, a second proof of service (in the Appendix).

To sum up:

- If a defendant appears in court, no additional service is necessary as long you hand them copies of the papers you filed and they are present when the judge signs the order.
- If no defendant appears, then you will need to have the papers and order (assuming the judge signs it) served on both defendants.
- Because this is such an important part of the case, we recommend that you have a professional process server carry out the service.

## D. How Your Case Proceeds After the TRO Hearing

Most disputes involving lenders and trustees are resolved shortly after a TRO is granted. By now, the reasons should be obvious. If it looks like you are going to win, most lenders will settle rather than go through years of expensive litigation and uncertainty.

*If your lender won't settle.* We can't possibly cover all the intricacies of a full-blown Superior Court trial. If your case goes this far, we suggest you hire a lawyer or be prepared to use *Represent Yourself in Court,* by Paul Bergman and Sara J. Berman-Barrett (Nolo Press) as well as to become familiar with basic legal research techniques.

Barring your lender's willingness to settle, here's how your case will proceed. First, the court will schedule a preliminary injunction hearing within two weeks of the TRO being issued (regardless of who won) and request that you and the lender submit further pleadings and evidence to prove your respective positions. If the court issues a preliminary injunction at or following that hearing, you will probably be able to settle quickly because your lender won't be able to foreclose until the case is resolved. On the other hand, if the court doesn't issue a preliminary injunction, you are still entitled to press ahead with the lawsuit, but your lender will be allowed to complete its foreclosure. At the preliminary injunction hearing, the court may establish deadlines for discovery (written and oral questions of opposing witnesses and examination of documents). Finally, the case will go to trial. The few foreclosure lawsuits that go to trial usually involve serious allegations of lender fraud, where a lender is in danger of losing and incurring a large money judgment or punitive damages. Depending on the backlog in your county's Superior Court calendar, the trial will occur within two to three years after you filed suit. The preliminary injunction will enjoin the foreclosure until the trial date.

# 9

# BANKRUPTCY

**B**ankruptcy is a powerful remedy for people who are over their heads in debt. It may also be used to temporarily stop a foreclosure, but for how long depends on a number of factors discussed in this chapter. If you need more information or believe that you want to file for bankruptcy, consult one or more of the additional resources listed in Section D.

For many people, bankruptcy can be a very difficult step to take. It tends to conjure up feelings of failure, shame and guilt. But be assured that bankruptcy is a legitimate and viable strategy if you're in a severe financial crisis. Bankruptcy is about new beginnings. It is designed to help you resolve your financial problems under the supervision of a bankruptcy court and get a fresh financial start on life.

## A. File for Bankruptcy and Stop the Foreclosure

Without question, filing for bankruptcy is your most dramatic option for delaying a foreclosure. The fact that you file for bankruptcy gives rise to a federal court order effective that same day. Called an Order for Relief (commonly referred to as the "automatic stay"), the order requires that your foreclosing trustee, as well as all your other creditors, cease their collection-related activities. Once your foreclosing trustee learns of the bankruptcy filing, from the court or from you, the foreclosure is stopped dead in its tracks. The purpose of the automatic stay is to freeze your economic situation until a bankruptcy trustee (appointed by the bankruptcy court) can step in and do the following:

• decide whether or not bankruptcy is appropriate, and if so,

• distribute your property or income (depending on which type of bankruptcy you file; see Section B below) to your creditors to pay what you owe.

For most people, all it takes to file for bankruptcy is a one-page petition, a list of your creditors (including your foreclosing lender) and a $160–$175 filing fee. If you file no additional papers, the bankruptcy court will dismiss your bankruptcy case in 15 days. If, on the other hand, you file the additional papers needed to keep your bankruptcy case alive and ticking, you may delay the foreclosure for weeks, months or even permanently.

The rest of this chapter provides:

• an overview of how bankruptcy works

• some guidance on which type of bankruptcy is best for you, if any, and

• resources you can use to handle your own bankruptcy or at least educate yourself before you hire an attorney.

*Involuntary bankruptcy note.* Creditors have the right to file an involuntary bankruptcy against a debtor (which forces the debtor into bankruptcy). If an involuntary bankruptcy is filed against you, see a lawyer immediately.

## B. How Bankruptcy Works

Bankruptcy works in two entirely different ways, depending on the type you file. Liquidation bankruptcy—commonly known as Chapter 7 bankruptcy—requires that you give up (liquidate) nonessential items of property in exchange for cancellation of most of your debts. Chapter 7 bankruptcy is described in more detail in Section B3 below. In contrast, reorganization bankruptcy lets you keep your property but requires that you repay at least some of your debts over a three- to five-year period. The specific reorganization bankruptcies are Chapter 13 (for individuals), Chapter 12 (for farmers) and Chapter 11 (for businesses and, very rarely,

individuals). These types of bankruptcies are described in more detail in Sections B2, B4 and B5 respectively.

If, after reading Chapter 1 Section D, you decide to hold on to your real estate but cannot reinstate your loan before the scheduled foreclosure sale (see Chapter 3), a reorganization bankruptcy will give you additional time to do this as long as you resume your current payments. If you are willing to part with the real estate—perhaps because it is worth less than you owe on it—Chapter 7 bankruptcy may be your best choice. Unfortunately, it is usually impossible to keep real estate you aren't living in, and very difficult to keep your home, if you file for Chapter 7 while facing foreclosure. We explain why in Section B3 below.

### 1. How Bankruptcy Treats Debts

To understand how the different types of bankruptcy work, you first need information on how bankruptcy treats your debts. This is because some types of debts are paid before other types, and some types of debts can't be discharged in bankruptcy at all. Without this information, you can't decide whether or not bankruptcy is appropriate for you.

Bankruptcy categorizes every type of debt according to:

• whom the debt is owed (the type of creditor)

• whether a lien on your property secures repayment of the debt (the creditor has a right to get paid out of some or all of your property if you fail to pay the debt), and

• whether or not the debt can be discharged in bankruptcy.

#### a. Type of Creditor

When filling in the bankruptcy forms, you are asked to separate your debts into three groups: priority, secured and unsecured.

1) *Priority debts.* "Priority" debts, as the name implies, are a payment priority, whether the payment comes from your liquidated property (under Chapter 7) or as part of your repayment plan in a

reorganization bankruptcy. Priority debts include the following:

- taxes and other debts owed to the government
- alimony and child support
- wages, salaries and commissions owed employees or independent contractors (up to $4,000 per person) earned within 90 days before you file
- contributions you owe to an employee benefit plan
- money you owe farmers or fishermen (up to $4,000 per person), and
- money you owe someone (up to $1,800 per person) who made a deposit to purchase, lease or rent property or services from you for his personal use.

For most individual debtors, only the tax and support priority categories apply. For debtors who are or were engaged in a business, the other categories often apply as well.

2) *Secured debts.* A debt is secured (and the creditor to whom you owe money is a secured creditor) if the creditor can take some or all of your property if you don't make your payments. For example, your foreclosing lender is a secured creditor because its deed of trust gives it the right to force the sale of the property to satisfy the debt if you don't pay.

3) *Unsecured debts.* Unsecured debts aren't linked to any specific item of property. Failure to pay an unsecured debt may get you sued, but the creditor can't take any of your property unless the creditor has sued you and obtained a judgment, and then takes the necessary steps to enforce the judgement.

Most debts that people owe are unsecured, including credit card debts, medical and legal bills, student loans, most court judgments, back utility bills and department store charges. In bankruptcy, unsecured creditors are paid last, after priority creditors and secured creditors.

## b. Liens on the Property

Liens are discussed in detail in Chapter 1. To summarize, a lien is a legal claim against property for a specific amount of money. The most common type of lien is the one created by the deed of trust when you borrowed money against your home—either to purchase it or for other purposes (as in a home equity loan or second deed of trust). Other types of liens are:

- federal and state income tax liens (which when recorded apply to all the property you own, but typically are enforced only against your real estate)
- mechanic's liens (liens recorded against your property by contractors, or by those who provided the building supplies, for unpaid construction or repair services or supplies), and
- judgment liens (liens that judgment creditors can get against your real estate, personal property and business assets by recording the judgment with the appropriate agency).

The point of understanding liens in the context of how bankruptcy treats your debts is a simple one: all debts that are covered by appropriately recorded liens are considered to be secured, and those to whom these debts are owed are considered secured creditors, and, as mentioned above, are usually paid before unsecured creditors.

## c. Debts That Can Survive Bankruptcy

Most types of debts can be discharged in bankruptcy, but some remain and will have to be paid sooner or later. It is important to know what these debts are, since your decision to file for bankruptcy may be influenced by whether you will be able to discharge your major debts. If, for example, your major debt is a child support arrearage, you may decide not to file bankruptcy once you understand that this type of debt survives bankruptcy.

Debts that survive bankruptcy fall into two categories:

Category 1. Debts that will remain at the end of all bankruptcy cases. These debts include child support and alimony, most taxes, recent student loans that first became due fewer than seven years ago (plus the time you received any deferment or forebearance), court-ordered restitution or criminal fines, condominium and cooperative association dues or assessments, and debts for personal injuries or death to someone arising from your intoxicated driving.

Category 2. Debts that will remain at the end of a Chapter 7 bankruptcy case if the creditor files an objection in the bankruptcy court and the court rules the debt cannot be discharged. These debts include the following:

- debts incurred on the basis of fraud
- debts from willful or malicious injury to another
- debts from larceny (theft), breach of trust or embezzlement
- debts of $1,000 or more to any one creditor for luxury items purchased within 60 days of filing and cash advances in excess of $1,000 obtained within 60 days of filing, and
- debts arising from a marital settlement agreement or divorce decree (other than child support or alimony, which are in the first category).

Note: Reorganization bankruptcies have something called the "super discharge." If these Category 2 debts are unsecured, whatever balance remains when you have completed your repayment plan is wiped out.

## 2. Overview of Chapter 13 Bankruptcy

We explain Chapter 13 bankruptcy first because for most people facing foreclosure, it is the best (and perhaps the only) bankruptcy remedy.

*If property is owned by a business.* Chapter 13 can be used to stop a foreclosure only if you own the property in your own name. If you own your property as a corporation, partnership or limited liability company, you will need to file Chapter 11. See Section B5.

Chapter 13 allows you to pay personal or business-related debts over time without selling off your assets through liquidation. A Chapter 13 bankruptcy allows you at least three years and no more than five years to pay off as much of your debt as possible.

### a. Who Can File a Chapter 13 Bankruptcy

You may file for Chapter 13 bankruptcy if:

- you are an individual (including a married couple), sole proprietor or member of a partnership (a corporation, partnership or limited liability company itself cannot file a Chapter 13 bankruptcy)
- your secured debts do not exceed $750,000 and your unsecured debts do not exceed $250,000
- you can establish that your income over the next several years will be at least somewhat predictable, and
- your future income is likely to be high enough to both pay for your basic needs and pay a sufficient amount each month to satisfy Chapter 13 payment requirements.

### b. How Chapter 13 Bankruptcy Works

As part of your Chapter 13 bankruptcy filing, you describe your property, debts, essential expenses, current income and important financial transactions during the previous two years. You also must propose a plan to repay all or a portion of your debts from your disposable income—your current income less your essential expenses—over a three-to five-year period.

The bankruptcy court appoints a trustee to administer every Chapter 13 case. The Chapter 13 trustee's primary role is to:

- make sure your proposed plan is feasible and meets the requirements of the law
- advise you, other than on legal matters, and help you perform under your plan

- collect payments from you, typically on a monthly or bi-weekly basis
- disburse the money to your creditors, after deducting a trustee's fee (which may be as high as 10% of each payment), and
- maintain detailed accounting records that inform the court whether you have fulfilled your obligations under your plan.

As a general rule, your plan payments must be high enough to pay, over the period of your plan:

- 100% of all your priority debts (see Section B1 above)
- 100% of the arrearages (and interest) on your secured debts, such as your deed of trust, and
- an amount on your unsecured debts equal to the value of your nonexempt property (see Section B3 below). Be aware that some courts don't enforce this provision, while others won't approve a plan unless you intend to pay a sizeable portion of your unsecured debts.

*If your loan was signed before October 22, 1994.* You must pay interest on the arrearages while you cure the default. No law prescribes the exact interest rate, but most bankruptcy judges will require you to pay either the interest rate in your promissory note or the current market rate of interest. Of course, this is tantamount to paying interest on interest because each loan payment already includes interest. Unfortunately, this is the law. To relieve this inequity, Congress modified the interest requirement. If your loan was taken out after October 22, 1994, you do not have to pay interest on the arrears. (11 U.S.C. § 1323(e).)

If you successfully complete your plan, which may be modified from time to time depending on your circumstances, the remaining unsecured debts will be discharged except for those identified in Category 1, above.

### c. Can Your Lender Foreclose After You File for Chapter 13?

Although the automatic stay initially bars your lender from proceeding with the foreclosure (see Section A, above), your lender may file a written request (called a "motion for relief from the automatic stay") asking the bankruptcy court for permission to continue with it. The court is likely to grant this motion in these kinds of situations:

- your plan does not provide for payment of the arrearage on your deed of trust (or mortgage) within a reasonable time (depending on the judge, anywhere from 6 to 60 months)
- you fail to make the regular monthly payments on your mortgage or deed of trust after filing
- you fail to make your plan payments on time and modification of your plan isn't possible
- you fail to maintain adequate insurance on the property or maintain it in reasonable condition, or
- the judge refuses to confirm your plan and dismisses your case (you can file again, but you risk angering the judge and perhaps suffering worse consequences down the road).

With the help of a bankruptcy attorney, you should be able to defeat your lender's motion for relief from the automatic stay and fend off the foreclosure if you can immediately cure the problems that led to the filing of the motion in the first place.

---

**CHAPTER 13 CAN HELP IF YOU FACE A BALLOON PAYMENT**

Chapter 13 allows you to pay a balloon payment (final loan payment) over time. (11 U.S.C. § 322(c)(2).) Let's say your promissory note calls for a balloon payment of $35,000, which is due in 14 months. You may propose to pay the $35,000 over the 36-month duration of your Chapter 13 plan.

### d. If You Realize Chapter 13 Isn't Right for You After You File

If for some reason you are unable to complete your Chapter 13 plan, you can voluntarily dismiss the case or convert it to another chapter—almost always Chapter 7. If, when you convert to Chapter 7, you've already cured the arrearage through plan payments you have been making, and you've stayed current on your loan payments, you may be able to keep your property. That will depend on how much equity you have in it. (See Section B3d below for help in determining your equity.) If you haven't cured your arrearage or you haven't remained current, then most likely the lender will seek to have the stay lifted and proceed with the foreclosure.

## 3. Overview of Chapter 7 Bankruptcy

As a general rule, people facing foreclosure are rarely able to hang on to their real estate in a Chapter 7 bankruptcy. You will have a particularly difficult time keeping real estate you don't live in; the trustee is sure to sell it to pay your unsecured creditors if there's any equity in it.

A Chapter 7 bankruptcy is the traditional form of bankruptcy, commonly referred to as a "straight" or "liquidation" bankruptcy. As we have emphasized throughout this chapter, Chapter 7 isn't a good remedy if you're trying to hold on to your real estate. But if you are willing to let it go, Chapter 7 may be very helpful in getting your finances in order.

### a. Who Can File a Chapter 7 Bankruptcy

A Chapter 7 bankruptcy may be filed by virtually any person or business organization, such as a sole proprietorship, corporation, partnership or limited liability company. If you file as an individual, you can represent yourself.

### b. How Chapter 7 Bankruptcy Works

The basic idea behind a Chapter 7 bankruptcy is that you're entitled to keep certain items of property which are legally considered "exempt" from liquidation. (See Section B3e below for more on exempt property.) A Chapter 7 trustee who is appointed by the court to oversee your case assumes control of, and sells, your nonexempt assets for the benefit of your unsecured creditors. (The trustee can "abandon" assets he or she feels are valueless or too expensive or cumbersome to liquidate.) The Chapter 7 trustee distributes the proceeds of the sale of your nonexempt assets to your unsecured creditors.

All debts that remain unpaid are no longer your personal responsibility (except for debts that survive bankruptcy). In legal jargon, they are discharged. Your case is normally completed in three to six months with usually just one visit to the court or trustee's office. After that, you are not allowed to file another Chapter 7 bankruptcy for six years.

Once you file your bankruptcy papers, you can't sell any nonexempt property without the court's consent. You will, however, be allowed to maintain control of your exempt property and any property and income you acquire after you file bankruptcy.

*If you are a partnership, corporation or limited liability company in Chapter 7.* If your real or personal property is held in the name of a partnership, corporation or limited liability company, an attorney must represent the entity during the bankruptcy proceedings under the California Unauthorized Practice of Law Statutes. All business activity must cease once the bankruptcy is filed and all business assets must be turned over to the Chapter 7 trustee. In rare circumstances, the court may grant permission for the Chapter 7 trustee to continue to operate your business (for example, if it's a hotel or car wash), until it can be sold. All income derived from the business after filing Chapter 7 will be used to pay your creditors.

### c. Can You Save Property in Foreclosure by Filing Chapter 7 Bankruptcy?

In most cases, the answer is no. If you file for bankruptcy when facing a foreclosure, you have to deal with the arrearage that led to the foreclosure in the first place. Chapter 7 bankruptcy has no procedure to handle the repayment of your arrearage—or any other debts—over time. Rather, your nonexempt property is liquidated and your creditors are paid in a particular order required by the Bankruptcy Code—which will probably leave the arrearage unpaid. Even if the arrearage could be paid in your Chapter 7 bankruptcy case, your lender will not want to wait—given that payment is not guaranteed. Therefore, the bankruptcy court will most likely let the foreclosure proceed—unless the bankruptcy trustee decides to sell the property herself.

The Chapter 7 trustee is likely to sell the property herself when the property has equity that can be used to pay some of your unsecured creditors. For real estate you don't live in, this decision would depend on whether you have any equity in it. (See subsection d below.) If a sale would pay off your lender and other lienholders and still produce a surplus, the trustee will sell the property. Otherwise, the trustee will abandon it (relinquish any control over it), which almost always means the foreclosing lender will get the automatic stay lifted and proceed with the foreclosure.

### d. Calculate Your Nonexempt Equity Using Bankruptcy Equity Worksheet

Your equity is the difference between what your property is worth and what you have to pay others before you see a dime. Your non-exempt equity is your equity minus your homestead exemption. If there is anything left over, the trustee will probably sell your home and distribute that amount to your unsecured creditors.

For a rough estimate of the amount of non-exempt equity you have in your home, fill out the Bankruptcy Equity Worksheet below.

### Worksheet Instructions

1. *Estimated sales price of your home.* In a bankruptcy sale, a typical home goes for 20–30% less than it would in a normal sale. The trustee knows this and may take it into account when deciding whether or not to sell your home. However, the trustee is not required to use this discounted value and may use the full market value of your home in deciding whether to take it. To be on the safe side, put your home's full estimated sales price on this line. To get a rough idea of what your home is worth, you might ask a real estate agent, hire an appraiser or look at comparable properties in your area.

### BANKRUPTCY EQUITY WORKSHEET

| | |
|---|---|
| 1. Estimated sales price of your home | $ |
| 2. Estimated costs of sale | |
|    a. Costs of sale of your home (approximately 5% of sale price) | $ |
|    b. Amount owed on real estate loan(s) | $ |
|    c. Outstanding liens, taxes and priority debts | $ |
| 3. Subtotal (add lines 2a, b and c) | $ |
| 4. Estimated equity (lines 1 - 3) | $ |
| 5. Homestead exemption | $ |
| 6. Estimated nonexempt equity (lines 4 - 5) | $ |

2a. *Costs of sale of your home.* Costs of sale vary, but tend to be about 5% of the sales price. The trustee does not have to subtract the costs of sale in determining whether to take your home, but many do.

2b. *Amount owed on real estate loans.* Enter the amount needed to pay off your loans and any other liens that are secured by your home as collateral. If you can't come up with a reasonably reliable estimate, contact each lender and ask how much you'll need to pay off its loan.

2c. *Outstanding liens and taxes and priority debts.* Fill in the total of all unpaid liens—claims against your home that have been recorded at the county recorder's office and priority debts. See Section B1 above for more on liens and priority debts. Incidentally, judgment liens may be removed as part of the Chapter 7 bankruptcy process if they prevent you from receiving your homestead allowance.

If you aren't sure whether there are liens on your home, visit the county recorder's office or contact the customer service department of a local title insurance company for assistance.

3. *Subtotal.* Add up lines 2a, b and c.

4. *Estimated equity.* Subtract the subtotal from the estimated sales price of your home. For bankruptcy purposes, this is the equity in your property—that is, the amount your house will sell for, less what must be paid to others from the proceeds before you see anything.

5. *Homestead exemption.* Fill in the amount of your homestead exemption. If you are single and not disabled, your exemption is $50,000. For families, your exemption is $75,000, if no other member has a homestead. If you are 55 or older, your exemption is $100,000 if you are single and earn under $15,000, or married and earn under $20,000. If you are over 65 years old, or physically or mentally disabled, your exemption is $100,000.

6. *Estimated nonexempt equity.* Subtract the homestead exemption from your estimated equity (4 - 5). Here's how to understand your calculations of estimated nonexempt equity:

• If the amount is less than zero: Your estimate shows that all of your equity is exempt. If your

estimate is correct, the trustee won't sell your home because the proceeds would go to your foreclosing lender, any junior lienholders and you (your homestead exemption), with nothing left over to pay your unsecured creditors. In that situation, the trustee will simply file a Notice of Abandonment and allow you to keep your home. Of course, in that event, you will still need to deal with your foreclosing lender and negotiate a resolution of the default in order to avoid a foreclosure.

If the amount is greater than zero: You have nonexempt equity in your home and the trustee is likely to sell your home to pay off your unsecured creditors. If you find yourself in this predicament, don't file Chapter 7 bankruptcy. Consider a reorganization bankruptcy instead.

*The Bankruptcy Equity Worksheet is for estimate purposes only.* The bankruptcy trustee may challenge the market value you claim and determine that your residence is worth more than you think. Depending on your homestead amount, this could mean the difference between keeping your home and losing it.

### e. Understanding the Homestead Exemption

There are two lists of property that may be considered exempt when filing bankruptcy in California. You must choose exemptions from one list or the other—no mixing and matching is allowed. Most people who have equity in their homes choose the list set out in Code of Civil Procedure § 704.140. That is because it provides the following exemptions for an owner-occupied dwelling of between one and four units, including mobile home, boat or condominium:

- $50,000 if you are single and not disabled
- $75,000 if you are part of a family
- $100,000 if you are 65 or older, or are physically or mentally disabled, and
- $100,000 if you are 55 or older and earn less than $15,000 if single or less than $20,000 if married.

As previously mentioned, equity in those amounts is exempted from bankruptcy.

### Personal Property Exemptions Under Code of Civil Procedure § 704.710

- appliances, furnishings, food
- $2,000 ($3,000 if married) in bank deposits from Social Security
- $2,000 in building materials to repair home
- burial plots
- health aids
- $5,000 in jewelry, heirlooms and art

- $1,900 in motor vehicles
- personal injury lawsuits
- 75% of personal injury recovery installments
- wrongful death lawsuits
- 75% of wrongful death recovery installments
- AFDC, aid to blind, aged and disabled
- financial aid to students
- unemployment benefits
- union benefits due to labor disputes
- workers' compensation awards
- $5,000 ($10,000 if married) in tools, materials, instruments, uniforms, books, furnishings, equipment, vessel and motor vehicles
- 75% of public employee vacation installments
- 75% of wages received within 30 days of filing
- pensions, including public and private retirement benefits, IRAs and Keoughs
- disability or health insurance benefits
- unmatured life insurance benefits to $8,000, and
- fidelity bonds.

If you have little or no equity in your home, then you can use the other set of California exemptions, which are listed in Code of Civil Procedure § 703.140. Among other things, these exemptions include a $15,800 exemption to apply toward whatever property you want.

### f. Can Your Lender Foreclose After You File for Chapter 7?

In Chapter 7 bankruptcy, the automatic stay will keep your lender from foreclosing until:

- the Chapter 7 trustee decides not to sell your property
- your lender successfully asks the court to terminate the automatic stay (by filing a document called "motion seeking relief from the automatic stay")
- you receive a bankruptcy discharge (the stay is automatically lifted), or
- your case is dismissed (either by the bankruptcy court or upon your request).

The most likely scenario is that your lender will file a Motion for Relief from the Automatic Stay shortly after you file your Chapter 7 and the court will grant it unless there is equity in the home that the trustee can capture in a quick sale. Either way, you will probably lose your home.

### g. Converting From Chapter 7 to Chapter 13

If you file a Chapter 7 bankruptcy and later discover that Chapter 13 is the better option, you can usually convert your case to Chapter 13. As discussed in Section B2 above, Chapter 13 will allow you to pay your debts out of your future income. You will not be required to give up your property as long as you stay current on your mortgage and successfully complete a plan that pays off your arrearage within a reasonable time.

Your right to convert is absolute as long as you did not previously convert from Chapter 13 to Chapter 7. Note, however, that if you missed your regular loan payments on your real property after you filed Chapter 7, some courts will require that you make the missed payments before your Chapter 13 plan can be approved.

---

**"CHAPTER 20" BANKRUPTCY**

A strategy that may seem attractive but isn't likely to work is referred to as "Chapter 20." First, you file for Chapter 7 to get rid of your dischargeable debts and your personal liability for your secured loans. Immediately after you receive a Chapter 7 discharge, you file Chapter 13. You then pay off over time the deeds of trust and liens on your property and any remaining non-dischargeable debt. This approach will not save your house—since the foreclosure will usually be allowed to proceed in the Chapter 7 bankruptcy—but it may improve your overall debt situation if you are willing to let go of the house.

---

## 4. Overview of Chapter 12 Bankruptcy

*If you are not a family farmer.* Skip this section, as Chapter 12 bankruptcy is not an option.

A Chapter 12 bankruptcy is known as the "adjustment of debts of a family farmer with regular income" or, more commonly, the "family farmer bankruptcy." Congress enacted Chapter 12 in 1986 with the hope of slowing the burgeoning number of small farms in the United States being lost through foreclosure. A Chapter 12 allows you to keep your farm, reorganize your finances, make payments over three to five years and discharge the remaining debts not paid through the bankruptcy—except for debts that automatically survive bankruptcy. (See Section B1 above.)

Chapter 12 bankruptcy is largely modeled on Chapter 13 bankruptcy. (Read Section B2, above, for a detailed discussion of Chapter 13 bankruptcy.)

### a. Who Can File a Chapter 12 Bankruptcy?

Chapter 12 bankruptcy has very strict eligibility requirements. If you operate a family farm, you can use Chapter 12 only if:

• your total debts do not exceed $1.5 million
• at least 80% of your debts, excluding the debt associated with your home, arises from farming operations, and
• at least 50% of your income is based on farming operations.

A corporation or partnership (at least half owned by your family) that operates the farm may file Chapter 12 bankruptcy if 50% or more of your family's income is based on farming operations.

There are two key advantages of a Chapter 12 bankruptcy. First, you retain the right to continue operating your farm while in Chapter 12. Second, during your case, you can keep your farm and pay your foreclosing lender "the reasonable rent customary in the community where your property is located," regardless of the actual payment amount specified in your promissory note.

### b. Debtor-in-Possession in Chapter 12

While you are in Chapter 12 bankruptcy, you are called a "debtor-in-possession" or "DIP," and have full authority to operate your farm on a day-to-day basis. In other words, you do not need special permission from the bankruptcy court to conduct ordinary business or farm your land. Only special activities that fall outside the scope of ordinary farm business, such as selling off your farm or equipment, must be submitted to the bankruptcy court for approval.

The bankruptcy court appoints a trustee to administer every Chapter 12 case. The Chapter 12 trustee's primary role is to collect payments from you, typically on a monthly or bi-weekly basis. The trustee then disburses the money to your creditors, after deducting a small trustee's fee. The Chapter 12 trustee is also responsible for maintaining detailed accounting records that inform the court whether you are fulfilling your obligations under your plan.

In addition, the bankruptcy court may order a Chapter 12 trustee to look into your farm operations and determine if it is economically worthwhile for you to continue your farming business.

### c. When a Creditor Can Foreclose After You File for Chapter 12

Creditors may seek relief from the automatic stay (covered in Section A, above) anytime after you file Chapter 12. A common reason is because you have no equity in your farm, and a foreclosing lender claims you don't need the farm to carry out your Chapter 12 plan. With the help of a lawyer, you may be able to defeat your lender's motion—for example, by proving to the bankruptcy court that your farm is also your family residence. Most bankruptcy judges are sympathetic to farmers who also live on their farms.

## 5. Overview of Chapter 11 Bankruptcy

Chapter 11 bankruptcies are complex and costly and are very difficult to do without a lawyer. It is unlikely to be the remedy of choice for most readers of this book. Nevertheless, you should review this section to see if it applies to your situation.

### a. Who Can File a Chapter 11 Bankruptcy?

Chapter 11 reorganization is the most common bankruptcy chapter used for corporations, limited liability companies, and general and limited partnerships. It may also be used by individuals whose secured debts exceed $750,000 and unsecured debts exceed $250,000.

### b. What Happens in a Chapter 11 Bankruptcy?

A Chapter 11 bankruptcy can last anywhere from three months to three years, with six months as an average length.

During the Chapter 11, the debtor proposes a plan of reorganization to pay his creditors. Plans of reorganization vary greatly in length and complexity. A major bankruptcy may involve a plan of several hundred printed pages. In a simpler Chapter 11 reorganization, the plan may be only 15 or 20 typewritten pages. A copy of the proposed plan must be sent to all creditors affected by the plan. In a large bankruptcy, that could be thousands of creditors!

For all practical purposes, you are out of bankruptcy once your Chapter 11 plan of reorganization is confirmed by the court. A confirmed plan constitutes a binding contract and provides a new relationship between you and your creditors. Your payment of debt is limited to the schedule and amounts provided in your plan. If all goes as expected, you emerge from Chapter 11 bankruptcy still owning your real property. After confirmation, the bankruptcy court usually retains control of the bankruptcy case only to enforce your compliance with the terms of your plan.

In essence, you act as your own bankruptcy trustee in a Chapter 11 reorganization. You are called a "Debtor-in-Possession" or "DIP" for short. As a DIP, you continue to operate your business and manage your real estate, largely without interference from the bankruptcy court. You are free from paying all of your pre-petition debts until the Chapter 11 is over.

You are expected in Chapter 11 to negotiate with your creditors a reorganization (restructure) of your financial affairs. Your negotiations result in an acceptable plan of reorganization to restructure your finances and repay your creditors in full or part.

Some individuals and small businesses choose not to file Chapter 11 reorganizations because of the complexity and costs involved, including high filing fees (currently $800) and substantial attorney fees. In addition, you must pay a quarterly fee to the U.S. Trustee's Office (a percentage of your post-petition disbursements, often several hundreds or thousands of dollars) until your case is closed.

### c. When a Creditor Can Foreclose After You File for Chapter 11

Although your lender is "stayed" from pursuing foreclosure, it may file a Motion for Relief from the Automatic Stay, asking the court to allow it to proceed with foreclosure. (Automatic stays are covered in more detail in Section B2, above.)

Your lender may argue that it should be entitled to relief from stay because you have no equity in your property—that is, your property is worth less than your loan. However, this sole argument will not convince a judge to allow your lender to foreclose. Even if you have no equity in your property, your property may still be necessary for your reorganization. In other words, you may be able to sell or refinance your property in the future (presumably after it appreciates in value and builds up some equity) and use the proceeds to pay your creditors.

If your lender seeks relief from stay during your bankruptcy because it has not received regular loan payments during the Chapter 11 bankruptcy, relief will not be granted. Under most circumstances, a secured creditor is not entitled to loan payments during the Chapter 11 bankruptcy.

Lenders typically seek relief from an automatic stay if they believe the collateral securing its loan (your property) is not being adequately protected. In other words, your lender could argue that its secured position is deteriorating if your property is decreasing in value. For example, perhaps the property is uninsured, you failed to pay property taxes or you are not maintaining the property.

If your real estate is your only asset, a Motion for Relief from Automatic Stay may be equivalent to asking the court to short-circuit your reorganization and liquidate your entire estate. Because of this, much of the litigation associated with Chapter 11 centers around whether your property is necessary for your reorganization. Bankruptcy courts are reluctant to grant such a motion until you have had an opportunity to see if your property can be sold or refinanced, or your loan restructured, especially during the first 120 days of your case.

## C. Which Bankruptcy Is Right for You?

Now that you have an overview of the different types of bankruptcy, you can consider which type might be best for you. The accompanying sidebar lists additional resources to help you make this decision.

If you want to keep your real estate, you should file a reorganization bankruptcy. For just about everyone this will be a Chapter 13 bankruptcy, or for farmers, a Chapter 12 bankruptcy. If you don't qualify for Chapter 13 because your debts are too high, you should speak with an attorney about the possibility of filing Chapter 11.

If you don't qualify for a reorganization bankruptcy—because you don't have enough income to make all required payments under the plan—then your only choice will be Chapter 7. This means you will definitely lose real estate you're not living in, and probably your home as well, unless you can negotiate a solution with your lender (see Chapter 5).

If the question of saving your real estate is no longer an issue, there are advantages and drawbacks to bankruptcy. The best resource to help you make that decision is *Money Troubles: Legal Strategies to Cope With Your Debts*, by Robin Leonard (Nolo Press). (See sidebar.)

## D. Additional Resources

Although this chapter provides adequate information to help you understand your options, it cannot possibly give all the information you need to actually file for bankruptcy. For that, you should consult the references listed in the accompanying sidebar, and if you wish (or your situation is too complex), a bankruptcy lawyer. Keep in mind that bankruptcy often requires a lot of negotiating—with your creditors, the bankruptcy trustee and the bankruptcy judge.

---

### BANKRUPTCY RESOURCES FROM NOLO PRESS

If you decide to handle your own bankruptcy, or want more information on the step-by-step process, Nolo Press publishes several bankruptcy aids:

*How to File for Bankruptcy*, by Stephen Elias, Albin Renauer and Robin Leonard, contains all the information necessary for you (as long as you are not a business entity) to decide whether or not to file for Chapter 7 bankruptcy, and instructions on how to do it yourself.

*Chapter 13 Bankruptcy: Repay Your Debts*, by Robin Leonard, can help you decide whether or not to file Chapter 13 bankruptcy. It provides step-by-step instructions on how file your own Chapter 13 bankruptcy.

*Money Troubles: Legal Strategies to Cope With Your Debts*, by Robin Leonard, covers how to negotiate with your creditors, deal with bill collectors, handle lawsuits, assess whether or not to file bankruptcy, handle exempt property and rebuild your credit.

These resources are available in many libraries and most bookstores. Or, to order directly from Nolo Press, see the catalog at the back of this book or contact Nolo Press online at www.nolo.com.

*chapter*

# 10

# HOW TO SELL YOUR PROPERTY QUICKLY TO STOP FORECLOSURE

**F**or some readers, selling your property may be the most efficient strategy for stopping foreclosure. However, selling your property can be time-consuming and stressful under normal circumstances, let alone with a foreclosure pending. Nevertheless, this chapter explains how you can sell your property at the best price possible before you lose it in a foreclosure sale.

If you decide to sell your house, we highly recommend you read *For Sale by Owner* by George Devine (Nolo Press). It explains in detail the ins and outs of selling your home, including disclosures, tax liability and real estate sale agreements. Order information is at the back of this book.

## A. Deciding Whether to Sell Your Property

There are some definite advantages to selling your property: you get rid of a financial burden and you preserve your credit rating. On the other hand, there may be much better ways to handle an impending foreclosure. Before you even consider putting your property on the market, carefully read Chapter 1, Section D. There you'll have a chance to assess whether or not to keep your property and to evaluate your options if you decide to give it up.

---

### PROBLEMS SELLING PROPERTY IN FORECLOSURE

If you decide to sell your property during the foreclosure, you will need to be sensitive to your time limitations. Above all, there's the ticking foreclosure clock to consider. In a normal market, most properties sell within six months. Unfortunately, you're likely to have less than 90 days to find a buyer and complete the transaction. Most lenders won't give you extra time to sell your property. Be especially cautious of these important issues:

• You may have difficulty getting a sales price high enough to pay your loans. Ideally, you want to receive enough funds to pay off all your underlying loans and perhaps leave a little for yourself. Unfortunately, this won't be possible if you have negative equity—if your property is worth less than the balance of your loan. In that situation, you'll need to obtain your lender's approval before selling your property for less than what you owe (called a "short sale"). See Section H for more on short sales.

• Selling may not solve your financial problems. Your financial crisis may require more drastic measures than selling your property. If this is your situation, read about bankruptcy (in Chapter 9) before deciding whether to sell your property.

• You may need to get your lender's permission. If you are involved in a short sale situation (see Section H) or if the close of escrow will extend out beyond the scheduled foreclosure sale, you will need your lender's permission.

• There may be adverse tax consequences. You may face potential tax liability if you sell your property; see Chapter 1, Section D5 for an overview of tax issues involved in selling your house. Here are the rules in a nutshell:

  – If you make a profit on the sale, you may have to pay capital gain taxes on the profit. However, you may be able to postpone this tax liability if you sell your primary residence and purchase another one within 24 months or you are over 55 and meet the requirements for this one time exemption.

  – If you sell your property for less than the amount due on your loan and your lender accepts that amount in satisfaction of your debt, you may be liable for paying taxes on the amount your lender forgave (see Section H2). If you are considering selling your property, consult with a CPA or tax consultant.

## B. Hire a Real Estate Agent

Because of the pending foreclosure, it is almost always advisable to use a real estate agent. An agent's experience in marketing foreclosure properties, screening and qualifying buyers, handling negotiations and promptly closing escrows will be invaluable to you as time runs out. Your job is to find a real estate agent who can help you sell your property at a reasonable price within the limited time left before the foreclosure sale.

Also, if you find an agent who is experienced (or specializes) in properties in foreclosure, they will appreciate the urgency of not just finding a buyer but closing escrow as quickly as possible. After all, agents understand that the only way they will collect their commission is if escrow closes before the foreclosure sale. If you know any real estate agents, ask them for a referral to someone with experience in selling properties in foreclosure. Friends, relatives and business acquaintances may also steer you in the right direction. Title companies and local newspapers are also good resources.

*If you decide to sell your property without an agent.* We again suggest you read *For Sale by Owner*, by George Devine (Nolo Press). It is the sine qua non of do-it-yourself real estate books.

### 1. Interview Real Estate Agents

Look for an experienced real estate agent who has successfully sold properties in foreclosure. An experienced agent can also negotiate with your lender over a possible "short sale" or a brief postponement of the foreclosure sale (to allow a pending escrow to close), if it becomes necessary.

Even though you're in a hurry, it behooves you to interview several agents rather than hiring the first one who comes your way. Here are several questions you should ask prospective real estate agents:

- *Will the agent place your property in the Multiple Listing Service (MLS)?* The MLS book and related computer services list and describe properties currently on the market. This is the largest and most frequently used resource for agents looking for properties for sale. The MLS is published weekly and distributed only to real estate agents. Once you select an agent, she will immediately list your property in the MLS. In that way, a broad range of agents and their potential buyers will learn of your property's availability, price and features.

- *Does the agent have specific experience selling properties in foreclosure?* Also find out if the agent has negotiated any "short payoffs" with lenders or extensions of foreclosure sales (to allow a pending escrow to close). Ask for references and get specific details on how quickly the agent sold the property and whether it was at or near asking price.

- *How much does the agent think your property will sell for?* Watch out for an agent who gives you an unrealistically high estimate to ensure getting the listing. You don't have time to let your property sit on the market before you drop the price.

- *How much will the agent charge?* Most real estate agents set their commissions at approximately 6% of the sales price of the property, although some agents may be willing to negotiate the commission rate, especially if you agree on a lesser level of services. You will pay the commission out of the sales price. For example, if your property sells for $150,000, you'd pay your real estate agent $9,000 at the 6% commission rate. In most cases, your agent will split the commission evenly with the buyer's agent (which is no additional cost to you).

- *How will the agent market your property in the limited time left before the foreclosure sale?* In addition to the usual ways properties are marketed (Section C, below), does your agent have other ways to market your property? (For example, posting a sign at a local factory, hospital or school; or perhaps offering a special discount to corporate relocation agencies for a referral. Ask your agent to be creative.)

- What services will the real estate agent provide? Will he or she help you fill out required disclosure forms? Recommend appraisers, inspectors and contractors, if needed? Negotiate with potential buyers and handle offers and counter-offers? Help qualify buyers for a loan? Open escrow, review escrow instructions, find a title insurance company, help remove contingencies and make sure escrow closes on time? But remember, as pointed out earlier, you may be able to negotiate a lower commission rate if you're willing to take on some of these services yourself.

## 2. Settle on a Listing Agreement

Once you find an agent, you'll need to enter into what's known as a "listing agreement". There are three types of listing agreements you should consider using:

- exclusive listing agreement
- exclusive agency agreement, or
- open listing agreement (non-exclusive).

As you'll see below, some of these arrangements are better for your real estate agent than for you. Remember that the listing agreement is negotiable. If you can't settle on an agreement that you feel comfortable with, consider finding another agent. Don't hesitate to insist on terms you're comfortable with, and to quickly move on if the agent won't cooperate.

### a. Exclusive Listing Agreement

Most people enter into an exclusive listing agreement (formally known as an Exclusive Authorization and Right to Sell). During the listing period—typically 90 days to six months, although it may be shorter if the property is already in foreclosure—your property is listed with only one agent. You agree to pay the full commission on the sales price, usually 6%, if your agent successfully sells the property during the listing period, even if someone other than the agent (including you!) finds a buyer. You must also pay the full commission if your agent finds a buyer who agrees to pay the full price but you decide not to sell.

*Example: Roy owns a $300,000 home in Palo Alto. Confronting foreclosure, Roy decides to list his home with an agent under an exclusive listing agreement. A month later, Roy's next door neighbor expresses an interest in buying Roy's home as a rental investment. Even if Roy and his neighbor seal the deal, Roy's agent will get the full commission of approximately $18,000.*

### b. Exclusive Agency Agreement

An exclusive agency agreement is really a misnomer. The only thing that makes it "exclusive" is that you agree to work with one agent at a time. Under this arrangement, you and your real estate agent simultaneously try to sell your property. You pay a commission only if your agent (not you) finds a buyer.

Most agents are reluctant to enter into this type of relationship, perhaps because of potential disputes over who found the buyer. If you select an agent who agrees to an agency agreement, you and your agent may want to weekly (or even daily) exchange lists of potential buyers each of you found.

### c. Open Listing Agreement

An open listing agreement resembles the exclusive agency agreement described in Section B2b, just above, but you ask more than one agent to simultaneously market your property. If you find the buyer yourself, you won't pay any commission.

Because real estate agents compete against you and each other to find a buyer (and get the commission), this type of listing is obviously the least popular among agents. Similarly, you may not want an open listing because the agents may not have enough incentive to find a buyer for your property. Remember, unlike a normal sales situation, with a pending foreclosure time is of the essence!

## 3. Negotiating the Listing Agreement

As with most other kinds of contracts, much of the listing agreement consists of standard clauses (boilerplate) which are seldom if ever modified, while some parts are negotiated on a sale-by-sale basis. Most agents are agreeable to negotiating changes to the listing agreement. After all, agents survive on obtaining listings and are appreciative of the time-sensitive needs of a property owner in foreclosure. However, if your agent balks at your proposed changes, you may be left with a difficult decision. Unless you are convinced that this agent is perfect for your situation, you may simply need to select someone else.

To protect your interests during the foreclosure, you should negotiate the following items:
- *Term of the listing:* Most agents suggest terms of from three to six months, which is too long given the time limitations of your foreclosure. The listing should be limited to 60 days or, if you do not have 60 days, it should terminate a minimum of five days before the scheduled foreclosure sale. If no buyer is found in time, you may still engineer one of the other strategies described in this book during the last five days, such as bankruptcy (See Chapter 9), or giving your lender a deed in lieu of foreclosure (See Chapter 11).
- *Commission to agent:* Listing agreements typically contain a standard clause providing that the commission is earned when the agent presents you an offer from a "ready, willing and able"

buyer. Unfortunately, this means you could be liable for a commission even if escrow does not close in time to beat the foreclosure sale. To protect yourself, cross out the phrase "commission earned when agent presents an offer from a ready, willing and able buyer" and then type (or print) the phrase "no commission will be paid unless and until escrow closes prior to the foreclosure sale" on the blank lines near the end of the listing agreement or along the border of the agreement. Make sure your agent initials your changes. Further, have your agent agree that if the buyer pays you any portion of the sales price in the form of a promissory note (rather than cash), your agent will receive a promissory note for his or her proportionate share of the commission. Type (or print) the language on the blank lines near the end of the listing agreement or along the border of the agreement. Once again, make sure your agent initials the language.

*Consider raising your agent's commission for a quick sale.* Keep in mind that you are on a very short fuse with a foreclosure pending. Consider increasing the commission to motivate your agent to sell your property quickly. For example, you can offer a 7% commission if your property sells within the first 30 days and a 6$\frac{1}{2}$% commission if it sells within 60 days (if you still have 60 days before the sale).

- *Commission based on final sales price*: The listing agreement presented to you by your agent may contain a standard clause providing a 6% commission on the full sales price, even though you will probably end up negotiating a lower price with the buyer. State in the listing agreement (on the blank lines at the end or in the margin) that your agent's commission will be based on the final sales price established at the close of escrow.
- *Right to terminate*: To emphasize that you need your agent to be aggressive and market your property actively, specifically state in the listing

agreement that: "Seller has the right to terminate the agreement at any time (subject to five days prior written notice) if Seller determines, in his/her sole discretion, that the agent is not handling the sale of the property properly."

- *Marketing plan*: You are hiring a real estate agent to take advantage of his or her professional marketing ability, affiliation with the multiple listing service and capability for mass advertising. It is a good idea to require that your real estate agent commit to a very specific marketing plan, which you should attach as an addendum to your listing agreement. For example, your lender should commit to a weekly classified ad in the Sunday newspaper, weekly open houses, listing in the MLS and on the Internet, weekly caravans for agents and a special display advertisement in a local magazine or newspaper. (See Section C.)
- *Additional services*: You'll probably need help to complete the real estate transaction quickly and correctly. Specifically state in the listing agreement that your agent will "assist Seller in qualifying buyers, negotiate offers and counter-offers, help the Buyer find a lender quickly, remove escrow contingencies and help escrow close promptly."

### 4. If You Have Problems With Your Real Estate Agent

Your agent stands to make thousands of dollars from selling your property. That alone should motivate him to aggressively market your property. If, however, you're dissatisfied with your agent's performance, immediately meet with him and discuss your specific concerns. A heart-to-heart meeting with your agent will likely resolve many of your concerns. If it doesn't, you may want to change agents quickly so you can still sell your property before time runs out.

If you decide to terminate the services of a real estate agent you no longer want to work with, ask him to end the agreement early. If you've signed a listing agreement that terminates on a specific date, ask him to end the listing early, simply on the

grounds that there are "irreconcilable differences" between you and your agent (meaning that you can no longer work together harmoniously). The agent may be unwilling to give up the commission, especially if you appear to have a buyer or another agent lined up. As an alternative, consider offering him a partial commission if your property sells by a certain date, a reimbursement for the agent's actual expenses, or a payment for hours worked on selling your property.

*Address right to terminate in the listing agreement.* In Section B2, just above, we suggest that your listing agreement give you the right to terminate the agreement if you decide that the agent is not properly handling the sale of the property.

## C. Implement a Plan to Sell Your Property

Just because you hire an agent to sell your property doesn't mean you can kick back and wait for a buyer to show up. Remember, you are facing foreclosure and don't have the luxury of waiting. You should be prepared to help your agent as much as possible, even though you are paying a commission. Ask your agent how you can help, and be prepared to do some of the leg work yourself. Here are some suggestions.

## 1. Classified Advertisements

Your goal should be to reach as many potential buyers as possible, with specific and appealing information about your property. You'll need to advertise within the shortest time possible and within your agent's advertising budget. But beware. Some real estate firms place big, splashy newspaper ads that advertise their company rather than your property. Or they describe your property in a "teaser" ad without listing its address. These ads may generate phone calls or walk-ins for the real estate office, but they won't help you. Request that your agent advertise your property in the real estate classified section of your local newspaper every Sunday. At the very least, your agent should commit to one classified ad every Sunday during the term of the listing agreement. If your agent's budget permits, weekdays can also be included.

If your community has a weekly "shopper" or neighborhood paper that is distributed for free, you may want to advertise there as an excellent compliment to your other advertising. Buyers looking for bargains often peruse papers such as these. If your agent won't commit to advertising in each of the small local papers or shoppers, consider spending your own money to advertise. Remember, you can't stop the foreclosure by just hoping your property will sell.

Your agent will undoubtedly volunteer to write the newspaper ad, but you should go over it before it is published. You want your ad to be clear and understandable, not full of confusing abbreviations, real estate jargon and misleading (often exaggerated) descriptions of the property.

You'll need to decide whether to mention that your property is in foreclosure. This is often a difficult decision for property owners, and there are arguments supporting either choice. Because mentioning the word "foreclosure" in an ad tends to bring out speculators who hope to get a bargain at your expense, we suggest you simply state "immediate sale," "reduced for quick sale," "owner anxious" or "all reasonable offers considered" and then see what happens.

## 2. "For Sale" Signs

All real estate firms have "for sale" signs and will proudly post them on your property. On open house days, your agent should also post signs throughout your neighborhood announcing an open house at your property. Nevertheless, you should stay on top of your agent and recommend that signs be posted at intersections near your property. If necessary, you can even help your agent put up the signs.

## 3. Fact Sheet (Flyer)

A fact sheet is usually a one-page flyer that shows a picture (preferably color) of your property. It lists the basic facts about your property and highlights its special features. If you hold an assumable loan with a substantial balance and a below market interest rate, be sure your agent points this out in your fact sheet.

Your real estate agent will distribute copies of your property fact sheet to other agents, and will pass them out at open houses. It is in your best interests to give copies to friends, co-workers, neighbors and business associates. You may want to leave copies in local stores and businesses (with the owners' permission). Finally, look into sending copies to relocation, housing or personnel departments of local corporations and universities, which often help relocating employees find housing. You may also place your fact sheet on real estate programs on local cable television shows and the Internet. Some of these services are free while others charge a nominal fee. Your agent should be familiar with which programs or Web sites are available and their comparative costs.

### 4. Open Houses

An open house is a specific day (typically Sunday) in which potential buyers are invited to inspect your property without a special appointment. You might think of an open house as a nuisance and a painful reminder of your financial straits. But don't underestimate the value of all those people traipsing through your home. Remember, all you need is just one of those visitors to make an offer to buy the property. If you want to avoid the aggravation of an open house, get the property ready (your agent can give you tips) and let your agent deal with the "lookie-lou's" while you spend the day elsewhere.

## D. Prepare Your Property for Sale

One of the most effective ways to sell your property is to make it attractive to buy: mow the lawn, keep the property tidy, place plants and flowers in strategic locations. Given the pending foreclosure, it does not make sense to spend a lot of money and time on anything but minor improvements, such as a fresh coat of paint.

### 1. Make Disclosures Required by Law

With the help of your real estate agent, you'll complete several disclosure forms, which must be given to prospective buyers:

• *Real Estate Transfer Disclosure Statement.* You are responsible for disclosing all property defects you personally know about, no matter how insignificant (the roof leaks, your next door neighbors party loudly on weekends, the basement floor is cracked, there's dry rot around the windows, the refrigerator is on its last legs or whatever else you can think of). This disclosure effectively protects you from any later claim or lawsuit by the buyer based on failure to disclose.

• *Flood disclosure.* You must advise prospective buyers in writing if your property is in a flood hazard area. You can tell if your property is in a flood hazard zone if your lender required you to

obtain flood insurance when you bought your property. If you aren't sure whether your property is in a flood hazard area, ask your real estate agent to investigate or check with the Federal Emergency Management Agency (FEMA).

• *Seismic disclosures.* You must disclose in writing to potential buyers whether your property lies within any seismic zones. You must also specify if it has any known earthquake weaknesses. Check with your real estate agent or a local city or county planning department.

• *Fire hazards.* You must disclose in writing to prospective buyers if your property is located in an unincorporated area that the state has designated fire hazard area. Check with your real estate agent.

*If you have any doubts about the condition of your property.* Hire a contractor to inspect it. If the contractor finds problems, disclose them to all potential buyers. You can use the contractor's detailed written report to complete your disclosure form and you can also give copies of the inspector's report to potential buyers.

## E. Offers and Counter-Offers

Sooner or later, you will receive an offer to purchase your property. You may be relieved and perhaps a little nervous. Fortunately, there are standard methods to deal with offers, and your agent will help you through the steps. For starters, make sure your agent pre-qualifies the buyer.

### 1. Buyer Presents an Offer

The process starts when a prospective purchaser submits a written offer to purchase your property. The offer is contained in a document called a Real Estate Purchase Contract and Receipt for Deposit, commonly referred to as a "deposit receipt." The "deposit receipt" will contain several pages of detailed information, including the price and other financial terms. You should be particularly concerned that the price is sufficient to cover all of your debt and that the proposed escrow closing date is before the foreclosure sale. The offer will also include contingencies—events that must happen or else escrow won't close. For example, if the offer is contingent upon the buyer qualifying for financing or your property passing certain physical inspections, you should consider strict deadlines for removing those contingencies. On the other hand, if the offer is contingent upon something that will not likely occur before the foreclosure sale, such as the buyer first selling his property, you should reject the contingency. Make sure you review the deposit receipt carefully with your agent, paragraph by paragraph. Most deposit receipts give you a strict deadline in which to accept, reject or propose a counter-offer.

## 2. Making Counter-Offers

Although you are anxious to sell your property, you may find yourself facing an offer that doesn't quite satisfy your needs as to price or terms. You have the right to counter-offer to the buyer with terms that are acceptable to you. Work with your agent to write a counter-offer and present to the buyer and/or her agent as soon as possible. Although the offer may contain a deadline for a response, chances are you will want to respond sooner because of the shortage of time. Do not wait more than 36 hours to give a counter-offer. Once you have a potential buyer, keep the momentum moving forward.

Sometimes a buyer will submit a counter-offer to your counter-offer. In fact, sometimes the process can go on for numerous rounds of counter-offers. Don't be discouraged; a series of counter-offers is a sign that you are moving closer in your negotiations. Make it clear how long you're giving the potential buyer to accept your counter-offer. With a foreclosure pending, you should require that the buyer respond to your counter-offer within 24 hours.

Several important issues in the offer on which you might want to counter-offer are:

- *Price.* Most potential buyers expect you to counter on price, and will bid a little low precisely to see how you will counter. In fact, if your negotiating strategy is to stick with the price you've named, your agent should go out of her way to make this clear to the buyer before the offer is presented.

- *Financing.* If the offer contains financing terms you believe are impractical, or if the buyer wants you to accept a promissory note and deed of trust for a portion of the sales price and you don't want to, the counteroffer is your opportunity to change these provisions.

- *Occupancy.* If you're living in the property, the offer should give you a reasonable amount of time to move out after escrow closes. You may wish to lengthen the time of occupancy in your counter-offer.

- *Contingency of buyer selling property.* As mentioned, a contingency is an event that must happen before escrow can close (that is, the before the sale can be completed). Most contingencies are standard conditions in real estate transactions. However, other contingencies are problematic and could endanger the timely close of escrow. For example, a buyer may propose to purchase your property contingent on first selling the property he or she already owns. This contingency is never acceptable in a foreclosure scenario. It would be excruciatingly painful to lose your property at a foreclosure sale because you fruitlessly waited for a buyer to sell his or her property. Refuse to accept this term in your counter-offer. A buyer who really wants your property can seek short-term financing to complete the transaction.

- *Inspections.* Frequently, buyers want a detailed inspection of your property during the escrow, either by themselves or with a licensed property inspector. The purpose of the inspection is to determine whether there are any physical problems that would prohibit them from purchasing the property. If a buyer's offer allows too much time for inspections, shorten the time limits in your counter-offer. For example, the first inspection should be conducted within ten days of opening escrow and the final inspection the day before escrow closes.

- *Condition of the property.* Reiterate in your counter-offer that your property is being sold in its "as is" condition, without any warranties or representations. This claim will eliminate the condition of your property as an excuse for the buyer to delay the close of escrow. It will also protect you from a lawsuit if a buyer purchases your property and subsequently discovers defects. But keep in mind that the "as is" clause does not eliminate your obligation to disclose the physical condition of your property (see Section D above).

- *Close of escrow.* Escrows typically close in 30 to 60 days, but you may not have that much time before the foreclosure sale. To avoid this conflict, state in your counter-offer that escrow must close no later than a specific date (preferably at least five days before the scheduled trustee's sale) and specify that because "time is of the essence," there will be no extensions.

## 3. Accepting an Offer or Counter-Offer

Carefully review the buyer's offer and counter-offer, if there is one. All terms of the buyer's offer (or counter-offer) will stand unless you counter that they be eliminated or modified.

Be sure that all counter-offers show not only the date, but the exact local time (Pacific Daylight Time or Pacific Standard Time) of presentation and expiration. Once you and your agent have determined that all of the terms are acceptable to you (such as price, financing, closing of escrow), you can sign the offer or counter-offer and give it to your agent. Your agent should then deliver the buyer's offer to purchase (deposit receipt) to an escrow company and make sure that an escrow is opened immediately.

## 4. Back-up Offers

Most offers contain contingencies that may cancel the deal and leave you without a buyer, even though the foreclosure sale lurking around the corner. To avoid having to start all over if a deal falls through, you should accept "back-up" offers.

*Example: Tanja accepts an offer with a contingency that the buyer find acceptable financing within 30 days. She also accepts several back-up offers. As it turns out, the first buyer can't find financing within 30 days, so Tanja cancels the escrow and pursues the back-up offers.*

In the escrow instructions, you'll need to disclose to the buyer that you will be accepting back-up offers during the escrow period. Make sure that anyone making a back-up offer understands (in writing) that her offer will not be formally considered unless the pending escrow falls through.

# F. Proceeding Through Escrow to Closing

This section contains an overview of the escrow process, which begins with signing the purchase agreement and ends with transfer of ownership.

## 1. Working With the Escrow Officer

The escrow process consists of steps taken by an escrow officer (a person responsible for handling the details of the escrow), the buyer and the seller to fulfill the terms and conditions stated in the purchase agreement (deposit receipt). For example, you and/or the buyer will execute documents, clear title, inspect the property, pay off existing lienholders, obtain new financing and pay monies. The terms and conditions of the purchase are described in a document called escrow instructions.

After you've agreed to sell your property, your real estate agent will deliver the offer and any counter-offers to an escrow officer. Because of the pending foreclosure, you should understand the escrow process and closely monitor its progress. Promptly closing escrow involves detailed, picky and often overlapping steps.

## 2. Removing Contingencies

If the escrow instructions contains contingencies, such as the buyer obtaining the results of a physical inspection of the property, the escrow holder will make sure you and the buyer, with the help of your agents, remove them. During this period, you should contact the escrow officer at least once a week to make sure that the process is moving forward.

As you and the buyer satisfy or waive each contingency, they must be removed from the escrow by signing an escrow instruction stating that the particular contingency has been removed. Because of the pending foreclosure, sign a separate escrow instruction as each contingency is satisfied or waived. Have your agent monitor the timely removal of each contingency.

Buyers frequently need extra time to satisfy an escrow contingency. Without the extra time, the escrow would end (that is, the deal would fall through) unless buyer and seller agree to extend it. Any agreement to extend the time to meet a contingency (or to change any other term of the escrow) must be in writing and signed. If an extension threatens to extend the escrow beyond the date of the scheduled foreclosure sale—and the foreclosing lender refuses to temporarily postpone the sale date—you have no choice but to refuse the buyer's request for an extension.

If the buyer can't remove a contingency that jeopardizes the entire deal—for example, an inspection turns up a physical problem with the exterior of the property that may need to be repaired before the close of escrow—you should have the escrow officer issue a Seller's Demand for Removal of Contingencies to the buyer. This document requires the

buyer to either accept the property in its present condition or cancel the sale.

If, after trying in good faith, the buyer still can't resolve a contingency, the deal is over and you should immediately pursue any back-up offers.

## 3. Closing Escrow

Escrow closes when the escrow holder records a grant deed naming the buyer as the new owner of the property and issues checks to everyone entitled to be paid from the proceeds (such as your foreclosing lender and any other lienholders). You and the buyer—not necessarily together—must go to the escrow company to review and sign the closing documents. Your agent should make sure that the paperwork necessary for closing escrow is completed several days before the anticipated closing date.

# G. Special Rules for Dealing With Equity Purchasers

*If the buyer is not an equity purchaser.* This section does not apply if you receive an offer from a buyer who wants to:

- purchase your non-residential property
- live on the property as her personal residence, or
- purchase the property with a deed in lieu of foreclosure.

If you are selling your own home, you may receive an offer from what's known as an "equity purchaser." Equity purchasers are individuals (or occasionally companies) who purchase single-family residences (one to four family dwelling units, one of which is owner-occupied) on which a Notice of Default has been recorded. Equity purchasers don't intend to live in the property. Typically, they are interested in purchasing the property as an investment and plan to quickly re-sell or rent it.

Equity purchasers subscribe to publications that publish daily lists of properties in foreclosure. They usually want to purchase properties by offering a couple thousand dollars (for the equity) and promising to take over (and renegotiate) the loan with the foreclosing lender. Some equity purchasers also give the homeowner an option to buy back the property within one year, or allow them to rent the property for several months.

*Example: Sam owns a home in San Diego that is in foreclosure. Sam estimates that he has approximately $12,000 in equity. A few weeks before the trustee's sale, Sam is approached by Russell, who offers to purchase Sam's home for $1,000 plus takeover payments on the loan. Russell offers Sam the right to rent the home for six months and the right to purchase it back within one year for $5,000. Russell would be an equity purchaser.*

Most equity purchasers will contact you directly and avoid your real estate agent. Your agent can help you deal with equity purchasers. However, because an equity purchaser's offer typically will not include enough cash to allow your agent to receive a full commission, your agent may be naturally reluctant to negotiate with an equity purchaser. As a result, don't be surprised if your agent dissuades you from considering an offer from an equity purchaser. Keep in mind that there is nothing wrong with selling to an equity purchaser, as long as there is a "level playing field" and negotiations are fair and honest.

## 1.  Laws Regulating Equity Purchasers

Unfortunately, equity purchasers have been known to prey on homeowners in financial distress (especially the poor, elderly, and financially unsophisticated) by inducing them to sell their homes at a fraction of the fair market value. Because of the potential for abuse, California laws protect homeowners from unethical equity purchasers. The rules strictly regulate equity purchaser activities and

protect unsuspecting property owners in the throes of foreclosure.

The Home Equity Sales Contract Act protects you when selling your home to an equity purchaser. (CC § 1695 and following.) The laws protect you against deceit and misleading representations and prohibits unfair contractual terms. Most important, the laws give you an opportunity to cancel your sales contract within five days if you decide it is a bad deal. (Chapter 12, Section A gives an overview of how to look up the laws yourself.)

## 2.  Special Rules for Equity Purchase Contracts

Let's say you decide to sell to an equity purchaser. He or she must give you a written contract that conforms with numerous technicalities required by law. To be enforceable, the contract must:

- be in writing with letters in at least 10-point bold type (as discussed below, some notices must be in a larger type than the rest of the contract)
- be in the language you primarily used to negotiate the contract. For example, if you speak Spanish, the contract must be in Spanish (even if your deed of trust is in English)
- include the name, business address and telephone number of the equity purchaser
- state the address of your residence in foreclosure
- describe the total amount of money the equity purchaser will pay for your residence and provide a complete description of the terms of payment
- describe the terms of any proposed rental agreement if the equity purchaser is going to lease your residence back to you
- state the date and time at which possession will be transferred to the equity purchaser, and
- be completely filled out, signed and dated by both you and the equity purchaser before execution of the deed of trust conveying title to your property. This prevents an equity purchaser from inserting unreasonable terms in the blank spaces.

Even if you sign a contract with an equity purchaser, you have the right to back out by delivering a signed notice to the buyer. (CC § 1695.4.) Your right to cancel extends to midnight of the fifth business day following the day you signed the contract or 8:00 a.m. on the day scheduled for the foreclosure sale, whichever occurs first. The equity purchase contract must contain the following notice, placed near the space reserved for your signature, in at least 12-point bold type:

"**YOU MAY CANCEL THIS CONTRACT FOR THE SALE OF YOUR HOUSE WITHOUT PENALTY OF OBLIGATION AT ANY TIME BEFORE [DATE AND TIME OF DAY]. SEE THE ATTACHED NOTICE OF CANCELLATION FORM FOR AN EXPLANATION OF THIS RIGHT.**"

The equity purchase contract must be accompanied by a fill-in detachable form in duplicate, captioned "Notice of Cancellation" in a size equal to 10-point type if the contract is printed, or capital letters if the contract is typed. (CC § 1695.5.) A sample follows.

NOTICE OF CANCELLATION

THE CONTRACT WAS SIGNED ON [DATE CONTRACT WAS SIGNED].

YOU MAY CANCEL THIS CONTRACT FOR THE SALE OF YOUR HOUSE, WITHOUT ANY PENALTY OR OBLIGATION, AT ANY TIME BEFORE [DATE THAT IS FIVE (5) BUSINESS DAYS AFTER THE DATE THE CONTRACT WAS SIGNED].

TO CANCEL THIS TRANSACTION, PERSONALLY DELIVER A SIGNED AND DATED COPY OF THIS CANCELLATION NOTICE, OR SEND A TELEGRAM TO [NAME OF EQUITY PURCHASER] AT [ADDRESS] NOT LATER THAN [DATE FIVE BUSINESS DAYS AFTER THE DATE CONTRACT WAS SIGNED].

I HEREBY CANCEL THIS TRANSACTION AS OF _____, 199_.

_____

SELLER'S SIGNATURE

The equity purchaser must also include the following notice in the contract, in at least 14-point boldface type if the contract is printed, or in capital letters if the contract is typed:

**NOTICE REQUIRED BY CALIFORNIA LAW UNTIL YOUR RIGHT TO CANCEL THIS CONTRACT HAS ENDED, [name of equity purchaser] OR ANYONE WORKING FOR HIM/HER CANNOT ASK YOU TO SIGN A DEED OR ANY OTHER DOCUMENT.**

Until five business days have elapsed from the date you signed the contract, the equity purchaser cannot:

- accept a deed or any interest in your property from you
- record any documents, including the contract with the equity purchaser, a deed or any other document of conveyance
- sell or transfer any interest in your property to a third party
- take out a loan against your property, or
- pay you any money.

## 3. If the Equity Purchaser Violates the Law

By law, equity purchasers cannot make any untrue or misleading statements about the value of your residence or how much you'd receive after a foreclosure sale. Likewise, they must be truthful about all of the contract terms, your rights or obligations under the contract, and the purpose of all documents you sign.

If an equity purchaser buys your property and gives you an option to repurchase it, he or she may not place new deeds of trust or liens on your property or transfer title to a third party without your prior written consent.

*Illegal provisions make the equity purchase contract voidable at your option.* An equity purchase contract cannot contain provisions that limit the equity purchaser's liability or require arbitration of any dispute. Equity purchasers will be liable for any damages resulting from these illegal provisions.

You have the right to cancel the transaction within two years if the equity purchaser acted improperly (as described in this chapter). You must give the equity purchaser written notice of the violation and record a Notice of Rescission in the county recorder's office. The equity purchaser then has 20 days in which to deed your property back to you.

If the equity purchaser refuses to cancel the sale after the 20th day, or you subsequently discover that the equity purchaser took unconscionable advantage of you during the foreclosure process, you can file a lawsuit in Superior Court to cancel the contract. If this becomes necessary, find a lawyer to handle the lawsuit.

You may be allowed to recover your actual money damages plus reasonable attorney fees and costs. The court may also award punitive damages if the equity purchaser's conduct was intentional or malicious. In extreme case, an equity purchaser is subject to criminal punishment of a fine of at least $10,000 and imprisonment of up to one year.

## H. Arranging a "Short Sale" With Your Lender

The following section contains an overview of the short sale process. Most likely, your agent will handle the details of the transaction. Nevertheless, it will be helpful for you to understand the short sale and the procedures.

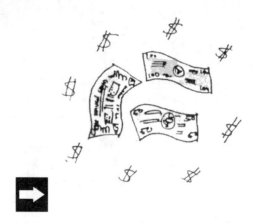

*If you have equity in your property.* A short sale only applies to property owners who don't have equity (or have negative equity) in their property. If you have equity in your property, skip this section.

You may run into a major stumbling block in selling your property if its market value has fallen below the amount you owe your lender. In this case, you have "negative equity"—in other words, you owe your lender more money than your property is worth. If you were to sell your property to avoid foreclosure, you'd have to add money into escrow to close the sale because your lender is entitled to full repayment of the loan. Assuming you can't afford to pay the lender the difference between the selling price and the loan balance, what is your alternative?

One of the best solutions is called a "short sale" or "short payoff." This procedure allows you to sell your property for as much as the market will bear. All of the net proceeds, minus escrow fees and real estate agents' commissions, go to your lender as payment in full. Your lender accepts a discounted payoff and reconveys (cancels) its deed of trust.

*Example: Susan purchased a home in Sacramento several years ago for $200,000 with a loan for $160,000 from Sacramento Thrift and Loan. Susan decided to sell her house to avoid foreclosure and was shocked to discover that the market value of her property had fallen to about $140,000. Sacramento Thrift agreed to a short sale and ultimately accepted $124,000 as payment in full, even though Susan's note still had a balance of approximately $152,000.*

A short sale is relatively straightforward if there aren't any junior lienholders encumbering your property. Unfortunately, things get more complicated when junior liens, tax liens or mechanic's liens encumber property. You have two choices:

- convince all senior and junior lienholders to accept a pro rata (proportionate percentage) share of the sale proceeds, or
- convince the junior lienholders to accept less than a pro rata share or nothing at all.

If the junior lienholder won't cooperate, you won't able to complete a short sale.

## 1. Will Your Lender Agree to a Short Sale?

If you're wondering why on earth your lender would agree to a short sale, consider it from your lender's perspective. If your lender takes back your property in foreclosure, it will absorb huge losses. Foreclosing and remarketing expenses, coupled with the decline in the real estate value, can total as much as 60% of the market value of the property at the time you financed it. Your lender probably won't receive any loan payments during the foreclosure. If a junior lienholder is foreclosing, it may have to bring the senior lienholder current to protect its junior deed of trust from being wiped out if the senior lienholder forecloses.

Many lenders do not readily admit they will agree to a short sale for fear that the practice might become widespread. However, when confronted with the expense of an imminent foreclosure, lenders will often agree to a short sale that will minimize their losses. But lenders rarely pre-approve short sales, so don't bother approaching your lender with hypothetical questions about accepting a short sale. The better approach is to accept an offer from a buyer (subject to your lender's approval), open escrow and then have your real estate agent submit the sale documents to your lender for approval.

## 2. Income Tax Liabilities With a Short Sale

If you go forward with a short sale, you may be liable for income taxes on the amount of your loan you are not paying back. When your lender releases you from debt, it is called "discharge of debt" and is considered taxable income by the IRS. For example, if your loan balance is $100,000, but your lender

accepts $80,000 as a short payoff, your $20,000 discharge of debt income is taxable.

Two IRS exceptions may relieve you of tax liability:

- *Bankruptcy exception.* If you file for bankruptcy, your debt will be relieved. (IRC § 108(a)(1)(A).)
- *Insolvency exception* (or the "balance sheet test"). If your secured and unsecured debt exceeds the value of your assets at the time of the short sale, the discharge of debt income may not be taxable. (IRC § 108(a)(1)(B).)

If you're interested in pursuing these exclusions, contact a CPA or tax consultant for further advice in this specialized area.

## 3. Overview of Short Sale Procedures

There are three steps to completing a short sale with your lender. Your real estate agent can help you with the details.

### a. Select a Listing Agent and Place Your Property on the Market

Follow the general instructions in Section B, above, to find an agent and list your property. Because your lender is not required to accept a short sale, advise potential buyers that any sale is subject to your lender's approval. Your agent should disclose this information in the Multiple Listing Service:

"The sale terms are subject to the consent of the lender. Please contact the listing agent for details."

The goal of a short sale is to price your property low enough that you can sell it before the foreclosure sale, yet high enough that your lender will accept the short payoff. Your real estate agent will help you get your property appraised and approximately priced.

*Have your property appraised.* Unlike a regular sale, most lenders require an appraisal for short sales. You'll either need to obtain a formal appraisal, or at the very least, letters from a minimum of three real estate agents, estimating the market value of your property (broker's price opinions). Your failure to get an appraisal could cause a delay in closing escrow.

## b.  Find a Buyer and Open Escrow

Once you receive an acceptable offer from a potential buyer, you'll need to add language in your counter-offer that protects you in the event your lender will not accept a short payoff:

"Seller advises Buyer of the need to obtain approval from lender to accept less than a full loan payoff to enable a sale to close at the offered price."

If the buyer accepts your counter-offer, your agent should immediately open escrow and include this same language in the escrow instructions.

## c.  Submit Short Sale Documents to Your Lender

As soon as you receive signed escrow instructions, your real estate agent should contact your lender's office and talk with someone who has authority to approve a short sale. Many institutional lenders now have individuals (or separate departments) specializing in short sales. The department may be called the "Short Payoff Department," "Loan Workout Department," "Loss Mitigation Department" or "Asset Management and Recovery Department."

Your agent will submit the following documents to the appropriate department or individual at your lender's office:

- a cover letter from your agent advising the lender of the buyer's offer to purchase your property and the need for a short payoff
- a copy of the listing agreement
- a letter from you authorizing your agent to negotiate on your behalf
- a copy of the signed offer or counter-offer from the buyer
- a copy of the escrow instructions
- a list of comparable sales in your neighborhood supporting the listing price (sometimes these can be found in the appraisal and broker's opinion letter)

- your tax returns from the last two years and bank statements from the last two months
- an estimated closing statement from the escrow officer, calculating the net proceeds to your lender upon close of escrow
- a copy of the escrow instructions, including all of the disclosure forms, and
- a "hardship letter" from you describing the specific circumstances causing the financial problems leading to the foreclosure. You should explain why you can't afford to pay the shortfall and give a sympathetic plea for compassion and help from your lender.

Your agent will need to convince your lender's representative that a short sale will cost the lender less than the costs of foreclosing your property (coupled with the market decline in value and the cost to resell it). If your lender sees a choice of losing upwards of 60% on a foreclosure versus losing only 20% to 30% on a short sale, he will be more inclined to make a common-sense business decision in your favor. To prepare for these discussions, you may find it helpful to break down the foreclosure costs.

*Example: Charles owns a property in Walnut Creek encumbered by a $100,000 loan. If his lender, Walnut Creek Savings, decides to foreclose, it will incur the following costs (calculated as a percentage of the loan):*

| | |
|---|---|
| *Loan balance:* | *100%* |
| *Market decline:* | *-20%* |
| *Foreclosure costs:* | *-05%* |
| *REO discount price:* | *-10%* |
| *Repairs:* | *-05%* |
| *Holding costs:* | *-08%* |
| *Adm & legal costs:* | *-03%* |
| *Sales costs:* | *-07%* |
| *Total:* | *-58%* |
| *NET TO LENDER:* | *<42%>* |

Your lender will probably want to make sure that there is no other viable solution to the problem. You and your real estate agent should emphasize that you have no resources to pay the shortfall and that your property is being sold for its true market value. (For an in-depth discussion of how to negotiate with your lender, see Chapter 5.)

# 11

# GIVING YOUR LENDER A DEED IN LIEU OF CLOSURE

**A**fter a lot of soul searching, you may come to the difficult conclusion that your property is just not worth keeping. It may become painfully obvious that no matter how much the property means to you and your family, you have no equity in it and you can't afford the regular payments. Let's say that other strategies described in this book won't work in your personal situation, but you still want to avoid a foreclosure sale and prevent any further damage to your credit.

Fortunately, there is a solution. You can voluntarily give your property to the foreclosing lender.

This will automatically stop the foreclosure. However, you must first get the lender's permission to do this. If the lender agrees, you will sign a Deed in Lieu of Foreclosure (deed in lieu), a document that transfers the property from you to your lender.

Provided your lender consents, you can give your lender a deed in lieu at any stage in the foreclosure—from the date you first missed a payment until the day of the foreclosure sale. Once your lender accepts the deed in lieu, the trustee must immediately terminate the foreclosure. Your lender will now own the property without completing the lengthy foreclosure process.

## A. Reasons to Use a Deed in Lieu

A deed in lieu may be your best strategy if you believe your property is not worth saving and most of the following match your circumstances:

- you either have no equity, or you have negative equity, in your property
- even if you stop the foreclosure, you cannot afford the scheduled loan payments
- you don't want a foreclosure on your credit report, and
- you've diligently, but unsuccessfully, tried to find a buyer for your property.

*Example: Peter owns a duplex in Santa Monica. The property is in foreclosure and there are approximately 30 days left before the trustee's sale. Peter has no equity in the property, can't afford the monthly payments and hasn't been able to locate a buyer. Under the circumstances, Peter contacts his lender and negotiates a deed in lieu of foreclosure. Once the lender accepts the deed in lieu from Peter, the foreclosure stops.*

You'll derive several benefits by giving your lender a deed in lieu rather than selling your property to a third party:

- *The foreclosure stops immediately.* Whether your lender is pursuing a judicial or nonjudicial foreclosure, it immediately stops once your lender accepts your deed in lieu. Your property will not be sold in a foreclosure sale.
- *You protect your credit rating.* Although missing payments and having foreclosure proceedings commence may damage your credit somewhat (if reported to the credit reporting agencies), a foreclosure sale may effectively ruin your credit for many years. However, a deed in lieu will not appear on your credit report; therefore a foreclosure sale would not appear, which may be crucial to you. You can explain to future creditors that you and your lender resolved the default with no need for a foreclosure sale.
- *Your lender cannot get a deficiency judgment.* If a judicial foreclosure is pending, deeding your property to your lender can give you immunity from any deficiency—the difference between the balance of the loan and the amount the property sells for at a foreclosure sale. (See Chapter 4, Section B11 for more on deficiency judgments.)

## B. Will Your Lender Accept a Deed in Lieu?

Unfortunately, many property owners mistakenly believe they can stop a foreclosure by giving a deed in lieu to the lender without its approval or by recording it in the county recorder's office without the lender's consent. However, neither of these actions has any legal significance. For the deed in lieu to be effective, your lender must willingly accept the deed in lieu and have it recorded in the county recorder's office (We cover the step-by-step procedures in Sections C and D, below.)

### 1. Advantages to Your Lender

A foreclosing lender that accepts a deed in lieu receives immediate title to your property with no additional costs or delays. Your lender's alternative is to pay foreclosure fees to a trustee or legal fees to attorneys, then wait four months (nonjudicial foreclosure) or up to three years (judicial foreclosure), to get the property.

Your lender also avoids the uncertainty of waiting to see if you're going to file a lawsuit to enjoin the trustee's sale, file bankruptcy or use some other strategy to stop the foreclosure.

### 2. Why Your Lender May Refuse a Deed in Lieu

Despite the many advantages of accepting a deed in lieu, your lender may prefer to proceed with a foreclosure. Your lender runs certain risks by accepting a deed in lieu. Here are the most common problems:

- Deeds of trust or liens encumbering your property are unaffected by the deed in lieu. If your lender forecloses, it will take the property subject to any existing senior deeds of trust and liens, which remain on the property. However, any junior deeds of trust and liens will be wiped out by the foreclosure sale. If your lender accepts a deed in lieu, junior deeds of trust and liens will remain on the property. For example, by accepting a deed in lieu, your foreclosing lender will have the obligation to bring junior loans current, resume scheduled payments and pay off lienholders when the loan comes due. Your property will be more difficult to sell because of the continuing obligations to junior lienholders. As a result, most lenders will not accept a deed in lieu unless there are no junior deeds of trust or liens encumbering the property.

- You could later try to set aside the deed in lieu. Although rare, former owners have had second thoughts and sued their lenders to set aside a deed in lieu, based upon theories of lender fraud or coercion. As a consequence, lenders are sometimes hesitant to accept deeds in lieu.

- Your lender may be concerned about inheriting liability if there are serious property problems. A lender may refuse a deed in lieu if your property has substantial physical problems (beyond general disrepair), such as toxic substances in the soil, structural weaknesses, a collapsing foundation, hillside erosion or boundary disputes. If the foreclosing lender voluntarily accepts title to your property, it could become liable for correcting the problems. In contrast, if your lender completes the foreclosure sale and sells the property to a third person, it would not be liable for the property's problems.

*If your lender won't accept a deed in lieu:* Don't panic. Consider selling your property at the best price you can get. (See Chapter 10.) If the proceeds won't cover your outstanding loan, you can approach your lender with a short sale, covered in Chapter 10, Section H.

## 3. HUD Deed in Lieu Program

If your loan is insured by the Federal Housing Administration (FHA), contact the U.S. Department of Housing and Urban Affairs (HUD) and ask about its deed in lieu program. HUD will encourage your lender to accept a deed in lieu if you meet three requirements:

1. You defaulted due to hardship basically beyond your control, such as illness, job loss, divorce or job transfer.

2. It is unlikely that you will be able to bring and keep your loan current.

3. No junior liens encumber your property or you can pay them off within 20 days of the date of your request for a deed in lieu.

If you don't meet the above criteria, HUD will discourage your lender from accepting a deed in lieu, so you'll have to pursue other options. (For general information on negotiating with HUD, see Chapter 5, Section D.)

## 4. Veterans Administration Deed in Lieu Program

If your loan is insured by the U.S. Department of Veteran Affairs (VA), contact the local VA office before delivering a deed in lieu to your lender. The VA must approve your deed in lieu before your lender can accept it.

The VA often gives approval if a deed in lieu will save time and money, and collection of the debt appears doubtful. The VA may require you to submit a financial statement along with a letter explaining why the VA should approve a deed in lieu.

According to the VA's Loan Servicing Guide, the VA will approve a deed in lieu under the following circumstances:

- You cannot afford your loan payments and your financial condition is unlikely to improve.

- You haven't succeeded in selling your property after reasonable exposure on the market.

- There are no junior liens or other deeds of trust on your property.

- The value of your property is the same or less than the balance of your loan.

- You agree in writing to be liable for any monetary loss the VA suffers by terminating the loan prematurely and re-selling your property. (Although this is a serious commitment on your part, in practice the VA rarely if ever chases veterans for the deficiencies. So, it does not appear to be a viable reason for avoiding the VA program.)

If the VA disapproves your deed in lieu, it will instruct your lender to proceed with the foreclosure. (For a general discussion on negotiating with the VA, read Chapter 5, Section E.)

## C. Negotiate Terms of the Deed in Lieu

Because your lender must consent to a deed in lieu, you will need to contact your lender by telephone or letter and request that it accept a deed in lieu rather than proceeding with the foreclosure. Instructions on how to reach and negotiate with the responsible person at your lender's office are in Chapter 5, Section A.

### 1. Issues to Address With Your Lender

If your lender is willing to accept a deed in lieu, negotiate the following issues together:

- *Will your lender cancel the note and deed of trust?* Your lender should sign the reconveyance (cancellation) on the back of your deed of trust and give it to you. Although technically unnecessary, it is a better policy to have your lender agree to return both your promissory note and the reconveyed deed of trust in exchange for your deed in lieu.

- *How will you deliver the deed?* Determine exactly who is authorized to accept the deed in lieu, and where. Typically, you simply hand your lender's representative the keys to your property along with a signed deed in lieu.

- *When will your lender take possession?* If you live on the property, your lender will probably allow you remain there for several months. Be sure to settle in advance the exact date you will voluntarily move out. As a condition of your continuing occupancy, agree to keep the property in good condition, to cooperate with potential buyers that want to inspect the property and to move out on the promised date. Typically, you won't have to pay for insurance, property taxes or rent during this occupancy period. If you don't live on the property, have your lender confirm in writing that it will assume responsibility for the tenant(s) leasing the property and that you will have no further responsibilities.

- *Will your lender correct your credit report?* Your lender should agree to promptly contact the three credit reporting agencies (Experian [formerly TRW], Transunion, and Equifax) and request that they remove from your credit report all references to foreclosure, including the Notice of Default and Notice of Sale.

- *Will your lender waive a deficiency judgment?* If a judicial foreclosure is pending, you are potentially liable for a deficiency judgment. Ask your lender to agree in writing to relieve you of all financial responsibility under your note and deed of trust, including back payments, attorney fees and foreclosure costs.

### 2. Get Agreement in Writing

Because the foreclosure clock is ticking, it is important to get your lender's written consent to a deed in lieu. Write a letter to your lender confirming that your lender agrees to accept a deed in lieu. Leave room at the bottom of the letter for your lender to indicate acceptance. A sample letter appears below.

October 23, 199X

Ms. Darlene Smith
Bundy Savings Bank
2323 State Street
Merced, CA

Re: Loan 65454, Secured by Property at
    27 Green Avenue, Stockton, CA

Dear Ms. Smith:

Your bank holds the first deed of trust securing a promissory note in the amount of $205,000 on the property listed above. On July 10, 199X, you started foreclosure proceedings by recording a Notice of Default in the county recorder's office. On October 12, 199X, you recorded a Notice of Trustee's Sale in the county recorder's office.

This letter confirms that I have agreed to sign, and you have agreed to accept, a deed in lieu of foreclosure on my property. You have also agreed to:

1.  Draft a deed in lieu of foreclosure and have it ready for me to sign no later than Friday, October 27, 199X.

2.  Advise the trustee to stop the foreclosure as soon as I sign the deed in lieu and deliver it to you.

3.  Promptly inform Experian, Transunion and Equifax to remove any reference to foreclosure on my credit reports.

4.  Permit me to occupy the property through January 15, 199X without paying rent, insurance or property taxes.

If this letter accurately reflects our agreement, please sign your name on the space provided below and return a copy to me.

Thank you for your anticipated cooperation in this matter.

Very truly yours,

Susan Temple
27 Green Avenue
Stockton, CA
209-555-2345

AGREED AND ACCEPTED TO:

By: _____

Authorized Officer
Bundy Savings Bank

## D. How to Prepare a Deed in Lieu of Foreclosure

After you negotiate the terms of the deed in lieu, your lender will probably prepare a deed in lieu for you to sign. If your lender does not have a blank deed in lieu, or you want to expedite the process, you can use the Deed in Lieu of Foreclosure form provided below and in the Appendix.

*A quitclaim deed may also be used.* Your lender may use a quitclaim deed, rather than a deed in lieu, to accomplish the same thing. If your lender uses a quitclaim deed, make sure the words "Deed in Lieu of Foreclosure" are printed or typed across the top of the form, above the words "Quitclaim Deed."

### 1. How to Fill in a Deed in Lieu

The following instructions are keyed to the sample Deed in Lieu of Foreclosure below. Preparing a deed in lieu isn't difficult, but pay attention to the details. One careless mistake could invalidate the whole document. If at all possible, you should type the information on the form.

## DEED IN LIEU OF FORECLOSURE

Recording requested by

❶

and when recorded mail
this deed and tax statement to:

❷

1. This transfer is exempt from the documentary transfer tax. ❸

2. This property is located in _____

    ☐ a. an unincorporated area

    ☐ b. the city of _____ ❹

3. For valuable consideration, receipt of which is hereby acknowledged, _____ ❺
hereby deeds to _____ ❻
      _____ , ❼

    in lieu of foreclosure, the following real property in the City of _____ ,
County of _____ , State of California: ❽
commonly known as _____

Date: _____

Date: _____

Date: _____

Date: _____

         ❾

ACKNOWLEDGMENT

State of _____ )

County of _____ )

On _____ , 19 ___ , before me, _____ , a notary public,
personally appeared_____ , personally known to me
or proved to me on the basis of satisfactory evidence to be the person(s) whose name is/are subscribed to this
instrument, and acknowledged to me that he/she/they executed the same in his/her/their authorized
capacity(ies) and that by his/her/their signature(s) on the instrument, the person(s) or the entity upon behalf of
which the person(s) acted, executed the instrument.

[NOTARY SEAL]    Signature of Notary Public

      ❶

### ❶ Recording information

Fill in your lender's correct name and address in the space below "Recording requested by." If you are not sure of the lender's exact legal name and address, contact your lender or the trustee before you fill in this information.

### ❷ Tax statements

Property tax statements should be mailed to the new owner, which is your foreclosing lender. Again, enter your lender's full legal name and correct address.

### ❸ Documentary transfer tax information

Local documentary transfer taxes are levied when real property is sold and a deed is recorded. In your case, however, the transfer should not be subject to this tax because you're deeding the property back to your lender, not selling it. You don't need to add anything.

### ❹ Location of the Property

Your property is located either in a city or an unincorporated area. Check the appropriate box and give the name of the city, if applicable.

### ❺ Identification of owners (grantors)

Here you fill in your name, along with the names of all owners of the property (who must sign the deed in lieu at the bottom). Use the full legal name for each owner, as listed in the original deed. Here are some guidelines:

- If you are single: It's a good idea to add the words "an unmarried person" after the name to show that a spouse wasn't mistakenly omitted. For example, "John Wong, an unmarried person."
- If any of the property owners are married: If both spouses are owners, list both of their names, followed by "husband and wife"—for example, "Adam Hart and Felicia Hart, husband and wife." If only one spouse owns the property, list the owner's name, followed by the words, "a married person, as his or her sole and separate property."

- If you hold title to the property as a business (other than a sole proprietorship): Specify the business entity after its name—"a corporation," "a partnership" or "a limited liability company." and the state it was formed. For example, "Sea-n-Shore, a California general partnership."
- If there are two or more owners: After you list all owners' names, designate how the owners hold title, such as "tenants in common," "joint tenants," or "husband and wife." If you aren't sure, look at the original deed for this information. For example, "Donald Martinez and Sonya Thomas, joint tenants."

### ❻ Words of transfer

Note that there are magical words that legally transfer your property to your lender: "hereby deeds to [name] in lieu of foreclosure." (The phrase "hereby quitclaims to" will also do the job.) This phrase establishes your intent to convey your property to your lender. Don't change the wording of this phrase; any changes could invalidate the deed in lieu.

### ❼ Identification of the new owner (grantee)

The deed in lieu must clearly identify the name of your foreclosing lender. Again, fill in your lender's exact legal name.

### ❽ Physical description of your property

The deed in lieu must identify the property being transferred. Start by filling in the city (cross out "city of" if the property is not within the city limits) and the county in which your property is located.

Next, you'll need to fill in the legal description, which includes some pretty strange-sounding terms. The easiest way is to copy the legal description from your old deed. If you can't find your old deed, you should be able to get a copy from your escrow company, a local title insurance company or your lender. Or you can visit the county recorder's office in the county where your property is located to obtain a copy.

*Don't make any typographical errors.* Double-check what you've filled in by having someone read the legal description from your old deed out loud while you follow along reading the deed in lieu you've prepared.

Although not required, it is helpful to fill in the street address of your property after the words "commonly known as." For example, "2345 State Street, Stockton, California."

### ❾ Date, signature and acknowledgment

All owners must sign the deed in lieu in the presence of a notary public. A notary simply confirms that each signature is genuine and that you signed the document in his or her presence. If you don't know a notary, contact your lender; most lenders have notaries in their offices. Everyone signing should bring a valid picture ID, such as a driver's license or passport.

Enter the date that you are signing the deed in lieu. The deed in lieu is effective from the date of delivery, which is presumed to be the date of execution (signing).

All owners (grantors) of the property, and their spouses (even if not on the deed) must sign the deed in lieu for it to be valid. Each person must sign his or her name exactly as it is listed earlier in the deed in lieu.

## 2. Deliver the Deed in Lieu to Your Lender

Make a copy of the signed and notarized deed in lieu for your records and deliver the original document to your lender. Ask for a signed receipt for the deed in lieu. Remember, your lender must accept the deed in lieu for it to be effective. Request that the lender advise the trustee to stop the foreclosure. You should also telephone the trustee the next day and confirm that the foreclosure has been canceled.

## 3. Get the Canceled Promissory Note and Reconveyed Deed of Trust

In exchange for delivering the deed in lieu, your lender should return to you your original promissory note and deed of trust. Again, ask for a signed receipt from your lender.

## 4. Make Sure the Deed in Lieu Is Recorded

Once your lender receives your deed in lieu, it should record it in the county recorder's office. Although it is entirely okay to just deliver the deed without recording it, recordation will make the transfer of title official and give public notice that you have given up all rights, title and interest to your property. We suggest you follow up with your lender in a couple days to confirm that the deed in lieu was recorded and to request a copy for your records.

# 12

# HELP BEYOND THIS BOOK

**T**his book describes judicial and nonjudicial foreclosures and various strategies for stopping foreclosure, but it doesn't cover everything. At some point you may need more information or assistance this book doesn't provide. You may need to turn to:

- a real estate lawyer who can provide legal information, advice or legal representation. (See Section A3.)
- a foreclosure consultant, who can assist in negotiating with your lender or refinancing your property. (See Section B), or
- the law library, an excellent source for additional information on any particular issue raised in the course of your foreclosure. (See Section C.)

## A. Real Estate Lawyers

Throughout this book, we've suggested that you see an attorney if you find yourself in a complex or difficult situation. While very few lawyers specialize in foreclosure, most real estate attorneys have a working knowledge of foreclosure and can be more helpful than a general practitioner. Here are some of the things a real estate lawyer can do for you:

- negotiate with your lender
- help you assess your financial situation, especially in the context of filing for bankruptcy (You will want to hire an attorney who specializes in bankruptcy if you decide to file.)
- prepare papers for filing a lawsuit in court to enjoin (stop) a foreclosure
- represent you in court
- coach you on how to prepare legal papers
- coach you on appearing in court, and

- answer your legal questions.

Real estate lawyers generally charge about $150 to $300 per hour depending on geographical regions and the lawyer's experience. Real estate attorneys tend to charge more than general practitioners because of their specialized knowledge.

## 1. How to Find a Real Estate Lawyer

There are several ways to find a real estate lawyer suited to your particular situation:

- *Personal referrals:* This is your best approach. If you know someone who was pleased with the services of a real estate lawyer, call that lawyer first. If he or she doesn't handle foreclosure matters, ask for a recommendation of someone else who's experienced and competent.
- *Telephone directory* (yellow pages): Most telephone directories have a separate listing for real estate attorneys. In addition, many attorneys advertise free consultations in which they will answer questions and help you determine whether they can help you.
- *Legal clinic:* Many law schools sponsor legal clinics and provide free legal advice to consumers. Some legal clinics offer free services to low- to moderate-income people while others limit their programs to very-low-income people. Make sure that the legal clinic has experienced real estate attorneys available to help you.
- *Group legal plans:* Some unions, employers and consumer action organizations offer group plans to their members or employees, who can obtain comprehensive legal assistance free or for low rates. If you're a member of such a plan, check with it first to see if they have lawyers on their panel who are experienced with real estate matters.

- *Pre-paid legal insurance:* Pre-paid "legal insurance" plans offer some services for a low monthly fee and charge more for additional or different work. That means that participating lawyers may use the plan as a way to get clients, who are attracted by the low-cost basic services, and then sell them more expensive services. If you're considering joining such a plan to get the help you need, make sure the plan has real estate attorneys available and find out if it costs extra to consult with a real estate attorney. If the plan offers extensive free advice with an experienced real estate attorney, your initial membership fee may be worth the consultation you receive, even if you use it only once. You can always join a plan for a specific service and then not renew.

Note that there's no guarantee that the real estate lawyers available through these plans are of the best caliber; sometimes they aren't. As with any consumer transaction, check it out carefully before signing up. Ask about the plan's complaint system, whether you get to choose your lawyer and whether or not the lawyer will represent you in court.
- *Chain discount law firms:* Firms such as Hyatt Legal Services or Jacoby & Meyers routinely offer legal advice on real estate matters. You can call and ask about their basic fees, and probably get an initial consultation for about $50 to $150.
- *Lawyer referral panels:* Most county bar associations will give you the names of real estate attorneys who practice in your area. But bar associations usually provide only minimal screening for the attorneys listed, which means those who participate may not be the most experienced or competent. You may find a skilled real estate attorney willing to work for a reasonable fee this way, but take the time to check out the credentials and foreclosure experience of the person to whom you're referred.

---

**LEGAL ADVICE OVER THE TELEPHONE**

If you are seeking legal advice on foreclosure, you may want to consult Tele-Lawyer, a company that offers legal advice over the phone. You can talk to a lawyer who specializes in real estate for about $3 a minute. The average call lasts about 14 minutes and costs about $42.

If the lawyer can't answer your foreclosure question, he or she may be willing to research it—for free—and get back to you. But most questions can be answered immediately because Tele-Lawyer provides its lawyers with a large computer database designed to help them answer common questions quickly.

You can reach Tele-Lawyer at:

800-835-3529 (charge to Visa or MasterCard)

900-654-3000 (charge appears on your phone bill)

---

## 2. What to Look for in a Real Estate Lawyer

Once you have the names of a few real estate lawyers, do some screening before you commit yourself to hiring one. It's important that you be as comfortable as possible with any lawyer you hire. When making an appointment, ask to talk directly to the lawyer. If you can't, this may give you your first hint as to how accessible the lawyer will be later. If you're told that a paralegal will be handling the routine aspects of your case under the supervision of a lawyer, you may be satisfied with that arrangement.

If you do talk directly to a prospective lawyer, ask some specific questions about foreclosure. Do you get clear, concise answers? If not, try someone else. If the lawyer says little except to suggest that he or she can handle the problem (for a substantial fee, of course), watch out. You're talking with someone who doesn't know the answer and won't admit it (common), or someone who pulls rank on the basis of professional standing.

Once you find a real estate lawyer you like, make an hour-long appointment to discuss your situation fully. Most attorneys will not charge for this initial consultation. Your goal at the initial conference is to find out what the lawyer recommends and how much it will cost. Go home and think about the lawyer's suggestions. If they don't make complete sense or you have reservations, call someone else.

## 3. Hiring a Real Estate Lawyer as a Legal Coach

If it does not make economic sense for you to turn your case over to an attorney to fight your foreclosure, you may still want to hire one on an hourly basis as a "legal coach," to give you occasional advice.

Attorneys have traditionally either assumed overall responsibility for a client's case or declined representation. However, due to a combination of economics, time demands of modern law practice and increased competition from foreclosure consultants, paralegals (trained attorney assistants), accountants and other professionals, you may be able to locate a real estate lawyer who is willing to act as your legal coach.

Your legal coach may do legal research if you need it, suggest techniques to resolve problems as they arise, clarify a confusing law, inform you of time deadlines or suggest ways to make your arguments more persuasive. He or she will not, however, take over your case unless you specifically agree that that's what you want.

As you go through the foreclosure process and the different options available to stop the foreclosure, there are many opportunities to consult with a legal coach. But don't consult a coach until you read through all relevant sections of this book. You may find that this book addresses questions you would normally pay a lawyer to answer or points you in a direction to easily find the answers on your own.

## B. Using a Foreclosure Consultant

During foreclosure (either judicial or nonjudicial), you may be contacted by someone claiming to be a "foreclosure consultant." A foreclosure consultant is an individual who, for a fee, offers to help you stop the foreclosure.

Some of the services a foreclosure consultant may offer include:

- counseling you on your debt situation
- negotiating with your lender
- arranging for an extension of the period in which you must cure the default or reinstate the loan
- arranging to extend or postpone the trustee's sale
- providing you general advice while you are in foreclosure
- helping you obtain refinancing of your property
- finding an attorney to handle a lawsuit against your lender, and
- assisting in filing bankruptcy.

By law, a foreclosure consultant must have a current California real estate brokers license, and be bonded in an amount equal to at least twice the fair market value of your property (CC § 2945.11). If you are approached by a foreclosure consultant, you should ask to see his license and bond before proceeding any further.

A good foreclosure consultant can provide a valuable service when you appear doomed to lose your property in foreclosure. On the other hand, unscrupulous consultants can be a dangerous waste of precious time, cost you money you don't have and further disrupt your already damaged relationship with your lender.

Unfortunately, some dishonest consultants have been known to use illegal schemes and other unreasonable commercial practices to improperly obtain money or place liens on property. Property owners in financial distress (especially the poor, elderly, and financially unsophisticated) are vulnerable to foreclosure consultants who induce them to pay large sums of money to avoid foreclosure. The purpose of this section is to help you distinguish between honest consultants and crooked ones.

---

### WHO IS NOT A FORECLOSURE CONSULTANT

Of course, not everyone who approaches you is a foreclosure consultant or covered by laws regulating foreclosure consultants. The following are not considered foreclosure consultants:

- lawyers rendering advice in the course of their practice
- licensed check sellers or cashiers
- licensed real estate brokers or sales people who make direct loans, or sell your residence in foreclosure without claiming any interest in the property
- licensed accountants acting in that capacity
- people acting under the express authority of the Department of Housing and Urban Development or other department of the United States of America or State of California
- people who are owed an obligation secured by a deed of trust encumbering a residence
- personal property brokers, commercial finance lenders or anyone else licensed to make loans, and
- any person or entity doing business as a bank, savings bank, trust company, savings and loan association, credit union, insurance company, title company or escrow company.
(CC § 2945.1)

---

### 1. California Foreclosure Consultant Act

A series of laws, designed to protect unsuspecting property owners, regulate foreclosure consultants' business conduct. A consultant is expected to negotiate with your lender, but he cannot legally:

- demand, charge or collect any fee or compensation from you until after the consultant performs every service he contracted to perform
- charge a fee which exceeds 10% per year of the amount of any loan he makes or obtains for you

- take any wage assignment, any type of lien on your property (such as a deed of trust) or any other type of security for payment
- receive any compensation from a third party without first disclosing it in writing to you
- acquire any ownership interest in your property which is in foreclosure
- take a power of attorney, except to inspect documents on your behalf, or
- induce you to enter into any contract that does not comply with or waives any of the above requirements. (CC § 2945.4)

If the foreclosure consultant fails to comply with any of these requirements, you can and should immediately fire the consultant.

## 2. Foreclosure Consultant Must Provide Written Contract

Before a foreclosure consultant can perform any service for you, she must give you a written contract. If your contract doesn't meet the letter of the law, you don't have to sign it.

In the past, some consultants have attempted to circumvent these restrictions by including a waiver of conditions in the contract. However, take heart in knowing that such a waiver in a consultant contract is considered void and unenforceable. (CC § 2945.5.) Any provision in the contract that attempts to limit the liability of the consultant's representatives or employees is also void. (CC § 2945.10(a).)

---

**CONTRACT REQUIREMENTS**

Under California Civil Code Section 2945, a foreclosure consultant's contract must:

- contain the name and address of the foreclosure consultant
- fully disclose the exact nature of the services to be provided by the consultant
- fully disclose the total amount of compensation to be paid, and when it is to be paid
- be dated and signed by you (The date you signed the contract must be on the first page of the contract and in the same size type as generally used in the contract)
- include a notice advising you of your right to cancel in a conspicuous location, in a size equal to at least 10-point boldface type
- include the following notice in at least 14-point boldface type:

## NOTICE REQUIRED BY CALIFORNIA LAW.

_____

**[name] or anyone working for him or her CANNOT:**
**(1) Take any money from you or ask you for money until** _____
**[name] has completely finished doing everything he or she said he or she would do; and**
**(2) Ask you to sign or have you sign any lien, deed of trust, or deed.**

---

### RECEIVING THE NOTICE OF CANCELLATION

The contract must be accompanied by a separate form entitled Notice of Cancellation, which must be easily detachable and contain in at least 10-point type the following language:

#### NOTICE OF CANCELLATION

To cancel this transaction, mail or deliver a signed and dated copy of this cancellation notice, or any other written notice, or send a telegram to

_____
[NAME OF FORECLOSURE CONSULTANT]

at _____
[ADDRESS]

NOT LATER THAN MIDNIGHT OF

_____.
[DATE]

I hereby cancel this transaction

_____.
[DATE]

_____
Owner's signature

---

#### a. How to Cancel a Contract

Once you sign a contract with a foreclosure consultant, you have three days in which to cancel the contract (midnight of the third business day after signing). (CC § 2945.2(a).)

The cancellation must be in writing, but it need not be in a particular form. For example, you could simply write a one-sentence letter advising the consultant that you were canceling the contract. Although not required to do so, you should mail a copy of your cancellation notice by certified mail, return receipt requested. Remember to keep a copy for your records.

#### b. How to Terminate a Contract

If you believe that a foreclosure consultant has violated any of the restrictions required by law, you have the right to immediately terminate the contract. You may also file a lawsuit against the con-

sultant for all damages resulting from any statement made or act committed during the services he performed on your behalf, along with attorney fees.

If the consultant's conduct is found to be intentional or malicious, you can also recover punitive damages up to three times the compensation received by the consultant. (CC § 2945.6(a).) A consultant who is found to have violated these restrictions also may be punished by a fine of not more than $10,000 and imprisonment of not more than one year. (CC § 2945.7).)

## C. The Law Library and Legal Research

Often, you can handle a problem yourself if you're willing to do some research in a law library. The trick is to know what kinds of information you can find there. Sometimes, what you need to know isn't written down. For instance, if you want to know whether you can successfully sell or refinance your property before the foreclosure sale, you can't find out by going to the law library. You'll probably have to talk to a real estate agent or mortgage broker.

Here, briefly, are the basic steps of researching legal questions.

### 1. Find a Law Library That's Open to the Public

Public law libraries are often found in county courthouses, public law schools and state capitals. If you can't find one, ask a public library reference librarian, court clerk or lawyer, or look in the yellow pages of your telephone book.

### 2. Use a Good Legal Research Resource

To find the answer to a legal question, or look up a statute or case, you need some guidance in basic legal research techniques. Any of the following resources that may be available in your law library will tell you how to do legal research:

- *Legal Research: How to Find and Understand the Law*, by Stephen Elias and Susan Levinkind (Nolo Press, see order information at the back of the book)
- *Legal Research Made Easy: A Roadmap Through the Law Library Maze*, by Nolo Press and Robert Berring (Nolo Press/Legal Star Video, see order information at the back of the book)
- *How to Find the Law*, by Morris Cohen, Robert Berring and Kent Olson (West Publishing)
- *The Legal Research Manual: A Game Plan for Legal Research and Analysis*, by Christopher and Jill Wren (A-R Editions), or
- *Introduction to Legal Research: A Layperson's Guide to Finding the Law*, by Al Coco (West Publishing).

To find legal resources online, get a copy of *Law on the Net* by James Evans (Nolo Press).

## 3. Use Other Background Resources

For general discussions of foreclosure issues, there are several other good real estate books, in order of priority:

- *Current Law of California Real Estate* (2nd ed.) by Harvey D. Miller and Marvin B. Starr, is the most famous and comprehensive treatise on real estate law. It has separate sections on judicial and nonjudicial foreclosures.
- *Real Estate Law in California*, by Bowman and Milligan (Prentice-Hall, 8th ed.) is a useful and readable book that contains extensive discussions on judicial and nonjudicial foreclosure.
- *California Real Estate Law and Practice*, by Don Augustine and Stanton H. Zarrow (Matthew Bender), is a multi-volume reference work, with a separate section on foreclosure.
- *California Jurisprudence* (usually abbreviated as *Cal Jur*) is a legal encyclopedia for California (West Publishing) and contains a separate section on foreclosure.
- *Summary of California Law* (9th ed.) by Bernard Witkin is the leading authority on California

law. There is an abbreviated section on real estate law and a brief discussion on foreclosure.

## 4. Find and Read Relevant Statutes

After consulting a background resource, you may need to read a particular statute for yourself. In California, the statutes are called "codes" and are contained in a series of books. Two companies publish the California Codes:

- West's Annotated California Codes (West Publishing), or
- Deering's Annotated California Codes (Deering Publishing).

The relevant statutes for judicial foreclosure can be found in:

- Sections 2889, 2903-2905, 2911, 2931 of the Civil Code, and
- Sections 337, 360, 379, 389, 392, 580, 680, 701, 716, 725, 726, 728, 729, 744 of the Code of Civil Procedure.

The relevant statutes for nonjudicial foreclosure are centrally located in Section 2924 of the Civil Code.

---

**OBTAINING STATUTES FROM THE INTERNET**

These and other California statutes may be obtained online at the following Web site: http://www.leginfo.ca.gov/. Even if you download the statutes, however, you will ultimately want to take your research to a law library to avail yourself of the many tools that are available there and not on the Web, including the annotations that follow each statute in the hardcover annotated codes described below.

---

After you read the statute in the hardcover portion of the book, turn to the very back of the book. There should be an insert pamphlet (called a pocket part) for the current year that contains amendments since the hardcover volume was published. Look to see if the statute is in the pocket part as well.

When you first read a statute, you'll probably be totally confused, if not in tears. Relax. No one understands these statutes as they're written. You can go to the pages that follow the statute and read its interpretation, or go directly to cases (court opinions) that have interpreted the statute.

## 5.  Find and Read Relevant Cases

To fully understand the statutes, it's usually necessary to read one or more cases (court decisions) that have dealt with how the particular statute applies to situations like yours.

These decisions can be found in the following:

* *California Reports* (Bancroft-Whitney) contain Supreme Court cases only.
* *Appellate Reports* (Bancroft-Whitney) covers Appellate Court cases only, and
* *California Reporter* (West Publishing) covers both Supreme Court and Appellate Court cases.

---

### FINDING CASES ON THE INTERNET

California cases decided during the past several are available on the World Wide Web. However, to fully research case authority on your issue, you will also have to visit a law library and use the cases and updating tools that are collected there but not available online.

Once you find a relevant case or two, you can also find similar cases by using cross-reference tools known as digests and Shepards. These are explained in *Legal Research: How to Find and Understand the Law*, by Stephen Elias and Susan Levinkind (Nolo Press) and other legal research texts.

# GLOSSARY

**Acceleration.** A clause in your promissory note that allows your lender to demand the immediate payment of the balance of your loan (rather than date your note is due) because you defaulted on your promissory note or deed of trust.

**Accounting.** A cause of action in a lawsuit in which you request that the court order a certified public accountant to audit your lender's books and records to determine the correct amount you owe your lender.

**Amortization.** Repayment of a promissory note over regular time intervals (such as monthly, quarterly, or annually) with equal payments of principal and interest so that at the end of the term of your loan, your debt will have been paid in full.

**Anti-deficiency laws.** State statutes providing that you are not liable to your lender for the shortage between the proceeds received at the foreclosure sale and the balance due on your loan. California is in the minority of states with anti-deficiency laws. In anti-deficiency states, if your lender conducts a nonjudicial foreclosure, you are not liable for the deficiency.

**Arrearage.** The past due balance on your promissory note, including interest, principal, late charges and attorney fees.

**Assignment.** Where a party to a contract transfers his/her rights and obligations under the contract to a third party.

**Assumption.** A clause in a deed of trust that requires the new owner of the property to become personally liable to the lender for the loan's repayment.

**Auction.** The final step in a foreclosure in which your property is sold at a public sale to the highest bidder. The person conducting the auction is called an "auctioneer."

**Automatic stay.** Immediately upon the filing of a bankruptcy petition in bankruptcy court, a federal injunction automatically arises which stops (stays) all debt collection actions, including foreclosure.

**Balloon payment.** The final lump-sum payment of principal due at the end of the term of a promissory note.

**Bankruptcy.** A proceeding authorized by federal law and carried out in the federal bankruptcy courts, which provide debtors with various kinds of relief from their debts.

**Beneficiary.** The individual (or company) named in a deed of trust that lends you money and is entitled to receive the payments. The deed of trust acts as written security that you will repay the promissory note. If the beneficiary (lender) is not repaid, it has the right to file foreclosure.

**Bid.** During the auction sale, offers received by potential purchasers to pay a designated price for your property which is communicated orally to the auctioneer. Bids usually must be backed up with cash (bids on credit are allowed only by the foreclosing lender).

**Bona fide purchaser for value ("BFP").** A purchaser of property who pays for it without notice of any suspicious circumstances that there may be something wrong with title to the property or the sales transaction.

**Bond.** A certificate issued by a bonding company for a specific amount of money at the beginning of a lawsuit to guarantee that the successful party will be compensated for losses resulting from the lawsuit if the bonding party eventually loses the lawsuit.

**Borrower.** The person or entity that borrows money.

**Collateral.** Real or personal property pledged as security for repayment of a loan.

**Complaint.** The initial document filed in the Superior Court (California) and served on the opposing party, which commences a lawsuit. The Complaint consists of a series of allegations ("causes of action") describing how the actions of the defendant(s) have damaged the plaintiff(s) (the party bringing the lawsuit).

**Conforming loan.** A loan that meets FNMA standards and guidelines. A lender can more readily sell a conforming loan.

**Conventional loans.** A real estate loan, usually from a bank or savings and loan association, not insured by the Federal Housing Agency or guaranteed by the Veterans Administration.

**Conveyance.** Transferring title of real property from one person to another by deed.

**Damages.** Monetary compensation recovered in Court by any person who has suffered a loss or injury because of the unlawful acts or negligence of another.

**Debtor.** In the context of bankruptcy, the individual, partnership, corporation or limited liability company that files bankruptcy.

**Debtor-in-possession.** In a Chapter 11 or 13 bankruptcy case, the Debtor remains in control of his/her assets during the pendency of the bankruptcy as opposed to a trustee taking control of assets.

**Declaratory relief.** A cause of action in a lawsuit in which the plaintiff(s) requests that the court determine the respective legal rights of the plaintiff(s) and defendant(s) with respect to a specific dispute.

**Deed.** A document in which ownership of real property is conveyed from one party to another.

**Deed in Lieu of Foreclosure.** A deed in which you convey your property to your lender instead of (in lieu of) your lender continuing the foreclosure.

**Deed of trust.** A three-party document in which you (as the trustor) pledge your property to a trustee as security for repayment of the promissory note to your lender (as the beneficiary).

**Default.** Your failure to comply with any of the terms and conditions of your promissory note and/or deed of trust.

**Defendant.** The party against whom a lawsuit has been filed.

**Deficiency.** The shortage between the balance of your unpaid loan and the proceeds received by your lender from the foreclosure sale.

**Deficiency judgment.** A judgment entered by a court against you for the shortage between the balance of your unpaid loan and the proceeds received by your lender from the foreclosure sale, or the fair market value of your property, whichever is greater.

**Due-on-sale clause.** A clause in your deed of trust which allows your lender to demand immediate payment of your entire loan upon sale of your property. This clause allows lenders to prevent subsequent purchasers from taking over the existing loan at lower than current market interest rates.

**Election of remedies.** California allows your lender to conduct a judicial and nonjudicial foreclosure simultaneously. However, your lender is required to eventually choose (elect) between a sheriff's sale (judicial foreclosure) or conducting a trustee's sale (nonjudicial foreclosure) itself.

**Encumbrance.** A lien recorded against real property, such as a deed of trust, mortgage, or judgment lien. Because it is a financial obligation, a lien is said to "burden" or "encumber" the property. If you sell or refinance your property, you will have to pay off the encumbrance.

**Equity.** The value of your property after deducting any outstanding liens and encumbrances.

**Equity of redemption.** Your right to save your property from foreclosure by paying off the entire debt, including interest and costs.

**Equity purchaser.** A person who offers to purchase your property in foreclosure by paying a nominal fee for your equity.

**Escrow.** A neutral third party responsible for processing the documents and monies in a real estate sales transaction.

**Estate.** In a bankruptcy context, the term used to describe the assets and liabilities of the debtor.

**Eviction.** The legal procedure to have a tenant removed from a property because the tenant has breached the lease, also known as an unlawful detainer lawsuit.

**Fair market value.** The price that a property would sell for in an open market between a willing buyer and a willing seller in an arms-length transaction. In a judicial foreclosure, a determination by the court as to the value of your property as of the date of the foreclosure sale.

**Forbearance.** The agreement by your lender to voluntarily refrain from foreclosing your property so that you may have more time to repay your loan. (Also known as a "standstill" or "workout" agreement.)

**Foreclosure.** The procedure in which your property is sold at a public auction to pay off your defaulted loan. There are two types of foreclosure in California, judicial and nonjudicial.

**Foreclosure consultant.** An individual who assists you while in foreclosure by negotiating with your lender and/or obtaining a refinance of the loan. Foreclosure consultants are regulated by law.

**Guarantor.** A person who becomes secondarily liable for another's debt.

**Impounds.** Additional payments collected by your lender (over and above your monthly payments of principal and interest), which are held by your lender and then used to make semi-annual payments for insurance and taxes on your property.

**Interest.** The cost of borrowing money from your lender. The interest rate is described in your promissory note as a yearly percentage of the loan.

**Irreparable injury.** Injury to you or your property that cannot be reasonably recovered in monetary damages, and which therefore must be received in some other form, such as an injunction.

**Joint tenancy.** A description of parties owning real property together, such as a husband and wife. Upon the death of either joint tenant, the deceased tenant's ownership interest is automatically transferred to the surviving tenant.

**Judgment.** A final decision by a court resolving the dispute between the plaintiff(s) and defendant(s) in a lawsuit and determining the rights and obligations of the parties.

**Judicial foreclosure.** The forced sale of real property, handled through a court proceeding.

**Junior.** A deed of trust recorded in the county recorder's office after a prior recorded deed of trust (called a "senior").

**Jurisdiction.** The authority of the court to decide a lawsuit with control over the property and the parties. In a foreclosure context, the superior court in the county in which the property is located has jurisdiction over the lawsuit.

**Lease.** An agreement between the owner of the property (called "landlord" or "lessor") and the person taking possession of the property (called "tenant" or "lessee") for a specific period of time (months or years) and in exchange for paying a specified amount of money ("rent").

**Lender.** The individual or entity that loans you money.

**Levy.** A seizure of real property by the sheriff or marshal for the purpose of conducting a foreclosure sale.

**Lien.** A document recorded against your property in the county recorder's office indicating that your property is security for the repayment of a debt or obligation. Liens are either voluntary (such as deeds of trust or mortgages) or involuntary (such as mechanic's liens, tax liens or judgment liens).

**Lienholder.** The person or entity holding a lien recorded against your property. A lienholder is "senior" if it is the first lien recorded against your property. All other lienholders subsequently recorded against your property are said to be "junior" lienholders.

**Liquidation.** The process in a Chapter 7 bankruptcy in which the trustee sells the non-exempt assets of the debtor to pay off creditors.

**Lis Pendens.** The latin phrase for "Notice of Pending Action," which is a document recorded in the county recorder's office warning that a lawsuit has been filed in the county courthouse involving title and/or possession to a particular property.

**Listing agreement.** Written agreement between a property owner and a real estate agent to sell the property at a certain price and terms in return for a commission.

**Mechanic's lien.** A lien recorded in the county recorder's office against your property by a contractor or sub-contractor when you fail to pay their bill for work done in connection with your property.

**Mortgage.** A two-party security document in which the property owner (mortgagor) pledge real property as security for repayment of the loan to the lender (mortgagee).

**Mortgagee.** The lender who receives the mortgage as security for repayment of the debt.

**Mortgagor.** The property owner who pledges his/her property as security for repayment of the debt.

**Negotiable.** The legal right of a holder to sell a promissory note to a third party, who then has the right to collect the payments.

**Nonjudicial foreclosure.** A five-step procedure, without the involvement of the court, resulting in a trustee conducting a public auction of your property and using the sale proceeds to repay your lender.

**Non-recourse.** A clause in a promissory note stating that the borrower is not personally liable to the lender if the borrower defaults on the loan.

**Note.** An abbreviation for promissory note.

**Notice.** Written or oral communication of information directly to a person or entity. Depending on the situation, written notice can be by personal delivery, mailing, posting it on the property, publishing it in a newspaper, or recording it in the county recorder's office.

**One-action rule.** Your lender is entitled to commence only one legal procedure to collect a secured debt, which by law is a foreclosure action if the promissory note is secured by a deed of trust.

**Owner-occupied.** When you live in the property you have pledged as security for the repayment of your loan.

**Permanent injunction.** A court order at the conclusion of a trial permanently preventing your lender from foreclosing your property.

**Plaintiff.** The aggrieved party that files a civil lawsuit.

**Plan of reorganization.** An agreement between the debtor and creditors, and approved by the bankruptcy court in a Chapter 11 case, for repayment of debts pursuant to a specific schedule.

**Posting.** Affixing a foreclosure notice to a post or wall on the property being foreclosed.

**Power of sale.** A right given to the trustee in your deed of trust to conduct a nonjudicial foreclosure of your property (rather than going through the lengthy process of a judicial foreclosure in court) in the event you default under your promissory note or deed of trust.

**Preliminary injunction.** A court order prohibiting your lender from foreclosing during the pendency of the lawsuit—that is, until the court can conduct a trial.

**Pre-payment penalty.** A clause in your promissory note that allows your lender to charge you a fee if you try to pay off your loan before its due date.

**Principal.** At any given time, the amount of money you owe your lender, not including interest.

**Private mortgage insurance.** Insurance obtained by your lender, but paid by you, which protects your lender in the event you default on your loan.

**Private sale.** A trustee's sale conducted in a nonjudicial foreclosure.

**Promissory note.** Your written promise to repay money that has been loaned to you.

**Purchase money.** Money loaned by the seller, or a third-party lender, used by the buyer to pay all or part of the purchase price of a property.

**Receiver.** A person appointed by the court to manage your property and collect the rents from your tenants during the pendency of a judicial foreclosure. By filing a judicial foreclosure action, your lender has the right to request that the court appoint a receiver for your property.

**Reconveyance.** Once your promissory note has been paid in full, the trustee will cancel the deed of trust, return the original document to you and record a reconveyance in the county recorder's office.

**Recording.** The procedure of filing documents in the county recorder's office in order to give public notice of real estate transactions. In this way, the recorder's office becomes a clearinghouse of information as to what liens (their amounts and priorities), transfers, deeds, reconveyances, easements, and similar documents are recorded against a particular property.

**Recourse.** A clause in a promissory note stating that the borrower is personally liable for payment of the loan.

**Redemption.** Your right to pay off the entire loan and have the foreclosure stopped.

**Redemption period.** A time period in which you take back your property by paying off the total balance of your loan. The time period is provided for by state statute.

**Refinance.** Paying off your existing loan(s) with funds obtained from a new loan on your property.

**Reinstatement period.** In a nonjudicial foreclosure, the three-month period beginning upon the issuance of the Notice of Default and ending five days before the trustee's sale, in which you can cure the default and stop the foreclosure by simply paying the arrearage on your loan.

**Rents and profits clause.** A clause in your deed of trust that allows your lender to collect the rents directly from your tenants if you default on your promissory note.

**REO (real estate owned).** Real property taken back by the lender after a foreclosure sale because no one else bid more than the lender's opening credit bid.

**Reorganization.** Efforts by a debtor during a chapter 11, 12 or 13 bankruptcy to restructure his/her assets and debts as part of a plan to repay creditors part or all of what is owed.

**Rescission.** The act of canceling a previously recorded document. In a foreclosure context, the trustee will "rescind" the Notice of Default or Notice of Trustee's Sale when you pay the arrears and bring your loan current.

**Sanction.** A monetary penalty charged by the court against the plaintiff or defendant for failing to follow court rules and regulations.

**Secondary market.** Informal markets in which lenders sell portfolios of their loans to investment groups, or other lenders, so that they can recycle the funds into more loans to new borrowers.

**Secured.** Promissory notes are either secured or unsecured. If your promissory note is secured, you have pledged your property as security to be sold (foreclosed) in the event you default under your promissory note.

**Security.** Property pledged by you to your lender to assure payment of your loan.

**Senior.** The lender with the earliest dated deed of trust recorded against your property, which therefore has priority over all subsequently recorded (junior) deeds of trust.

**Short sale.** (Also called "short pay".) Having your lender agree to accept less than the full balance of your loan when your property is sold.

**Sold-out junior.** A lender whose junior deed of trust was eliminated when a senior lender completed a foreclosure sale of your property.

**Specific performance.** An equitable remedy in which the court orders that a defendant perform the specific terms of a contract because monetary damages would be inadequate for the breach of that contract.

**Standstill agreement.** The agreement by your lender to voluntarily refrain from foreclosing your property so that you may have more time to repay your loan. (Also known as a "forbearance" or "workout" agreement.)

**Statutory redemption.** In a judicial foreclosure, your legal right to take back (redeem) your property after the foreclosure sale by paying the price your property sold for at the foreclosure sale.

**Temporary Restraining Order (TRO).** A court order prohibiting your lender from foreclosing for a brief period (i.e. two weeks) until the court can conduct a hearing to consider the issues in dispute. In the context of a pending foreclosure, a TRO enjoins your trustee and lender from continuing a nonjudicial foreclosure until the court can conduct a formal hearing.

**Tenant.** A party holding possession (without holding title) of real property for a specific period of time in exchange for paying rent during that period.

**Tenant-in-common.** A description of parties owning property together. In contrast to joint tenancy, upon death of either tenant-in-common, the deceased tenant's ownership interest is transferred to his next of kin, as opposed to the surviving tenant-in-common. Each tenant-in-common may encumber only his interest in the property, leaving the interest of the other tenant-in-common unencumbered.

**Tender.** An offer of money which is due in satisfaction of a claim, but without any stipulation or condition.

**Title insurance.** Insurance purchased by the buyer of property to insure that the buyer will become the actual owner of the property and that there are no liens recorded against the property other than disclosed in the insurance policy.

**Trustee.** The party that holds legal title to your property (by way of the deed of trust) as security for your repayment of your promissory note. The trustee's only responsibilities are to conduct the nonjudicial foreclosure, if necessary, and reconvey your deed of trust when you pay off the loan.

**Trustee's Deed Upon Sale.** The deed given by the trustee to the successful purchaser at the trustee's sale.

**Trustee's sale.** A public auction of your property conducted by the trustee (or auctioneer on behalf of the trustee) at the conclusion of a nonjudicial foreclosure.

**Trustor.** The legal name of the property owner who pledges her property as security for repayment of the loan to the lender. You would be the trustor if you signed a deed of trust pledging your property as security for a loan.

**Unlawful detainer.** A lawsuit by a landlord against a tenant who fails to pay rent or refuses to relinquish possession of real property upon the termination of the lease. If your property is sold at a trustee's sale, the new owner can file an unlawful detainer action to have you evicted.

**Unsecured.** Promissory notes are either secured or unsecured. If your promissory note is unsecured, you have not pledged any of your assets as security for repayment of the note. If your lender wants to recover the unpaid debt, it must file a lawsuit in court against you, rather than foreclosing.

**Venue.** The proper county to conduct a lawsuit. In a foreclosure context, venue is proper only in the county in which your property is located.

**Waste.** An abuse or destructive use of your property, including neglect to its land, structures, trees, gardens, and related improvements, in violation of your deed of trust. Although seldom used alone, waste of your property is a related cause for your lender conducting a foreclosure.

**Workout agreement.** The agreement by your lender to voluntarily refrain from foreclosing your property so that you may have more time to repay your loan. (Also known as a "forbearance" or "standstill" agreement.)

# APPENDIX

COMMUNICATIONS CHART

EQUITY WORKSHEET

PROMISSORY NOTE WORKSHEET

DEED OF TRUST WORKSHEET

NOTICE OF DEFAULT WORKSHEET

NOTICE OF TRUSTEE'S SALE WORKSHEET (NONJUDICIAL FORECLOSURE)

NOTICE OF SALE WORKSHEET (JUDICIAL FORECLOSURE)

BLANK LINED AND NUMBERED PAPER

SUMMONS

CIVIL CASE COVER SHEET

PROOF OF SERVICE

DEED IN LIEU OF FORECLOSURE

# COMMUNICATIONS CHART

Date of contact:                                              Time:

☐ Telephone        ☐ Letter        ☐ Fax        ☐ Meeting/location

Name of contact person:

Who initiated communication?

What we discussed:

Agreements we reached, if any:

---

Date of contact:                                              Time:

☐ Telephone        ☐ Letter        ☐ Fax        ☐ Meeting/location

Name of contact person:

Who initiated communication?

What we discussed:

Agreements we reached, if any:

---

Date of contact:                                              Time:

☐ Telephone        ☐ Letter        ☐ Fax        ☐ Meeting/location

Name of contact person:

Who initiated communication?

What we discussed:

Agreements we reached, if any:

## EQUITY WORKSHEET

1. Estimated sales price:

_____

2. List estimated costs of sale:

_____

   a. Real estate agent's commission (6% of sales price):

_____

   b. Closing costs (2% of estimated sales price):

_____

   c. Balance due on first deed of trust:

_____

   d. Balance due on additional deeds of trust:

_____

   e. Balance due on any other loans by property:

_____

   f. Missed payments on first deed of trust:

_____

   g. Missed payments and late fees on additional deeds of trust:

_____

   h. Any other liens:

_____

   i. Unpaid property taxes:

_____

   j. Foreclosure costs:

_____

3. Total estimated costs of sale:

_____

4. Your equity (1 – 3):

_____

## PROMISSORY NOTE WORKSHEET

Date note is signed:

Borrower(s):

Lender:

Principal amount borrowed:

Interest rate:

Term (number of months, years or other arrangement):

Payment frequency (monthly or other arrangement):

Commencement date (date payments begin):

Payment amount:

Is there a reference in the note to the deed of trust?

## DEED OF TRUST WORKSHEET

Date recorded: _____

Date signed: _____

Trustor: _____

Trustee: _____

Beneficiary: _____

County in which property is located: _____

Legal description: _____

Principal amount borrowed: _____

Date notarized: _____

Did you sign the deed of trust? yes/no _____

# NOTICE OF DEFAULT WORKSHEET (NONJUDICIAL FORECLOSURE)

ARE THE FOLLOWING CORRECT ON THE NOTICE OF DEFAULT,
AND CONSISTENT WITH INFORMATION ON YOUR PROMISSORY NOTE AND DEED OF TRUST?

| | | | |
|---|---|---|---|
| Name of trustor (you and any co-signers)? | ☐ No | ☐ Yes | Name: |
| Name of beneficiary (lender)? | ☐ No | ☐ Yes | Name: |
| Name of trustee? | ☐ No | ☐ Yes | Name: |
| Information about recording of deed of trust? | ☐ No | ☐ Yes | Date: |
| Legal description of the property? | Document No.: | | Book/Page No.: |
| Amount of original indebtedness? | | | |
| Amount in default? | ☐ No | ☐ Yes | Amount: |

RECORDING REQUIREMENTS

| | | | |
|---|---|---|---|
| Was the Notice of Default recorded in the recorder's office for the county in which your property is located? | ☐ No | ☐ Yes | When: |

MAILING REQUIREMENTS

| | | | |
|---|---|---|---|
| Was a copy of the Notice of Default mailed to you by certified or registered mail within ten business days of recording? | ☐ No | ☐ Yes | When: |
| Was a copy of the Notice of Default mailed to you by first-class mail within ten business days of recording? | ☐ No | ☐ Yes | When: |
| Within 30 days of recording, was a copy of the Notice mailed by first-class mail to everyone entitled to receive the Notice—including tenants, junior beneficiaries and anyone who recorded a Request for Notice? (You will need to call them and ask them if they received the Notice.) | ☐ No | ☐ Yes | When: |

PUBLICATION REQUIREMENTS

| | | | |
|---|---|---|---|
| If the trustee did not have your correct address, was the Notice of Default published in a newspaper of general circulation once a week for at least four weeks? (You have the right to ask the trustee to see its Affidavit of Publication and copies of the newspapers.) | ☐ No | ☐ Yes | 1st Date: |
| | | | 2nd Date: |
| | | | 3rd Date: |
| | | | 4th Date: |

## NOTICE OF TRUSTEE'S SALE WORKSHEET (NONJUDICIAL FORECLOSURE)

ARE THE FOLLOWING CORRECT ON THE NOTICE OF TRUSTEE'S SALE, AND CONSISTENT WITH INFORMATION ON YOUR NOTICE OF DEFAULT, PROMISSORY NOTE AND DEED OF TRUST?

| | | | |
|---|---|---|---|
| Name of trustor (you and any co-signers)? | ☐ No | ☐ Yes | Name: |
| Name of beneficiary (lender)? | ☐ No | ☐ Yes | Name: |
| Name of trustee? | ☐ No | ☐ Yes | Name: |
| Information about recording of deed of trust? | ☐ No | ☐ Yes | Date:<br>Document No.:<br>Book/Page No.: |
| Description of the property? | ☐ No | ☐ Yes | |
| Total amount of outstanding indebtedness? | ☐ No | ☐ Yes | Amount: |
| Date, time and location of sale? | ☐ No | ☐ Yes | Date:<br>Time:<br>Location: |
| Is the date of sale at least 20 calendar days from date the Notice of Sale was issued? | ☐ No | ☐ Yes | |

### MAILING REQUIREMENTS

| | | | |
|---|---|---|---|
| Did the trustee wait at least three months after recording a Notice of Default before mailing you a Notice of Sale? | ☐ No | ☐ Yes | When? |
| Was a copy of the Notice of Sale mailed to you by registered or certified mail at least 20 calendar days before the scheduled sale date? | ☐ No | ☐ Yes | When? |
| Was a copy of the Notice of Sale sent to you by first-class mail at least 20 days before the scheduled sale date? | ☐ No | ☐ Yes | When? |
| At least 20 days before the scheduled sale date, was a copy of the Notice of Sale sent by registered or certified mail to everyone entitled to receive notice— including tenants, junior beneficiaries and anyone who recorded a Request for Notice? (Ask the trustee for proof.) | ☐ No | ☐ Yes | When? |

### RECORDING REQUIREMENTS

| | | | |
|---|---|---|---|
| Was the Notice of Sale recorded in the county recorder's office where your property is located at least 14 days before the scheduled date? | ☐ No | ☐ Yes | When? |

# NOTICE OF TRUSTEE'S SALE WORKSHEET (NONJUDICIAL FORECLOSURE)

## PUBLICATION REQUIREMENTS

Before the sale date, was the Notice of Sale
published in a newspaper of general circulation
in the county where the property is located
three times over 20 days? (As the trustee for proof.)  ☐ No  ☐ Yes  1st Date:

2nd Date:

3rd Date:

## POSTING REQUIREMENTS

Was a copy of the Notice of Sale posted in
a public place?  ☐ No  ☐ Yes  Where?

Was a copy of the Notice of Sale posted
on your property?  ☐ No  ☐ Yes  Where?

# NOTICE OF SALE WORKSHEET (JUDICIAL FORECLOSURE)

## DID THE NOTICE OF SALE INCLUDE

|  |  |  | |
|---|---|---|---|
| Date of sale? | ☐ No | ☐ Yes | Date: |
| Time of sale? | ☐ No | ☐ Yes | Time: |
| Specific location of sale? | ☐ No | ☐ Yes | Location: |
| Correct legal description of the property, including the street address? | ☐ No | ☐ Yes | |
| Correct name and address of beneficiary (lender)? | ☐ No | ☐ Yes | |

## SERVICE AND MAILING REQUIREMENTS

|  |  |  | |
|---|---|---|---|
| Was the Notice of Sale mailed to you by first-class mail a minimum 20 calendar days before the scheduled sale date? | ☐ No | ☐ Yes | When? |
| Was the Notice of Sale personally served on you? | ☐ No | ☐ Yes | When? |
| At least 20 days before the scheduled sale date, was the Notice of Sale mailed by first class mail to everyone entitled to receive notice (including tenants and junior lienholders)? | ☐ No | ☐ Yes | When? |

## PUBLICATION REQUIREMENTS

|  |  |  | |
|---|---|---|---|
| Was the Notice of Sale published at least once a week over 3 weeks? | ☐ No | ☐ Yes | 1st Date: |
| | ☐ No | ☐ Yes | 2nd Date: |
| | ☐ No | ☐ Yes | 3rd Date: |
| Was the first publication date at least 20 calendar days before the scheduled sale date? | ☐ No | ☐ Yes | When? |
| Was the Notice of Sale published in a paper in the county where your property is located? | ☐ No | ☐ Yes | District: |

## POSTING REQUIREMENTS

|  |  |  | |
|---|---|---|---|
| Was the Notice of Sale posted in a public place? | ☐ No | ☐ Yes | Where? |
| Was the Notice of Sale posted on your front door or another conspicuous place? | ☐ No | ☐ Yes | Where? |

1
2
3
4
5
6
7
8
9
10
11
12
13
14
15
16
17
18
19
20
21
22
23
24
25
26
27
28

# SUMMONS
## (CITACION JUDICIAL)

**UNLAWFUL DETAINER—EVICTION**
*(PROCESO DE DESAHUCIO—EVICCION)*

Pilot Project—C.C.P. § 1167.2: Riverside Consolidated/Coordinated Courts and the Downey, El Cajon, and North Santa Barbara County Municipal Courts

**FOR COURT USE ONLY**
*(SOLO PARA USO DE LA CORTE)*

**NOTICE TO DEFENDANT:** *(Aviso a acusado)*

**YOU ARE BEING SUED BY PLAINTIFF:**
*(A Ud. le está demandando)*

| | |
|---|---|
| **THIS IS A COURT PROCEEDING IN WHICH THE PLAINTIFF SEEKS YOUR EVICTION FROM YOUR RESIDENCE.**<br><br>The plaintiff has requested that the court require you to post with the court a pretrial prospective rent deposit in the amount set below before the court permits you to have a trial of this case. Before the court orders you to post the amount, the court will hold a pretrial hearing. You will be informed by mail within the next few days when that hearing will be held.<br><br>A letter or phone call will not protect you. You have 5 calendar days after this summons is served on you to file at this court a written answer, motion, demurrer, and/or reply form. If you do not respond within 5 days, you still have a right to appear at the pretrial hearing and present oral argument and explain your side of the case. *(To calculate the 5 days, count Saturday and Sunday, but do not count other court holidays.)*<br><br>If you do not appear at the pretrial hearing or otherwise respond on time, you may lose the case, you may be evicted, and you may lose any pretrial rent deposit that you have deposited with the court. There are other legal requirements. You may want to call an attorney right away. If you do not know an attorney, you may call an attorney referral service or Legal Aid. | *ESTE ES UN PROCESO JUDICIAL EN EL QUE EL DEMANDANTE PODRÁ DESALOJARLO DE SU RESIDENCIA.*<br><br>El demandante solicita que el tribunal le exija pago previo al juicio del depósito de la futura renta, en el monto fijado más abajo. Antes de que se le permita ir a juicio, el tribunal llevará a cabo una audiencia previa al juicio. Dentro de los próximos dias, se le notificará por correo la fecha de dicha audiencia.<br><br>Ud. no podrá ampararse bajo una carta o un llamado telefónico. Tiene Ud. cinco dias calendario después de recibir esta citación, para presentar ante el tribunal una contestación por escrito, petición, excepción preventiva y/o formulario de respuesta. Si Ud. no respondiera dentro de los cinco dias, tendrá derecho a comparecer a una audiencia previa al juicio y presentar alegato oral para explicar su version del caso. (Para calcular los cinco dias, cuente sábados y domingos, pero no cuente otros dias de asueto judicial.)<br><br>Si no comparece a la audiencia previa al juicio o no responde a tiempo, Ud. puede perder el caso, puede ser desalojado y puede perder el depósito de la renta previa al juicio que Ud. haya depositado con el tribunal.<br><br>Hay otros requisitos legales. Puede Ud. descar llamar a un abogado immediatamente. Si Ud. tiene un abogado puede ponerse en contacto con un servicio de referencia a abogados o con asistencia legal (Legal Aid). |

The name and address of the court is: *(El nombre y dirección de la corte es)*

**CASE NUMBER:** *(Número del caso)*

**PRETRIAL RENT DEPOSIT DEMAND $** _____

The name, address, and telephone number of plaintiff's attorney, or plaintiff without an attorney, is:
*(El nombre, la dirección y el número de teléfono del abogado del demandante, o del demandante que no tiene abogado, es)*

DATE: _____ Clerk, by _____, Deputy
*(Fecha)* *(Actuario)* *(Delegado)*

[SEAL]

**NOTICE TO THE PERSON SERVED:** You are served

1. [ ] as an individual defendant.
2. [ ] as the person sued under the fictitious name of *(specify)*:
3. [ ] on behalf of *(specify)*:

   under: [ ] CCP 416.10 (corporation)     [ ] CCP 416.60 (minor)
   [ ] CCP 416.20 (defunct corporation)    [ ] CCP 416.70 (conservatee)
   [ ] CCP 416.40 (association or partnership)     [ ] CCP 416.90 (individual)
   [ ] other:

4. [ ] by personal delivery on *(date)*:
   (See reverse for Proof of Service)

Form Adopted by Rule 982
Judicial Council of California
982(a)(11S) [New July 1, 1995]

**SUMMONS — UNLAWFUL DETAINER (Pilot Project—C.C.P. § 1167.2)**

Code Civ. Proc., §§ 412.20, 1167

| PLAINTIFF *(Name)*: | CASE NUMBER: |
|---|---|
| DEFENDANT *(Name)*: | |

## PROOF OF SERVICE

1. At the time of service I was at least 18 years of age and not a party to this action, and **I served copies** of the *(specify documents)*:

2. a. Party served *(specify name of party as shown on the documents served)*:

   b. Person served: ☐ party in item 2a  ☐ other *(specify name and title or relationship to the party named in item 2a)*:

   c. Address:

3. I served the party named in item 2
   a. ☐ **by personally delivering** the copies on *(date)*:                          at *(time)*:
   b. ☐ **by leaving** the copies with or in the presence of *(name and title or relationship to person indicated in item 2b)*:

      (1) ☐ **(business)** a person at least 18 years of age apparently in charge at the office or usual place of business of the person served. I informed him or her of the general nature of the papers.
      (2) ☐ **(home)** a competent member of the household (at least 18 years of age) at the dwelling house or usual place of abode of the person served. I informed him or her of the general nature of the papers.
      (3) on *(date)*:                          at *(time)*:
      (4) ☐ A **declaration of diligence** is attached. *(Substituted service on natural person, minor, conservatee, or candidate.)*
   c. ☐ **by mailing** the copies to the person served, addressed as shown in item 2c, by first-class mail, postage prepaid,
      (1) on *(date)*:                          from *(city)*:
      (2) ☐ with two copies of the Notice and Acknowledgment of Receipt and a postage-paid return envelope addressed to me. *(Attach completed form.)*
      (3) ☐ to an address outside California with return receipt requested. *(Attach completed form.)*
   d. ☐ **by** causing copies to be mailed. A declaration of mailing is attached.
   e. ☐ **other** *(specify other manner of service and authorizing code section)*:

4. The "Notice to the Person Served" (on the summons) was completed as follows:
   a. ☐ as an individual defendant.
   b. ☐ as the person sued under the fictitious name of *(specify)*:
   c. ☐ on behalf of *(specify)*:
      under: ☐ CCP 416.10 (corporation)     ☐ CCP 416.60 (minor)      ☐ other:
             ☐ CCP 416.20 (defunct corporation)  ☐ CCP 416.70 (conservatee)
             ☐ CCP 416.40 (association or partnership)  ☐ CCP 416.90 (individual)

5. **Person serving** *(name, address, and telephone no.)*:

   a. **Fee** for service: $
   b. ☐ Not a registered California process server.
   c. ☐ Exempt from registration under B&P § 22350(b).
   d. ☐ Registered California process server.
      (1) ☐ Employee or independent contractor.
      (2) Registration no.:
      (3) County:

6. ☐ **I declare** under penalty of perjury under the laws of the State of California that the foregoing is true and correct.

7. ☐ **I am a California sheriff, marshal, or constable and I** certify that the foregoing is true and correct.

Date:

▶

_____
(SIGNATURE)

**PROOF OF SERVICE**
(Summons—Unlawful Detainer (Pilot Project—C.C.P. § 1167.2))

ATTORNEY OR PARTY WITHOUT ATTORNEY *(Name and Address)* :

TELEPHONE NO.:

*FOR COURT USE ONLY*

ATTORNEY FOR *(Name)* :

INSERT NAME OF COURT, JUDICIAL DISTRICT, AND BRANCH COURT, IF ANY:

CASE NAME:

## CIVIL CASE COVER SHEET
### (Case Cover Sheets)

CASE NUMBER:

1. ☐ Case category *(Insert code from list below for the ONE case type that best describes the case)*:

01 Abuse of Process
02 Administrative Agency Review
03 Antitrust/Unfair Business Practices
04 Asbestos
05 Asset Forfeiture
06 Breach of Contract/Warranty
07 Business Tort
08 Civil Rights *(Discrimination, False Arrest)*
09 Collections *(Money Owed, Open Book Accounts)*
10 Construction Defect
11 Contractual Arbitration
12 Declaratory Relief
13 Defamation *(Slander, Libel)*
14 Eminent Domain/Inverse Condemnation
15 Employment *(Labor Commissioner Appeals, EDD Actions, Wrongful Termination)*
16 Fraud
17 Injunctive Relief

18 Insurance Coverage/Subrogation
19 Intellectual Property
20 Enforcement of Judgment *(Sister State, Foreign, Out-of-Country Abstracts)*
21 Partnership and Corporate Governance
22 PI/PD/WD—Auto *(Personal Injury/Property Damage/ Wrongful Death)*
23 PI/PD/WD—Nonauto
24 Product Liability
25 Professional Negligence *(Medical or Legal Malpractice, etc.)*
26 Real Property *(Quiet Title)*
27 RICO
28 Securities Litigation
29 Tax Judgment
30 Toxic Tort/Environmental
31 Unlawful Detainer—Commercial
32 Unlawful Detainer—Residential
33 Wrongful Eviction
34 Other: _____

2. Type of remedies sought *(check all that apply)*:  a. ☐ Monetary  b. ☐ Nonmonetary  c. ☐ Punitive
3. Number of causes of action:
4. Is this a class action suit? ☐ Yes ☐ No

Date:

▶

. . . . . . . . . . . . . . . . . . . . . . . . . . . . . . . . . . . . . . . . .
(TYPE OR PRINT NAME)

(SIGNATURE OF PARTY OR ATTORNEY FOR PARTY)

### NOTE TO PLAINTIFF
- This cover sheet shall accompany each civil action or proceeding, except those filed in small claims court or filed under the Probate Code, Family Law Code, or Welfare and Institutions Code.
- File this cover sheet in addition to any cover sheet required by local court rule.
- Do not serve this cover sheet with the complaint.
- This cover sheet shall be used for statistical purposes only and shall have no effect on the assignment of the case.

Form Adopted by Rule 982.2
Judicial Council of California
982.2(b)(1) [New July 1, 1996]

**CIVIL CASE COVER SHEET**
**(Case Cover Sheets)**

| **PROOF OF SERVICE**<br>**(Summons)** | DATE: | TIME: | DEPT./DIV.: | CASE NUMBER: |
|---|---|---|---|---|

1. At the time of service I was at least 18 years of age and not a party to this action, and **I served copies** of the *(specify documents)*:

2. a. Party served *(specify name of party as shown on the documents served)*:

   b. Person served: ☐ party in item 2a  ☐ other *(specify name and title or relationship to the party named in item 2a)*:

   c. Address:

3. I served the party named in item 2
   a. ☐ **by personally delivering** the copies  (1) on *(date)*:  (2) at *(time)*:
   b. ☐ **by leaving** the copies with or in the presence of *(name and title or relationship to person indicated in item 2b)*:

      (1) ☐ **(business)** a person at least 18 years of age apparently in charge at the office or usual place of business of the person served. I informed him or her of the general nature of the papers.
      (2) ☐ **(home)** a competent member of the household (at least 18 years of age) at the dwelling house or usual place of abode of the person served. I informed him or her of the general nature of the papers.
      (3) on *(date)*:  (4) at *(time)*:
      (5) ☐ A **declaration of diligence** is attached. *(Substituted service on natural person, minor, conservatee, or candidate.)*
   c. ☐ **by mailing** the copies to the person served, addressed as shown in item 2c, by first-class mail, postage prepaid,
      (1) on *(date)*:  (2) from *(city)*:
      (3) ☐ with two copies of the Notice and Acknowledgment of Receipt and a postage-paid return envelope addressed to me.
      (4) ☐ to an address outside California with return receipt requested.  ◄ *(Attach completed form.)* ➧
   d. ☐ **by causing** copies to be mailed. A declaration of mailing is attached.
   e. ☐ **other** *(specify other manner of service and authorizing code section)*:

4. The "Notice to the Person Served" (on the summons) was completed as follows:
   a. ☐ as an individual defendant.
   b. ☐ as the person sued under the fictitious name of *(specify)*:
   c. ☐ on behalf of *(specify)*:
      under: ☐ CCP 416.10 (corporation)  ☐ CCP 416.60 (minor)  ☐ other:
             ☐ CCP 416.20 (defunct corporation)  ☐ CCP 416.70 (conservatee)
             ☐ CCP 416.40 (association or partnership)  ☐ CCP 416.90 (individual)

5. **Person serving** *(name, address, and telephone No.)*:
   a. **Fee** for service: $
   b. ☐ Not a registered California process server.
   c. ☐ Exempt from registration under B&P § 22350(b).
   d. ☐ Registered California process server.
      (1) ☐ Employee or independent contractor.
      (2) Registration No.:
      (3) County:

6. ☐ **I declare** under penalty of perjury under the laws of the State of California that the foregoing is true and correct.
7. ☐ **I am a California sheriff, marshal, or constable** and I certify that the foregoing is true and correct.

Date:

➤ _____
(SIGNATURE)

Recording requested by


and when recorded mail
this deed and tax statement to:



## DEED IN LIEU OF FORECLOSURE

1. This transfer is exempt from the documentary transfer tax.

2. This property is located in _____

   ☐ a. an unincorporated area

   ☐ b. the city of _____

3. For valuable consideration, receipt of which is hereby acknowledged, _____

   hereby deeds to _____

   _____ ,

   in lieu of foreclosure, the following real property in the City of _____ ,
   County of _____ , State of California:
   commonly known as _____

Date: _____

Date: _____

Date: _____

Date: _____

ACKNOWLEDGMENT

State of _____ )

County of _____ )


On _____ , 19 __ , before me, _____ , a notary public,
personally appeared _____ , personally known to me
or proved to me on the basis of satisfactory evidence to be the person(s) whose name is/are subscribed to this
instrument, and acknowledged to me that he/she/they executed the same in his/her/their authorized
capacity(ies) and that by his/her/their signature(s) on the instrument, the person(s) or the entity upon behalf of
which the person(s) acted, executed the instrument.



[NOTARY SEAL]   Signature of Notary Public

# INDEX

# N

# O

# P

# R

# CATALOG
## ...more from Nolo Press

|  | | EDITION | PRICE | CODE |
|---|---|---|---|---|
| **BUSINESS** | | | | |
| | Business Plans to Game Plans | 1st | $29.95 | GAME |
| | The California Nonprofit Corporation Handbook | 7th | $29.95 | NON |
| | The California Professional Corporation Handbook | 5th | $34.95 | PROF |
| | The Employer's Legal Handbook | 2nd | $29.95 | EMPL |
| | Form Your Own Limited Liability Company | 1st | $24.95 | LIAB |
| | Helping Employees Achieve Retirement Security | 1st | $16.95 | HEAR |
| ▣ | Hiring Independent Contractors: The Employer's Legal Guide, (Book w/Disk—PC) | 2nd | $29.95 | HICI |
| | How to Finance a Growing Business | 4th | $24.95 | GROW |
| ▣ | How to Form a CA Nonprofit Corp.—w/Corp. Records Binder & PC Disk | 1st | $49.95 | CNP |
| ▣ | How to Form a Nonprofit Corp., Book w/Disk (PC)—National Edition | 3rd | $39.95 | NNP |
| ▣ | How to Form Your Own Calif. Corp.—w/Corp. Records Binder & Disk—PC | 1st | $39.95 | CACI |
| | How to Form Your Own California Corporation | 8th | $29.95 | CCOR |
| ▣ | How to Form Your Own Florida Corporation, (Book w/Disk—PC) | 3rd | $39.95 | FLCO |
| ▣ | How to Form Your Own New York Corporation, (Book w/Disk—PC) | 3rd | $39.95 | NYCO |
| ▣ | How to Form Your Own Texas Corporation, (Book w/Disk—PC) | 4th | $39.95 | TCOR |
| | How to Handle Your Workers' Compensation Claim (California Edition) | 1st | $29.95 | WORK |
| | How to Market a Product for Under $500 | 1st | $29.95 | UN500 |
| | How to Mediate Your Dispute | 1st | $18.95 | MEDI |
| | How to Write a Business Plan | 4th | $21.95 | SBS |
| | The Independent Paralegal's Handbook | 4th | $29.95 | PARA |
| | Insuring the Bottom Line | 1st | $29.95 | BOTT |
| | Legal Guide for Starting & Running a Small Business, Vol. I | 3rd | $24.95 | RUNS |
| | Make Up Your Mind: Entrepreneurs Talk About Decision Making | 1st | $19.95 | MIND |

▣ Book with disk

| | EDITION | PRICE | CODE |
|---|---|---|---|
| Managing Generation X: How to Bring Out the Best in Young Talent | 1st | $19.95 | MANX |
| Marketing Without Advertising | 2nd | $19.00 | MWAD |
| Mastering Diversity: Managing for Success Under ADA and Other Anti-Discrimination Laws | 1st | $29.95 | MAST |
| ⊡ OSHA in the Real World: (Book w/Disk—PC) | 1st | $29.95 | OSHA |
| Pay For Results | 1st | $29.95 | PAY |
| ⊡ The Partnership Book: How to Write a Partnership Agreement, (Book w/Disk—PC) | 5th | $34.95 | PART |
| Rightful Termination | 1st | $29.95 | RITE |
| Sexual Harassment on the Job | 2nd | $18.95 | HARS |
| ⊡ Taking Care of Your Corporation, Vol. 1, (Book w/Disk—PC) | 1st | $26.95 | CORK |
| ⊡ Taking Care of Your Corporation, Vol. 2, (Book w/Disk—PC) | 1st | $39.95 | CORK2 |
| Tax Savvy for Small Business | 2nd | $26.95 | SAVVY |
| Trademark: How to Name Your Business & Product | 2nd | $29.95 | TRD |
| Workers' Comp for Employers | 2nd | $29.95 | CNTRL |
| Your Rights in the Workplace | 3rd | $19.95 | YRW |

## CONSUMER

| | EDITION | PRICE | CODE |
|---|---|---|---|
| Fed Up With the Legal System: What's Wrong & How to Fix It | 2nd | $9.95 | LEG |
| Glossary of Insurance Terms | 6th | $14.95 | GLINT |
| How to Insure Your Car | 1st | $12.95 | INCAR |
| How to Insure Your Home | 1st | $12.95 | INTRO |
| How to Insure Your Life | 1st | $12.95 | INLIF |
| How to Win Your Personal Injury Claim | 2nd | $24.95 | PICL |
| Nolo's Everyday Law Book | 1st | $21.95 | EVL |
| Nolo's Pocket Guide to California Law | 5th | $11.95 | CLAW |
| The Over 50 Insurance Survival Guide | 1st | $16.95 | OVER50 |
| Trouble-Free Travel...And What to Do When Things Go Wrong | 1st | $14.95 | TRAV |
| True Odds: How Risk Affects Your Everyday Life | 1st | $19.95 | TROD |
| What Do You Mean It's Not Covered? | 1st | $19.95 | COVER |

## ESTATE PLANNING & PROBATE

| | EDITION | PRICE | CODE |
|---|---|---|---|
| 8 Ways to Avoid Probate (Quick & Legal Series) | 1st | $15.95 | PRO8 |
| How to Probate an Estate (California Edition) | 9th | $34.95 | PAE |
| Make Your Own Living Trust | 2nd | $21.95 | LITR |
| ⊡ Nolo's Will Book, (Book w/Disk—PC) | 3rd | $24.95 | SWIL |
| Plan Your Estate | 3rd | $24.95 | NEST |
| The Quick and Legal Will Book | 1st | $15.95 | QUIC |
| Nolo's Law Form Kit: Wills | 1st | $14.95 | KWL |

⊡ Book with disk

|  | EDITION | PRICE | CODE |
|---|---|---|---|

## FAMILY MATTERS

| Title | Edition | Price | Code |
|---|---|---|---|
| A Legal Guide for Lesbian and Gay Couples | 9th | $24.95 | LG |
| California Marriage Law | 12th | $19.95 | MARR |
| Child Custody: Building Parenting Agreements that Work | 2nd | $24.95 | CUST |
| Divorce & Money: How to Make the Best Financial Decisions During Divorce | 3rd | $26.95 | DIMO |
| Get A Life: You Don't Need a Million to Retire Well | 1st | $18.95 | LIFE |
| The Guardianship Book (California Edition) | 2nd | $24.95 | GB |
| How to Adopt Your Stepchild in California | 4th | $22.95 | ADOP |
| How to Do Your Own Divorce in California | 21st | $24.95 | CDIV |
| How to Do Your Own Divorce in Texas | 6th | $19.95 | TDIV |
| How to Raise or Lower Child Support in California | 3rd | $18.95 | CHLD |
| The Living Together Kit | 8th | $24.95 | LTK |
| Nolo's Law Form Kit: Hiring Childcare & Household Help | 1st | $14.95 | KCHD |
| Nolo's Pocket Guide to Family Law | 4th | $14.95 | FLD |
| Practical Divorce Solutions | 1st | $14.95 | PDS |
| Smart Ways to Save Money During and After Divorce | 1st | $14.95 | SAVMO |

## GOING TO COURT

| Title | Edition | Price | Code |
|---|---|---|---|
| Collect Your Court Judgment (California Edition) | 3rd | $24.95 | JUDG |
| The Criminal Records Book (California Edition) | 5th | $21.95 | CRIM |
| How to Sue For Up to 25,000...and Win! | 2nd | $29.95 | MUNI |
| Everybody's Guide to Small Claims Court in California | 12th | $18.95 | CSCC |
| Everybody's Guide to Small Claims Court (National Edition) | 6th | $18.95 | NSCC |
| Fight Your Ticket ... and Win! (California Edition) | 6th | $19.95 | FYT |
| How to Change Your Name (California Edition) | 6th | $24.95 | NAME |
| Mad at Your Lawyer | 1st | $21.95 | MAD |
| Represent Yourself in Court: How to Prepare & Try a Winning Case | 1st | $29.95 | RYC |
| Taming the Lawyers | 1st | $19.95 | TAME |

## HOMEOWNERS, LANDLORDS & TENANTS

| Title | Edition | Price | Code |
|---|---|---|---|
| The Deeds Book (California Edition) | 4th | $16.95 | DEED |
| Dog Law | 2nd | $12.95 | DOG |
| ⬓ Every Landlord's Legal Guide (National Edition) | 1st | $34.95 | ELLI |
| For Sale by Owner (California Edition) | 2nd | $24.95 | FSBO |
| Homestead Your House (California Edition) | 8th | $9.95 | HOME |
| How to Buy a House in California | 4th | $24.95 | BHCA |
| The Landlord's Law Book, Vol. 1: Rights & Responsibilities (California Edition) | 5th | $34.95 | LBRT |
| The Landlord's Law Book, Vol. 2: Evictions (California Edition) | 6th | $34.95 | LBEV |

⬓ Book with disk

**CALL 800-992-6656 OR USE THE ORDER FORM IN THE BACK OF THE BOOK**

| | EDITION | PRICE | CODE |
|---|---|---|---|
| Leases & Rental Agreements (Quick & Legal Series) ........................................ 1st | | $18.95 | LEAR |
| Neighbor Law: Fences, Trees, Boundaries & Noise ................................................. 2nd | | $16.95 | NEI |
| Safe Homes, Safe Neighborhoods: Stopping Crime Where You Live ........................... 1st | | $14.95 | SAFE |
| Tenants' Rights (California Edition) ..................................................... 13th | | $19.95 | CTEN |

## HUMOR

| | EDITION | PRICE | CODE |
|---|---|---|---|
| 29 Reasons Not to Go to Law School ................................................. 1st | | $9.95 | 29R |
| Poetic Justice ............................................................................ 1st | | $9.95 | PJ |

## IMMIGRATION

| | EDITION | PRICE | CODE |
|---|---|---|---|
| How to Become a United States Citizen .................................. 5th | | $14.95 | CIT |
| How to Get a Green Card: Legal Ways to Stay in the U.S.A. ........................... 2nd | | $24.95 | GRN |
| U.S. Immigration Made Easy ................................................. 5th | | $39.95 | IMEZ |

## MONEY MATTERS

| | EDITION | PRICE | CODE |
|---|---|---|---|
| Building Your Nest Egg With Your 401(k) ..................................... 1st | | $16.95 | EGG |
| Chapter 13 Bankruptcy: Repay Your Debts .............................. 2nd | | $29.95 | CH13 |
| Credit Repair (Quick & Legal Series) ....................................... 1st | | $15.95 | CREP |
| How to File for Bankruptcy ................................................. 6th | | $26.95 | HFB |
| Money Troubles: Legal Strategies to Cope With Your Debts ................. 4th | | $19.95 | MT |
| Nolo's Law Form Kit: Personal Bankruptcy ............................... 1st | | $14.95 | KBNK |
| Simple Contracts for Personal Use ......................................... 2nd | | $16.95 | CONT |
| Stand Up to the IRS ........................................................ 3rd | | $24.95 | SIRS |
| The Under 40 Financial Planning Guide ................................... 1st | | $19.95 | UN40 |

## PATENTS AND COPYRIGHTS

| | EDITION | PRICE | CODE |
|---|---|---|---|
| The Copyright Handbook: How to Protect and Use Written Works ........................... 3rd | | $24.95 | COHA |
| Copyright Your Software ................................................... 1st | | $39.95 | CYS |
| Patent, Copyright & Trademark: A Desk Reference to Intellectual Property Law ....... 1st | | $24.95 | PCTM |
| Patent It Yourself ......................................................... 5th | | $44.95 | PAT |
| ▣ Software Development: A Legal Guide (Book with disk—PC) .......................... 1st | | $44.95 | SFT |
| The Inventor's Notebook ................................................... 2nd | | $19.95 | INOT |

## RESEARCH & REFERENCE

| | EDITION | PRICE | CODE |
|---|---|---|---|
| ◎ Law on the Net, (Book w/CD-ROM—Windows/Macintosh) ........................................ 2nd | | $39.95 | LAWN |
| Legal Research: How to Find & Understand the Law ....................................... 4th | | $19.95 | LRES |
| Legal Research Made Easy (Video) ................................................. 1st | | $89.95 | LRME |

◎ Book with CD-ROM
▣ Book with disk

| | EDITION | PRICE | CODE |
|---|---|---|---|

## SENIORS

| | EDITION | PRICE | CODE |
|---|---|---|---|
| Beat the Nursing Home Trap | 2nd | $18.95 | ELD |
| Social Security, Medicare & Pensions | 6th | $19.95 | SOA |
| The Conservatorship Book (California Edition) | 2nd | $29.95 | CNSV |

## SOFTWARE

| | EDITION | PRICE | CODE |
|---|---|---|---|
| California Incorporator 2.0—DOS | 2.0 | $47.97 | INCI2 |
| Living Trust Maker 2.0—Macintosh | 2.0 | $47.97 | LTM2 |
| Living Trust Maker 2.0—Windows | 2.0 | $47.97 | LTWI2 |
| Small Business Legal Pro—Macintosh | 2.0 | $25.97 | SBM2 |
| Small Business Legal Pro—Windows | 2.0 | $25.97 | SBW2 |
| Small Business Legal Pro Deluxe CD—Windows/Macintosh CD-ROM | 2.0 | $35.97 | SBCD |
| Nolo's Partnership Maker 1.0—DOS | 1.0 | $47.97 | PAGI1 |
| Personal RecordKeeper 4.0—Macintosh | 4.0 | $29.97 | RKM4 |
| Personal RecordKeeper 4.0—Windows | 4.0 | $29.97 | RKP4 |
| Patent It Yourself 1.0—Windows | 1.0 | $149.97 | PYW1 |
| WillMaker 6.0—Macintosh | 6.0 | $29.97 | WM6 |
| WillMaker 6.0—Windows | 6.0 | $29.97 | WIW6 |

# SPECIAL UPGRADE OFFER

## Get 25% off the latest edition of your Nolo book.

It's important to have the most current legal information. Because laws and legal procedures change often, we update our books regularly. To help keep you up-to-date we are extending this special upgrade offer. Cut out and mail the title portion of the cover of your old Nolo book and we'll give you 25% off the retail price of the NEW EDITION of that book when you purchase directly from us. For more information call us at **1-800-992-6656**. This offer is to individuals only.

⌹ Book with disk

## ORDER FORM

| Code | Quantity | Title | Unit price | Total |
|------|----------|-------|------------|-------|
|      |          |       |            |       |
|      |          |       |            |       |
|      |          |       |            |       |
|      |          |       |            |       |
|      |          |       |            |       |
|      |          |       |            |       |

Subtotal

California residents add Sales Tax

Basic Shipping (*$6.00 for 1 item; $7.00 for 2 or more*)

UPS RUSH delivery $7.50–any size order*

TOTAL

Name

Address

(UPS to street address, Priority Mail to P.O. boxes)       * Delivered in 3 business days from receipt of order.
S.F. Bay Area use regular shipping.

## FOR FASTER SERVICE, USE YOUR CREDIT CARD AND OUR TOLL-FREE NUMBERS

| | |
|---|---|
| Order 24 hours a day | 1-800-992-6656 |
| Fax your order | 1-800-645-0895 |
| e-mail | cs@nolo.com |
| General Information | 1-510-549-1976 |
| Customer Service | 1-800-728-3555, Mon.-Fri. 9am-5pm, PST |

## METHOD OF PAYMENT

☐ Check enclosed

☐ VISA    ☐ MasterCard    ☐ Discover Card    ☐ American Express

Account #                                    Expiration Date

Authorizing Signature

Daytime Phone

PRICES SUBJECT TO CHANGE.

## VISIT OUR OUTLET STORES!

You'll find our complete line of books and software, all at a discount.

**BERKELEY**
950 Parker Street
Berkeley, CA 94710
1-510-704-2248

**SAN JOSE**
111 N. Market Street, #115
San Jose, CA 95113
1-408-271-7240

## VISIT US ONLINE!

on the INTERNET — www.nolo.com

## N O L O   P R E S S   9 5 0   P A R K E R   S T . ,   B E R K E L E Y ,   C A   9 4 7 1 0